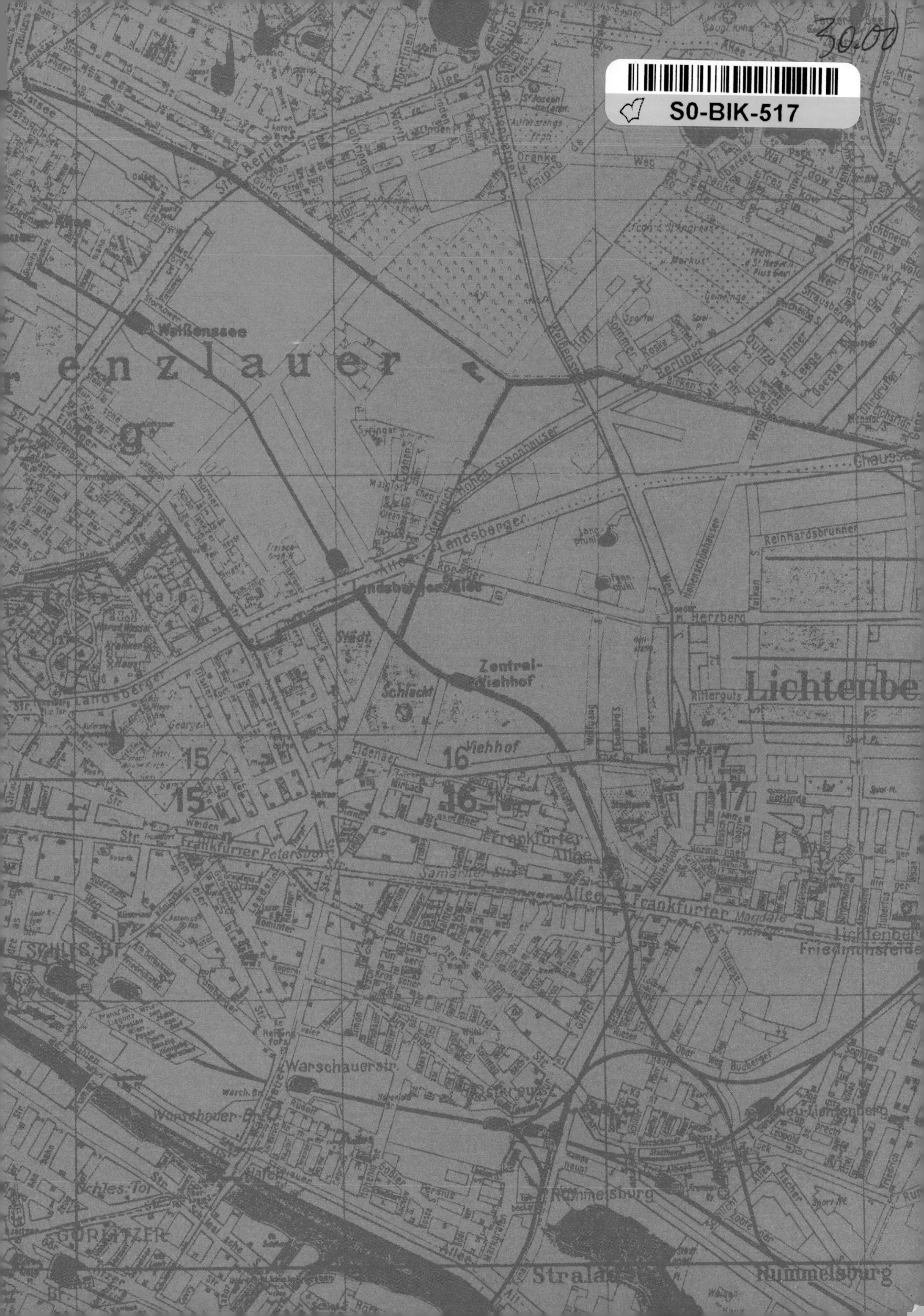
Weißensee
enzlauer
g
Landsberger Allee
Zentral-Viehhof
Schlacht
Viehhof
Lichtenbe
Reinhardsbrunner
Herzberg
Chaussee
15
16
17
Frankfurter Allee
Samariter Str.
Warschauer Str.
Warschauer Br.
Neu-Lichtenberg
Rummelsburg
Stralau
Schles. Tor
Görlitzer

Berlin

CITY OF LIGHT

a work of fiction by
JASON LUTES

Berlin: City of Light was originally serialized in the comic book **Berlin**, in issues
17 through 22, published by Drawn & Quarterly.

The previous two volumes of this trilogy, **Berlin (Book One): City of Stones** and
Berlin (Book Two): City of Smoke, are available in many fine book and comic stores
or direct from the publisher's website.

Publication design: Michel Vrána and Jason Lutes.
The photograph appearing on pages 150–151 was taken by Lena Ganssmann.

ISBN 978-1-77046-327-1
First edition: September 2018
Printed in China
10 9 8 7 6 5 4 3 2 1

Cataloging data available from Library and Archives Canada.

Published in the USA by Drawn & Quarterly, a client publisher of
Farrar, Straus and Giroux
Orders: 888.330.8477

Published in the Canada by Drawn & Quarterly, a client publisher of
Raincoast Books
Orders: 800.663.5714

Published in the UK by Drawn & Quarterly, a client publisher of
Publishers Group UK
Orders: info@pguk.co.uk

drawnandquarterly.com

Berlin

BOOK THREE

1

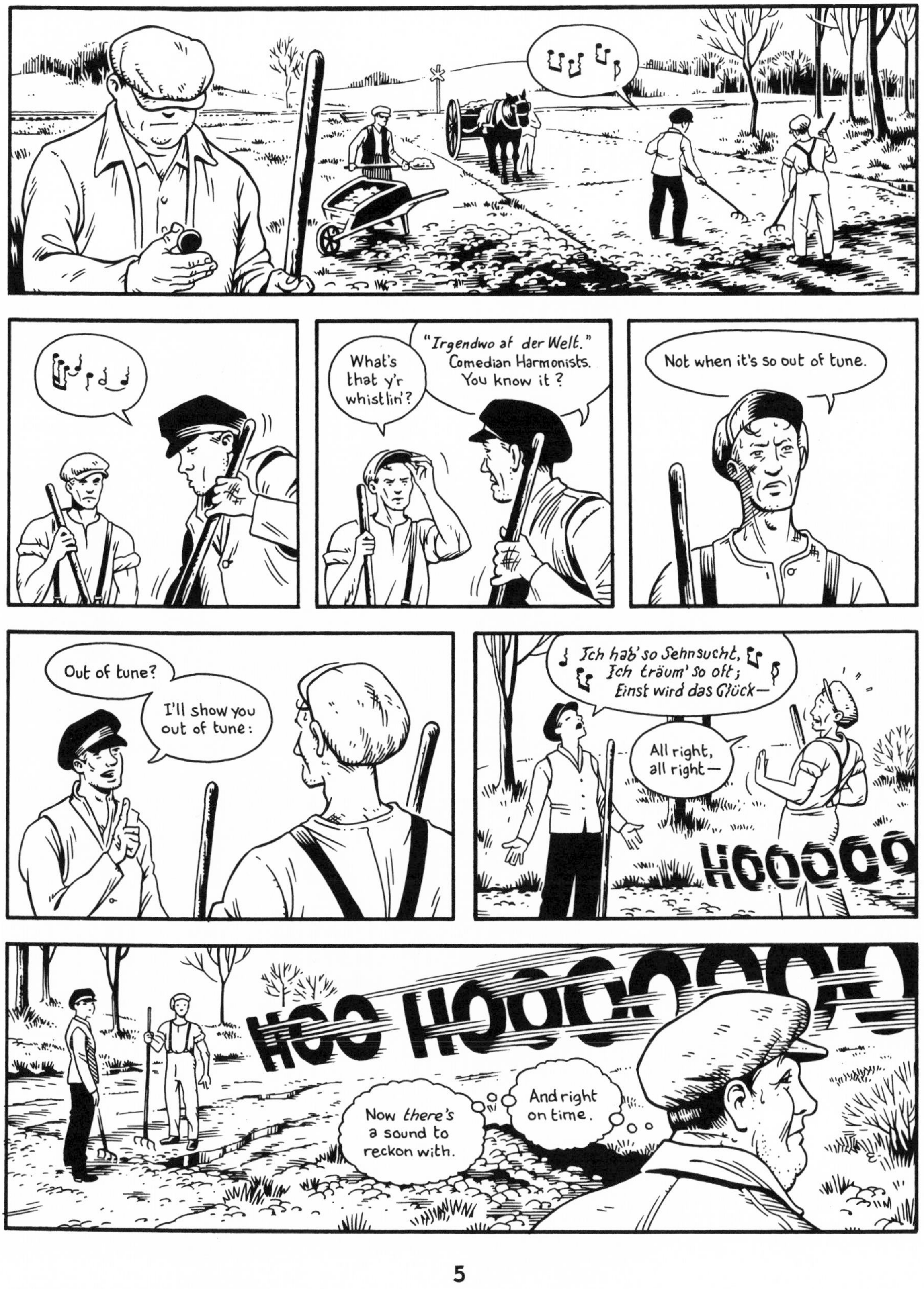
What's that y'r whistlin'?
"Irgendwo af der Welt." Comedian Harmonists. You know it?
Not when it's so out of tune.
Out of tune?
I'll show you out of tune:
Ich hab' so Sehnsucht, Ich träum' so oft; Einst wird das Glück—
All right, all right—
HOOOOO
HOO HOOOOOOO
Now *there's* a sound to reckon with.
And right on time.

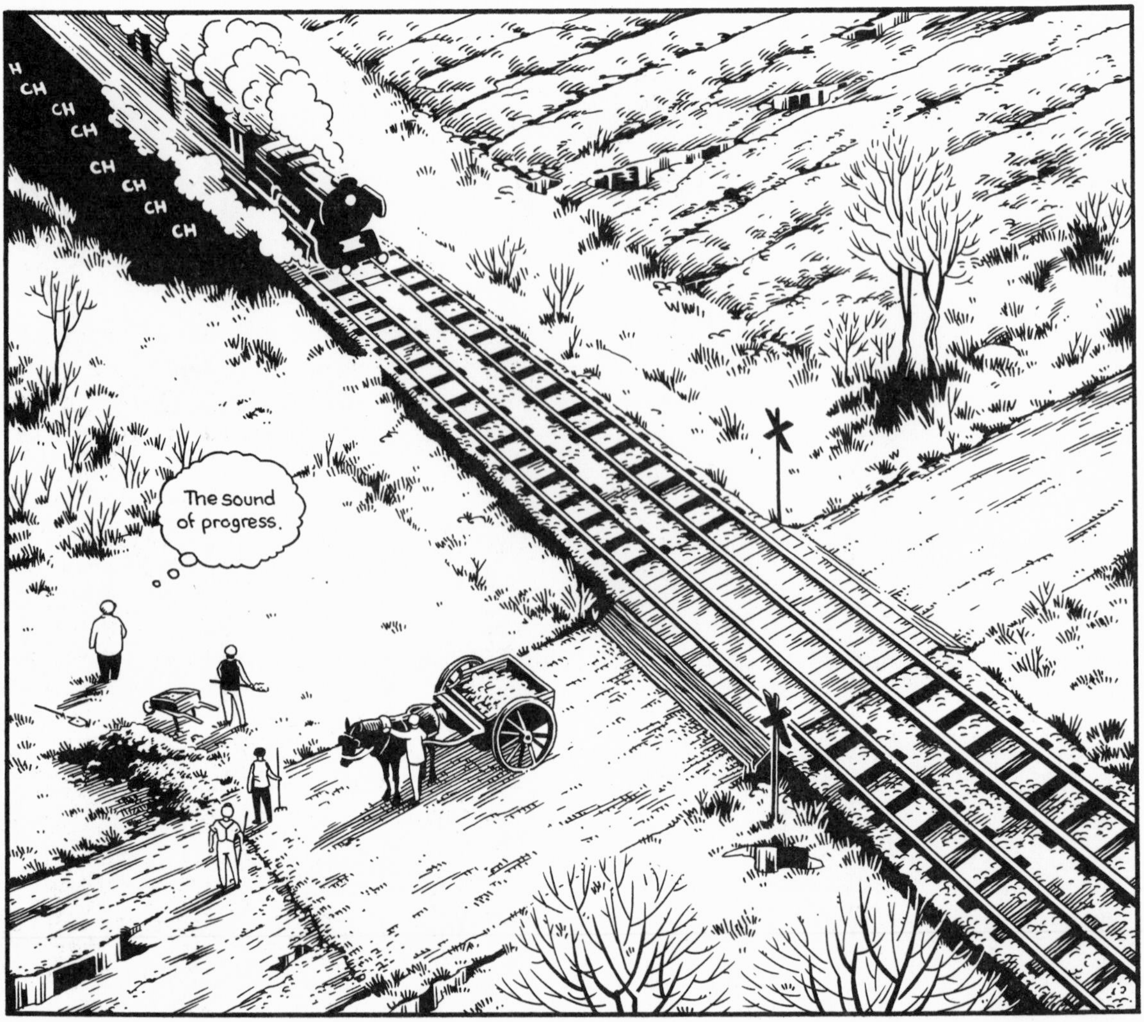
H
CH
CH
CH
CH
CH
CH
CH
The sound of progress.

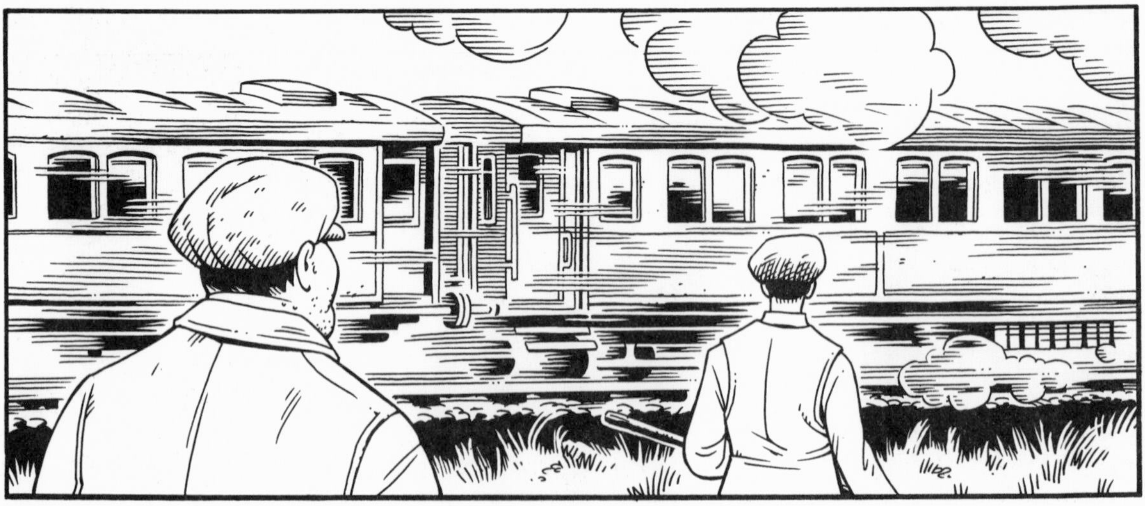

CH CH CH CH CH CH CH CH CH CH CH CH
CH CH CH
CH CH CH
CH CH CH
RAP
RAP
RAP
CH CH CH CH CH CH CH CH CH CH CH CH

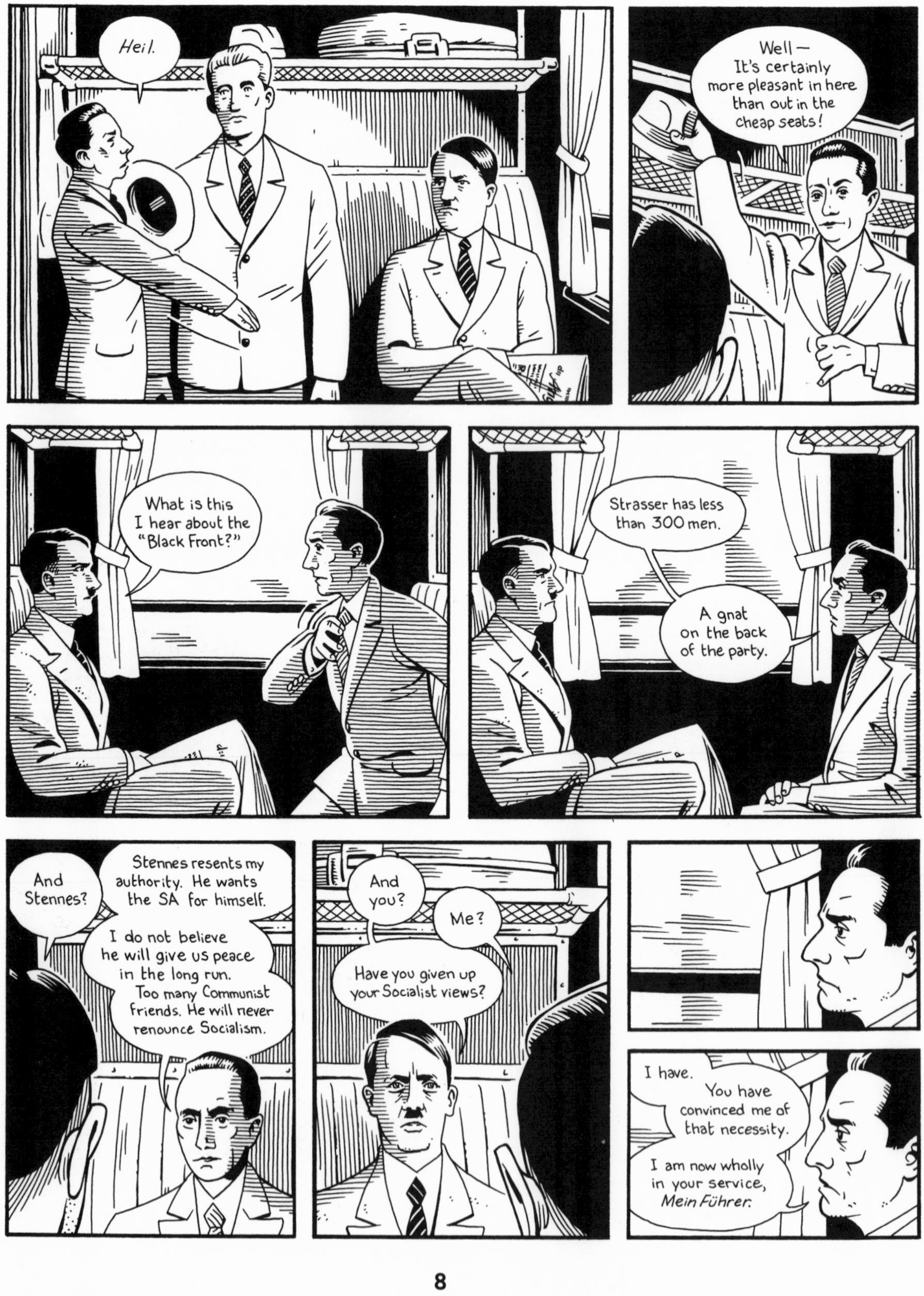
Heil.
Well — It's certainly more pleasant in here than out in the cheap seats!
What is this I hear about the "Black Front?"
Strasser has less than 300 men.
A gnat on the back of the party.
And Stennes?
Stennes resents my authority. He wants the SA for himself.
I do not believe he will give us peace in the long run.
Too many Communist friends. He will never renounce Socialism.
And you?
Me?
Have you given up your Socialist views?
I have.
You have convinced me of that necessity.
I am now wholly in your service, *Mein Führer.*

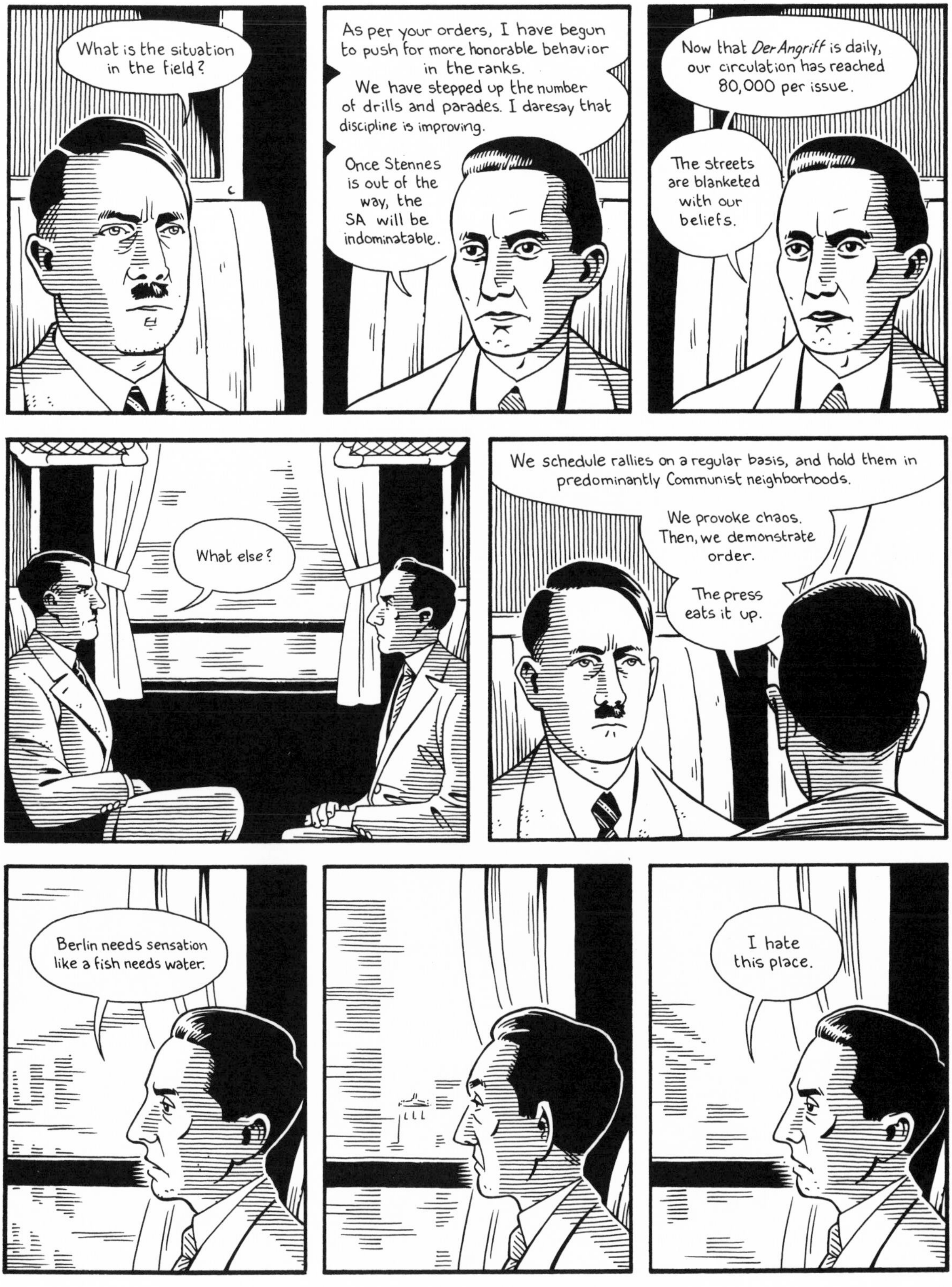
What is the situation in the field?
As per your orders, I have begun to push for more honorable behavior in the ranks. We have stepped up the number of drills and parades. I daresay that discipline is improving.
Once Stennes is out of the way, the SA will be indominatable.
Now that *Der Angriff* is daily, our circulation has reached 80,000 per issue.
The streets are blanketed with our beliefs.
What else?
We schedule rallies on a regular basis, and hold them in predominantly Communist neighborhoods.
We provoke chaos. Then, we demonstrate order.
The press eats it up.
Berlin needs sensation like a fish needs water.
I hate this place.

CITY OF LIGHT

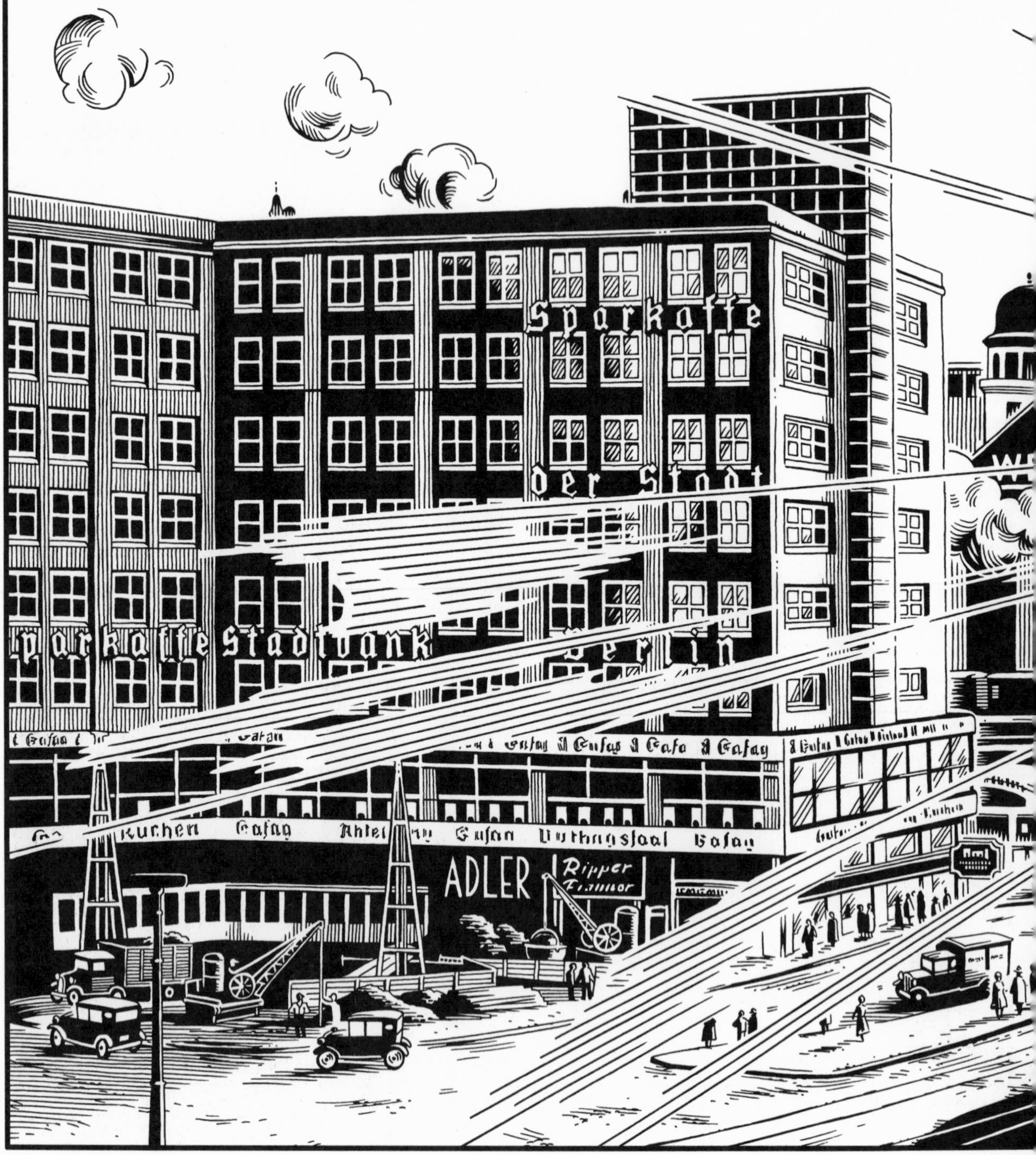

Sparkaffe
der Stadt
Kuchen
ADLER

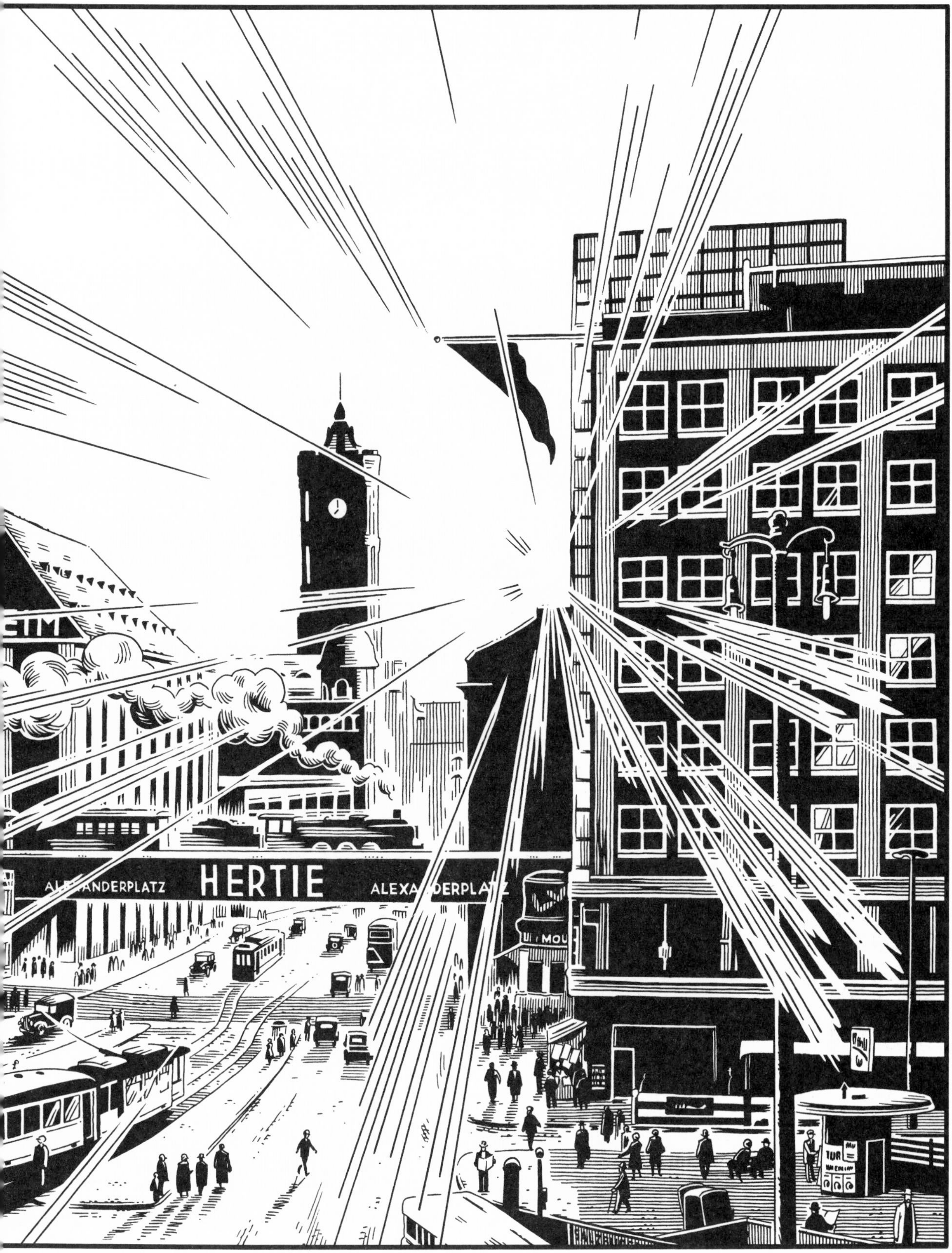

HERTIE
ALEXANDERPLATZ

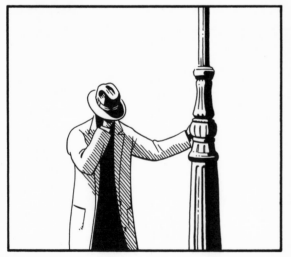

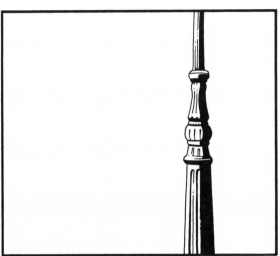

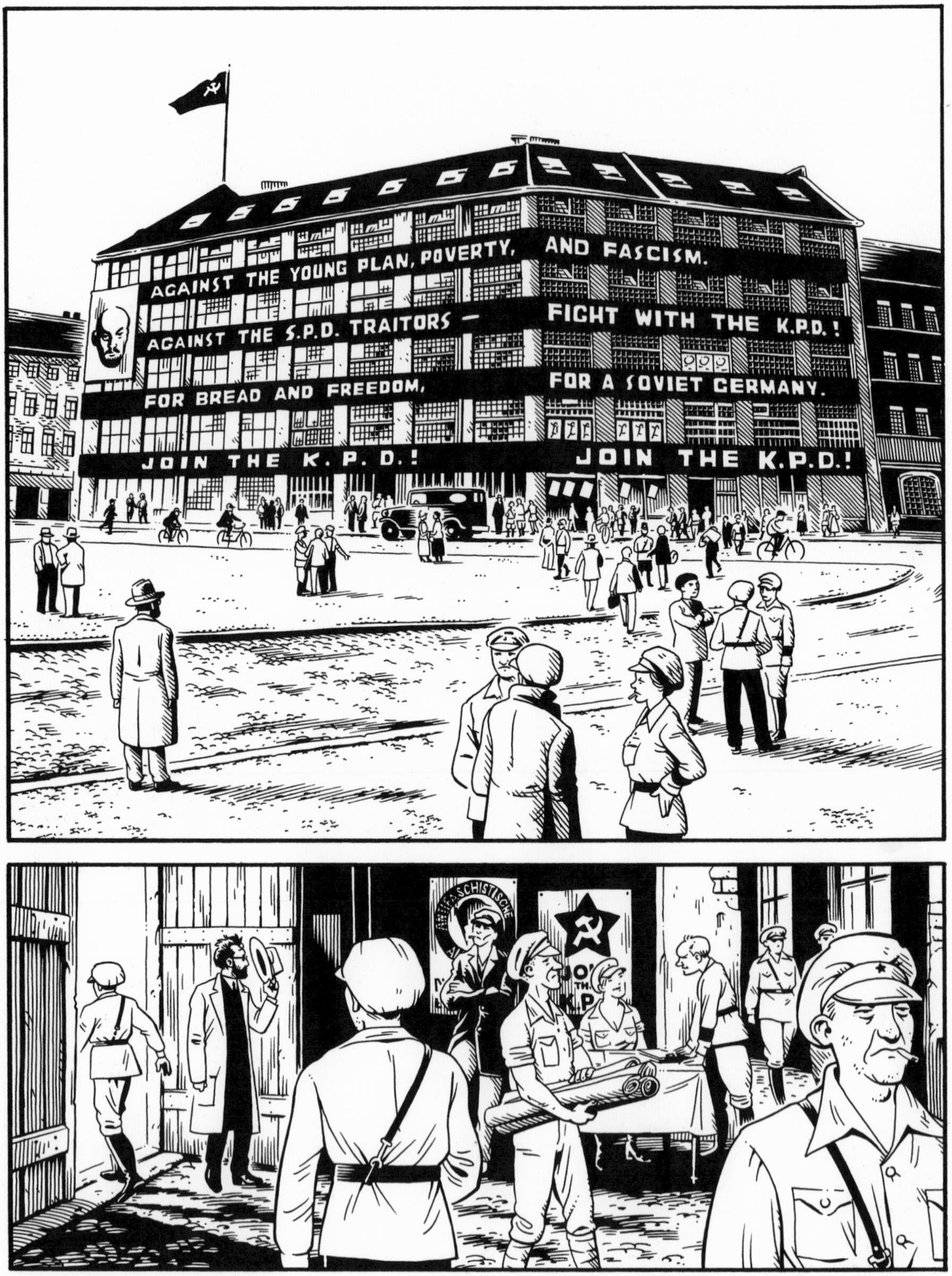
AGAINST THE YOUNG PLAN, POVERTY, AND FASCISM.
AGAINST THE S.P.D. TRAITORS — FIGHT WITH THE K.P.D.!
FOR BREAD AND FREEDOM, FOR A SOVIET GERMANY.
JOIN THE K.P.D.!
JOIN THE K.P.D.!

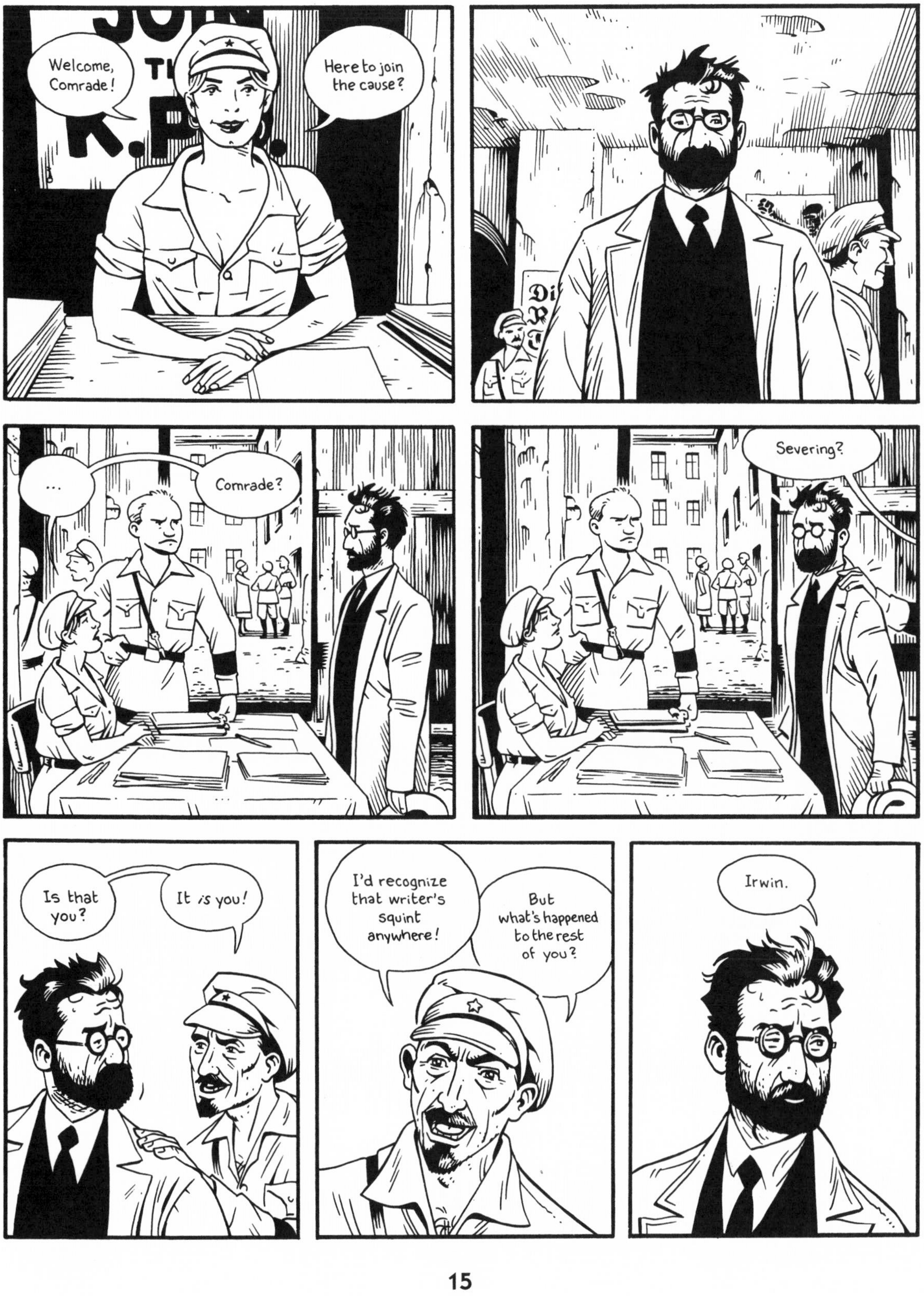
Welcome, Comrade!
Here to join the cause?
...
Comrade?
Severing?
Is that you?
It *is* you!
I'd recognize that writer's squint anywhere!
But what's happened to the rest of you?
Irwin.

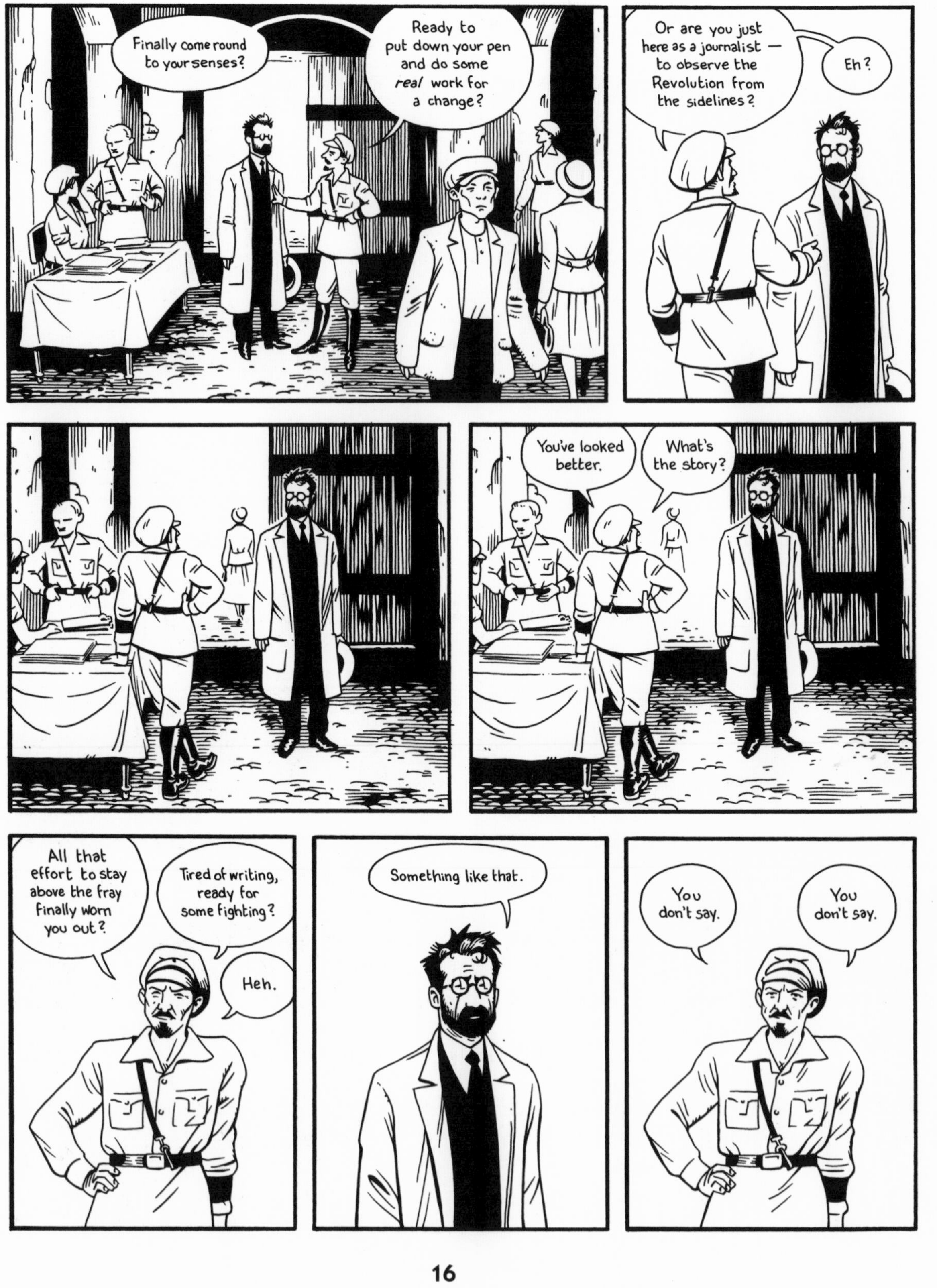
Finally come round to your senses?
Ready to put down your pen and do some *real* work for a change?
Or are you just here as a journalist — to observe the Revolution from the sidelines?
Eh?
You've looked better.
What's the story?
All that effort to stay above the fray finally worn you out?
Tired of writing, ready for some fighting?
Heh.
Something like that.
You don't say.
You don't say.

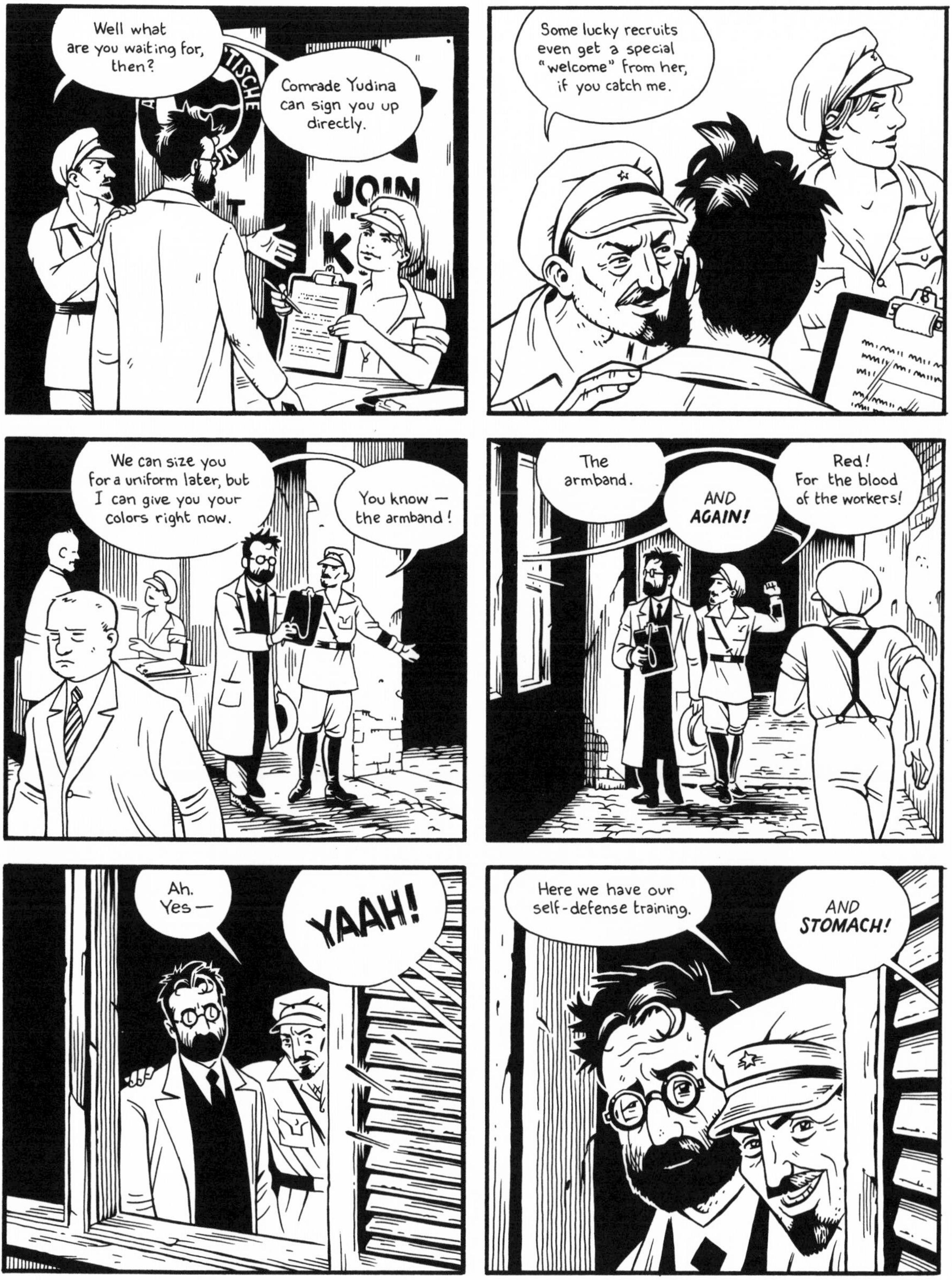
Well what are you waiting for, then?
Comrade Yudina can sign you up directly.
JOIN
Some lucky recruits even get a special "welcome" from her, if you catch me.
We can size you for a uniform later, but I can give you your colors right now.
You know — the armband!
The armband.
AND AGAIN!
Red! For the blood of the workers!
Ah. Yes —
YAAH!
Here we have our self-defense training.
AND STOMACH!

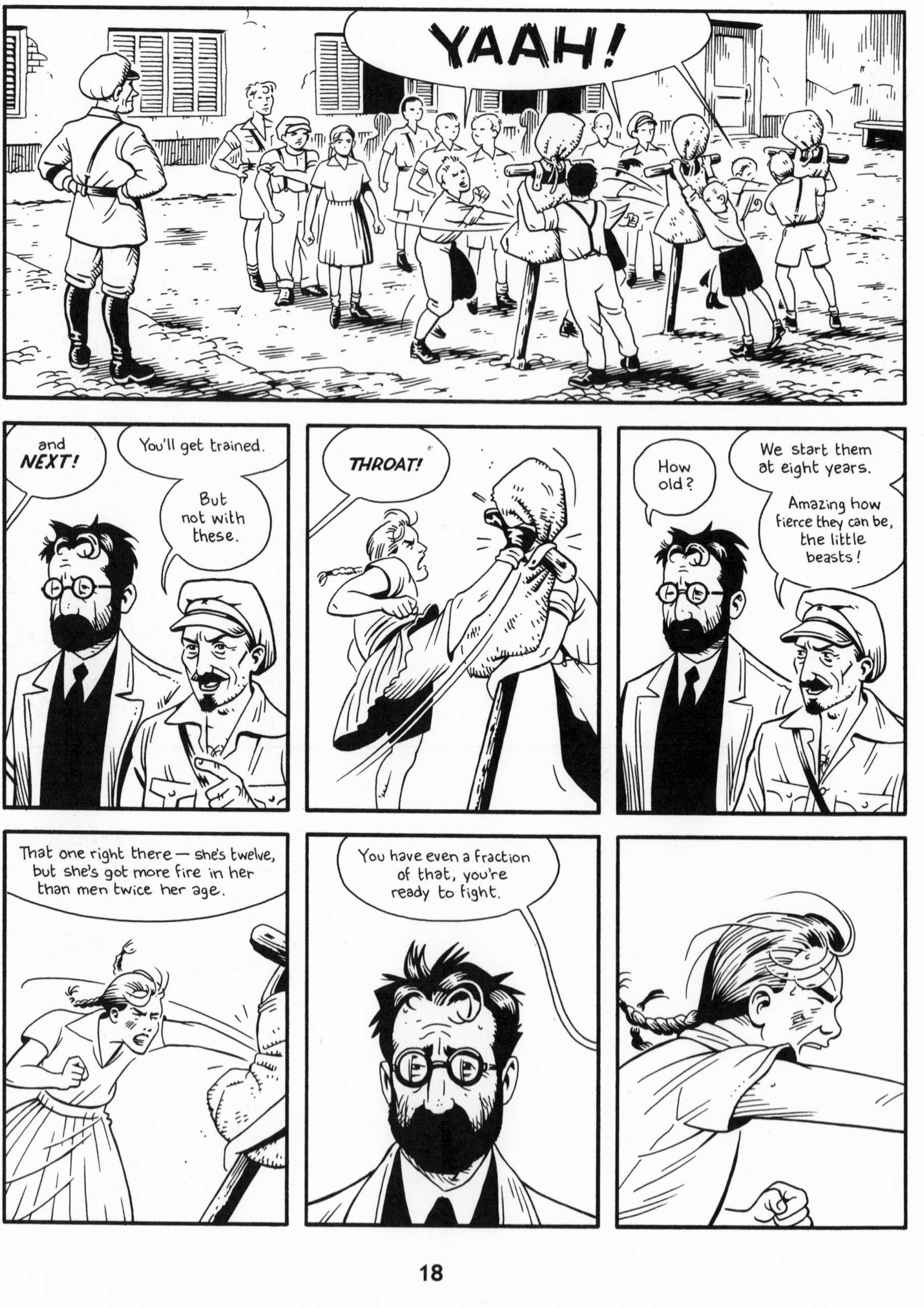
YAAH!
and NEXT!
You'll get trained.
But not with these.
THROAT!
How old?
We start them at eight years.
Amazing how fierce they can be, the little beasts!
That one right there — she's twelve, but she's got more fire in her than men twice her age.
You have even a fraction of that, you're ready to fight.

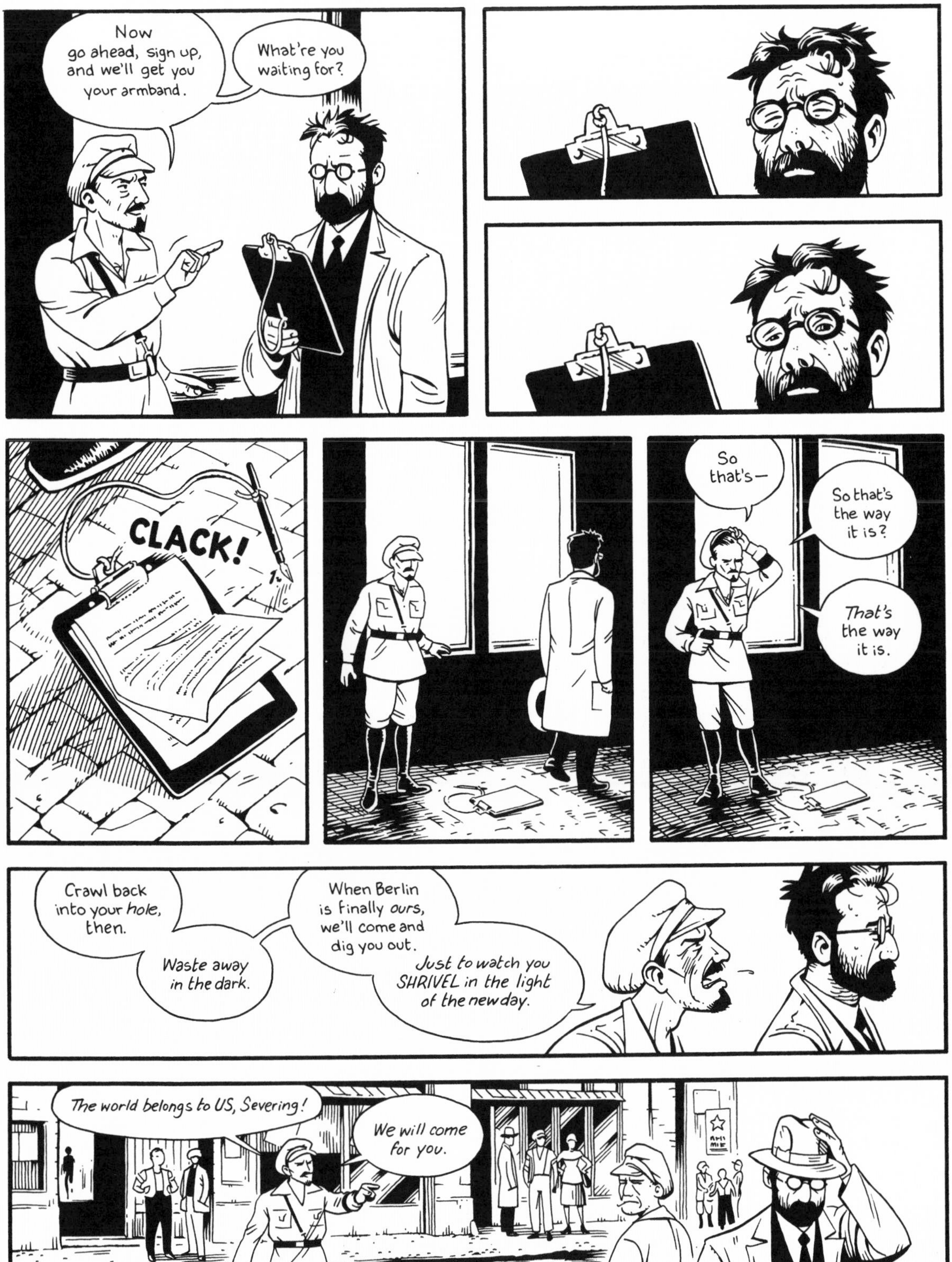
Now go ahead, sign up, and we'll get you your armband.
What're you waiting for?
CLACK!
So that's—
So that's the way it is?
That's the way it is.
Crawl back into your hole, then.
Waste away in the dark.
When Berlin is finally ours, we'll come and dig you out.
Just to watch you SHRIVEL in the light of the new day.
The world belongs to US, Severing!
We will come for you.

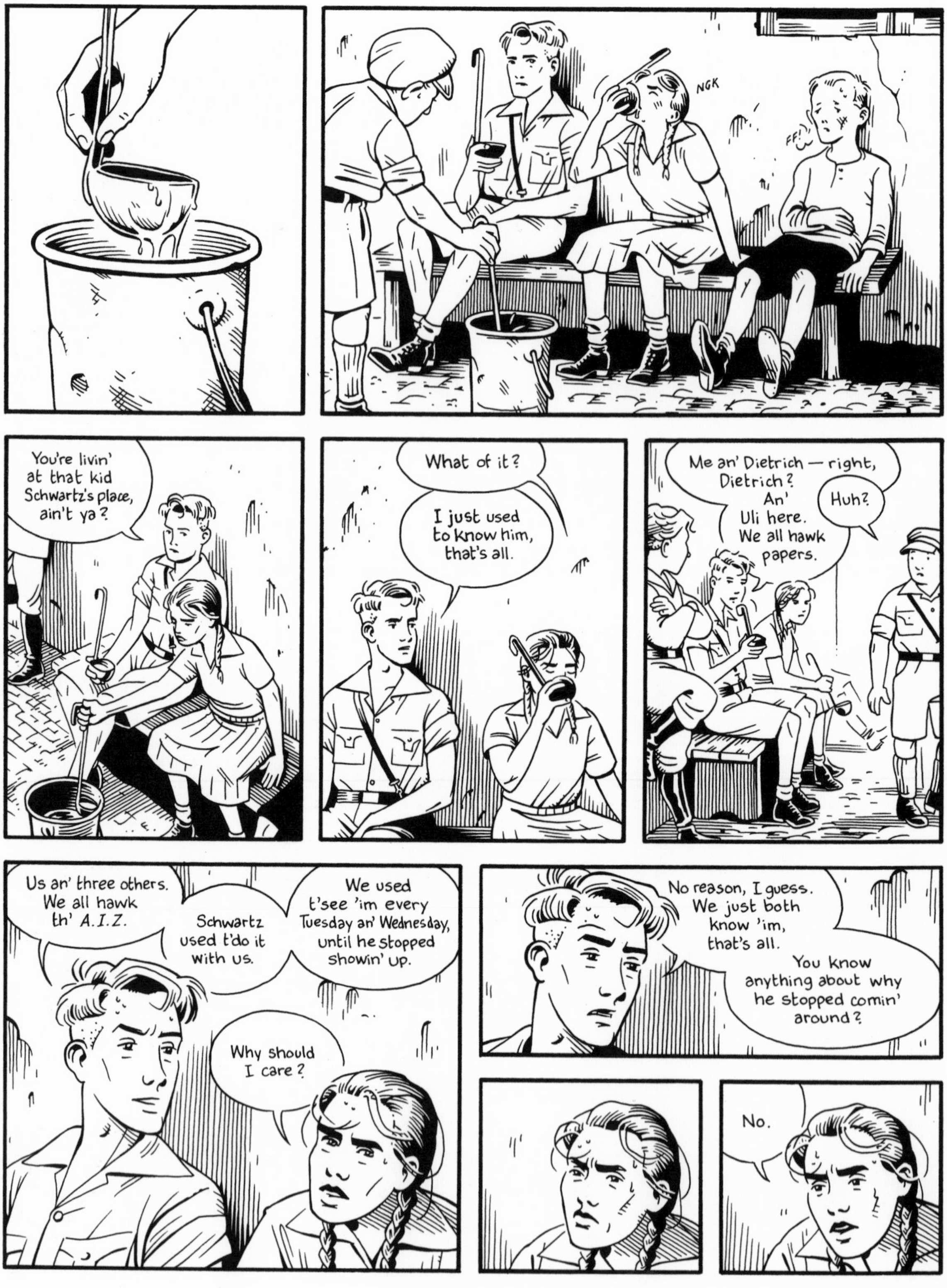
NGK
FF!
You're livin' at that kid Schwartz's place, ain't ya?
What of it?
I just used to know him, that's all.
Me an' Dietrich — right, Dietrich? An' Uli here. We all hawk papers.
Huh?
Us an' three others. We all hawk th' A.I.Z.
Schwartz used t'do it with us.
We used t'see 'im every Tuesday an' Wednesday, until he stopped showin' up.
Why should I care?
No reason, I guess. We just both know 'im, that's all.
You know anything about why he stopped comin' around?
No.

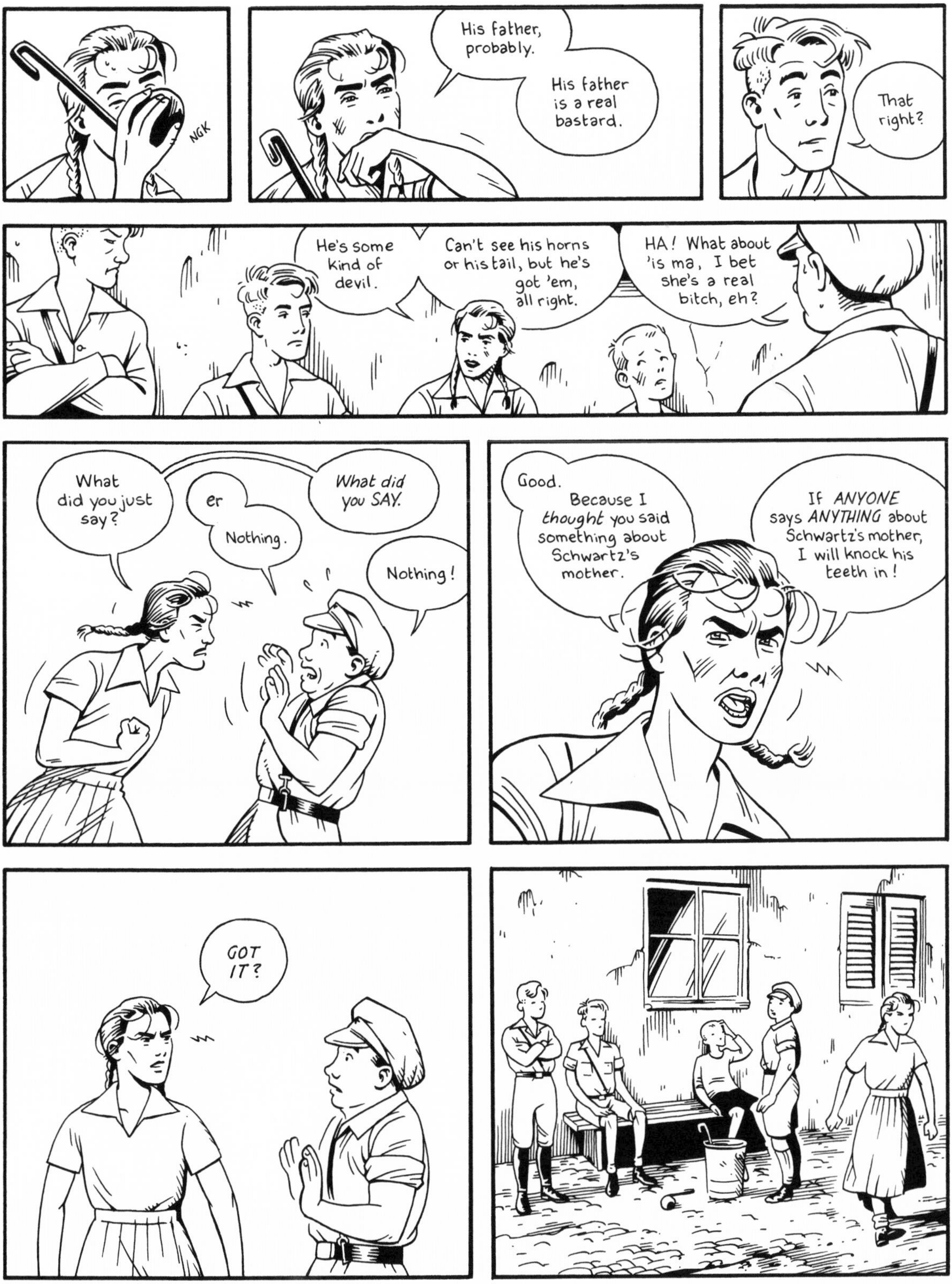
NGK
His father, probably.
His father is a real bastard.
That right?
He's some kind of devil.
Can't see his horns or his tail, but he's got 'em, all right.
HA! What about 'is ma, I bet she's a real bitch, eh?
What did you just say?
er
Nothing.
What did you SAY.
Nothing!
Good.
Because I thought you said something about Schwartz's mother.
If ANYONE says ANYTHING about Schwartz's mother, I will knock his teeth in!
GOT IT?

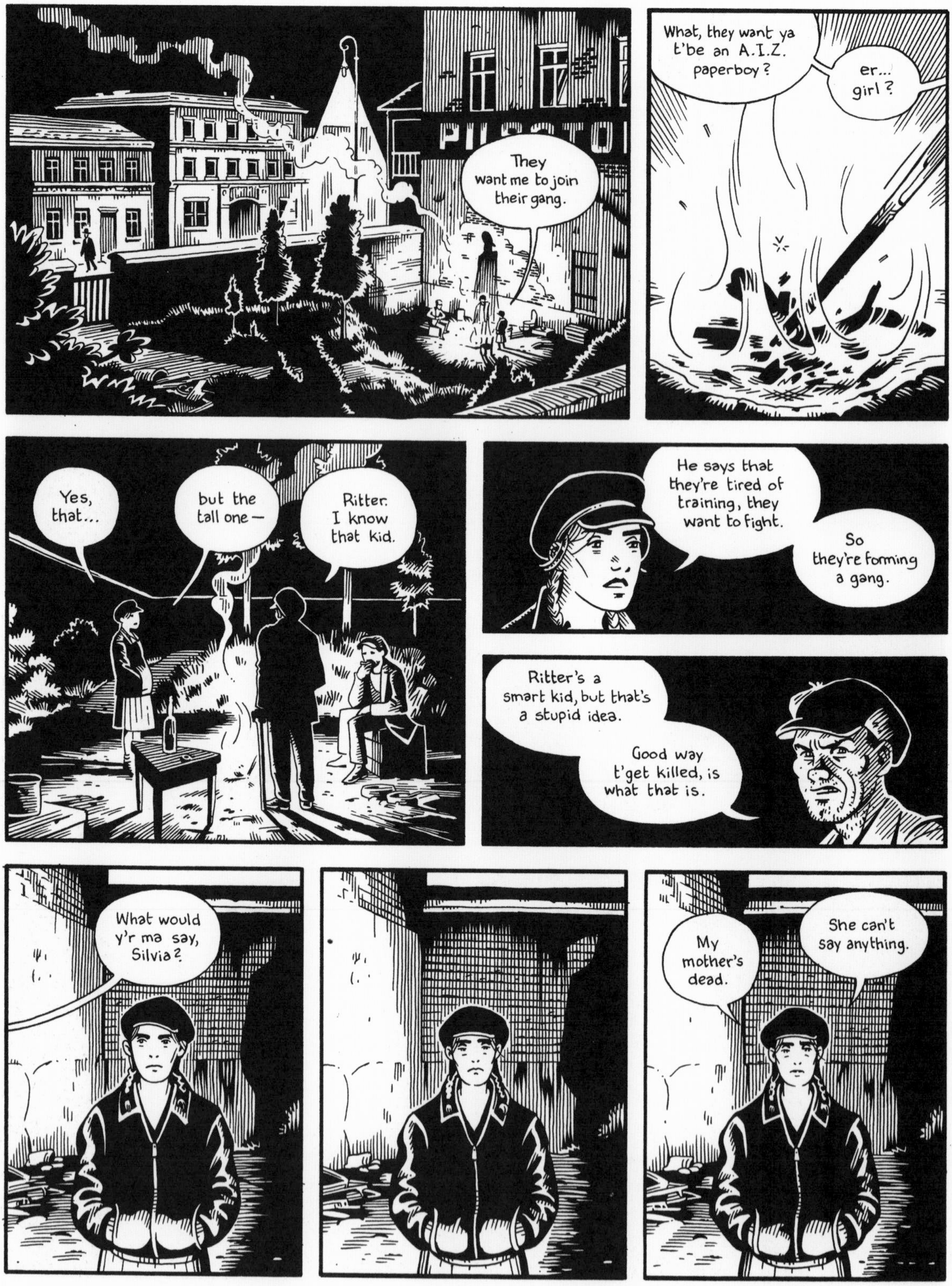
They want me to join their gang.
What, they want ya t'be an A.I.Z. paperboy?
er... girl?
Yes, that...
but the tall one—
Ritter. I know that kid.
He says that they're tired of training, they want to fight.
So they're forming a gang.
Ritter's a smart kid, but that's a stupid idea.
Good way t'get killed, is what that is.
What would y'r ma say, Silvia?
My mother's dead.
She can't say anything.

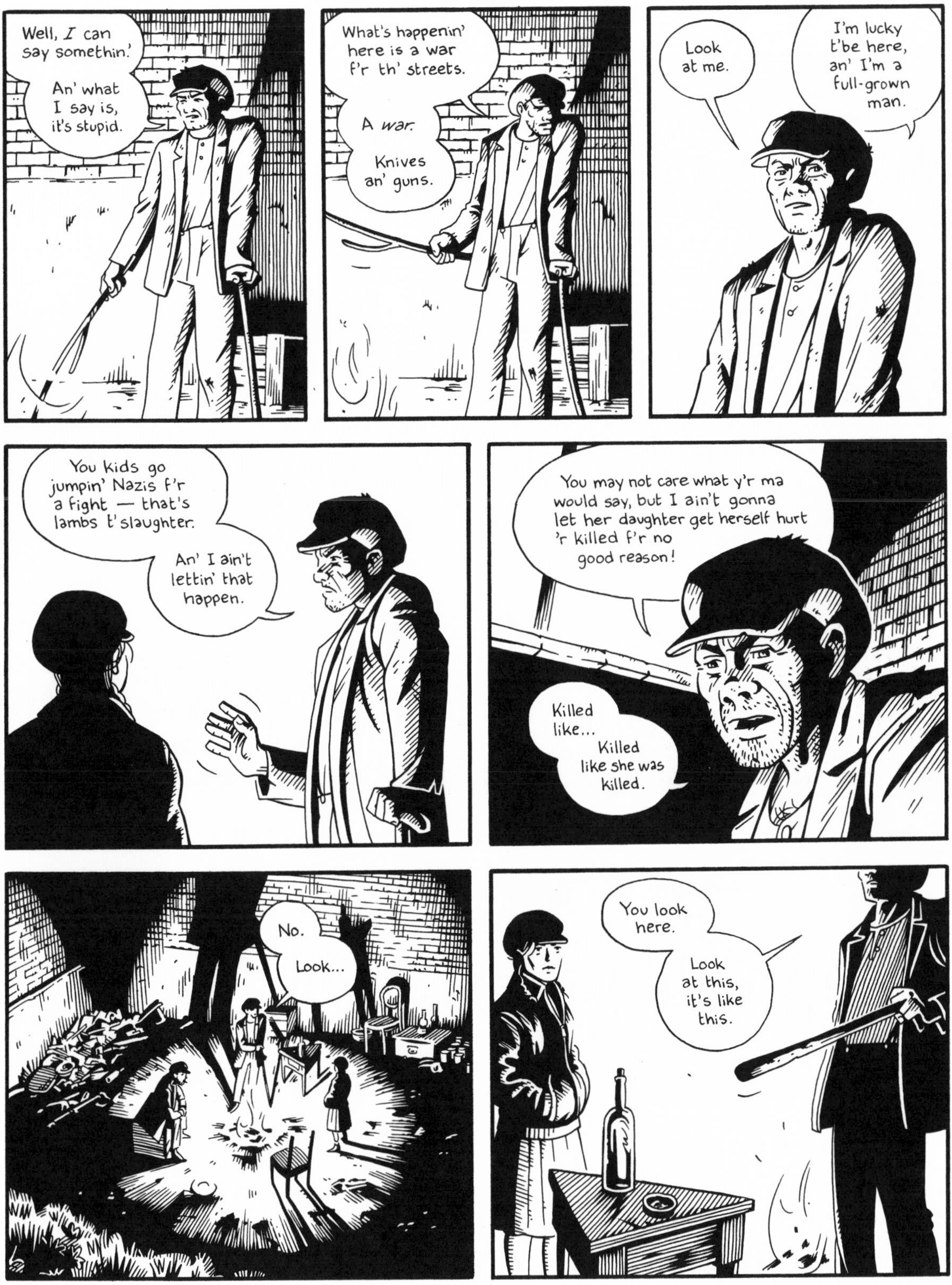
Well, *I* can say somethin.'
An' what I say is, it's stupid.
What's happenin' here is a war f'r th' streets.
A *war.*
Knives an' guns.
Look at me.
I'm lucky t'be here, an' I'm a full-grown man.
You kids go jumpin' Nazis f'r a fight — that's lambs t'slaughter.
An' I ain't lettin' that happen.
You may not care what y'r ma would say, but I ain't gonna let her daughter get herself hurt 'r killed f'r no good reason!
Killed like...
Killed like she was killed.
No.
Look...
You look here.
Look at this, it's like this.

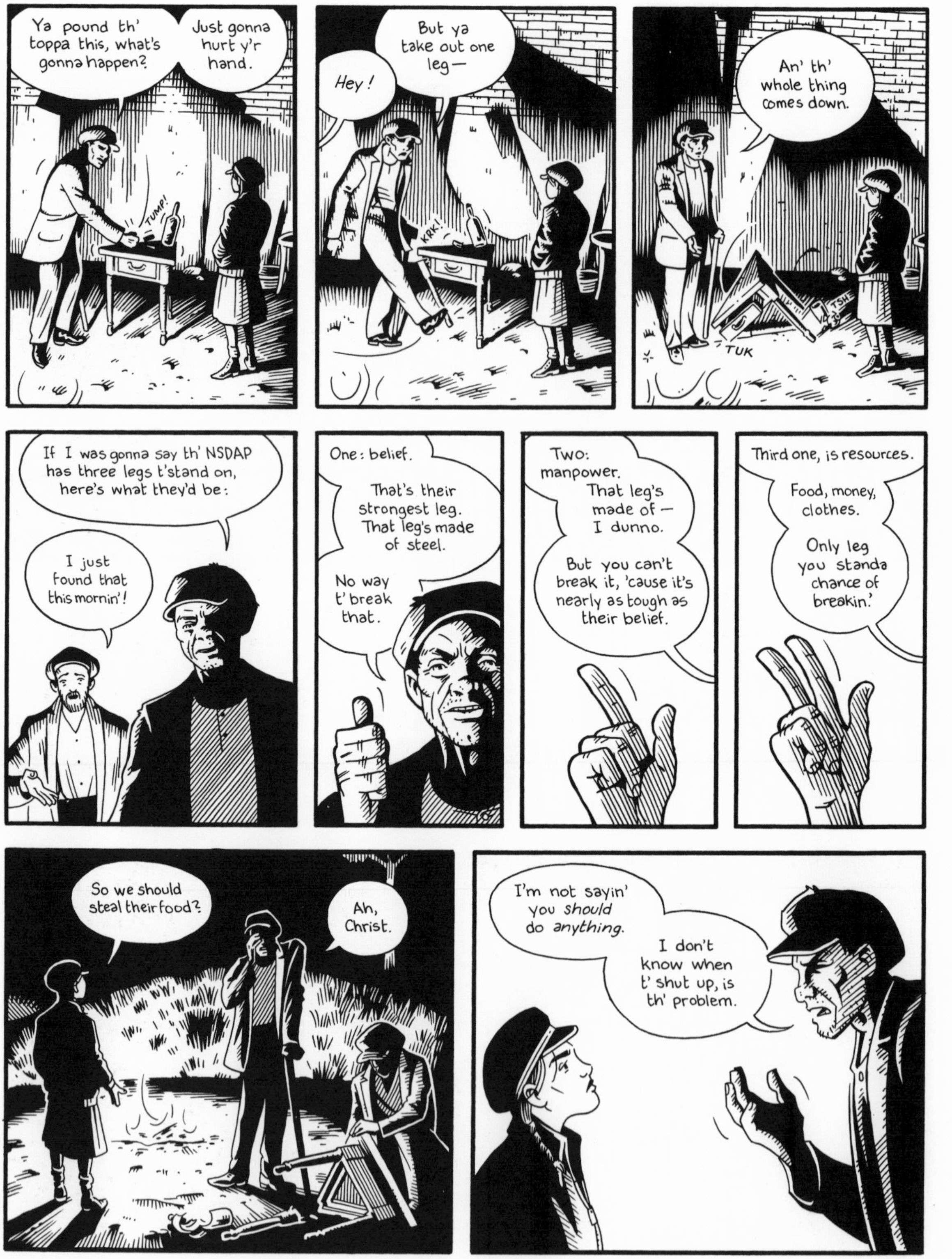
Ya pound th' toppa this, what's gonna happen?
Just gonna hurt y'r hand.
TUMP!
Hey!
But ya take out one leg—
KRK!
An' th' whole thing comes down.
TSH
TUK
If I was gonna say th' NSDAP has three legs t'stand on, here's what they'd be:
I just found that this mornin'!
One: belief.
That's their strongest leg. That leg's made of steel.
No way t' break that.
Two: manpower.
That leg's made of— I dunno.
But you can't break it, 'cause it's nearly as tough as their belief.
Third one, is resources.
Food, money, clothes.
Only leg you standa chance of breakin.'
So we should steal their food?
Ah, Christ.
I'm not sayin' you *should* do *anything*.
I don't know when t' shut up, is th' problem.

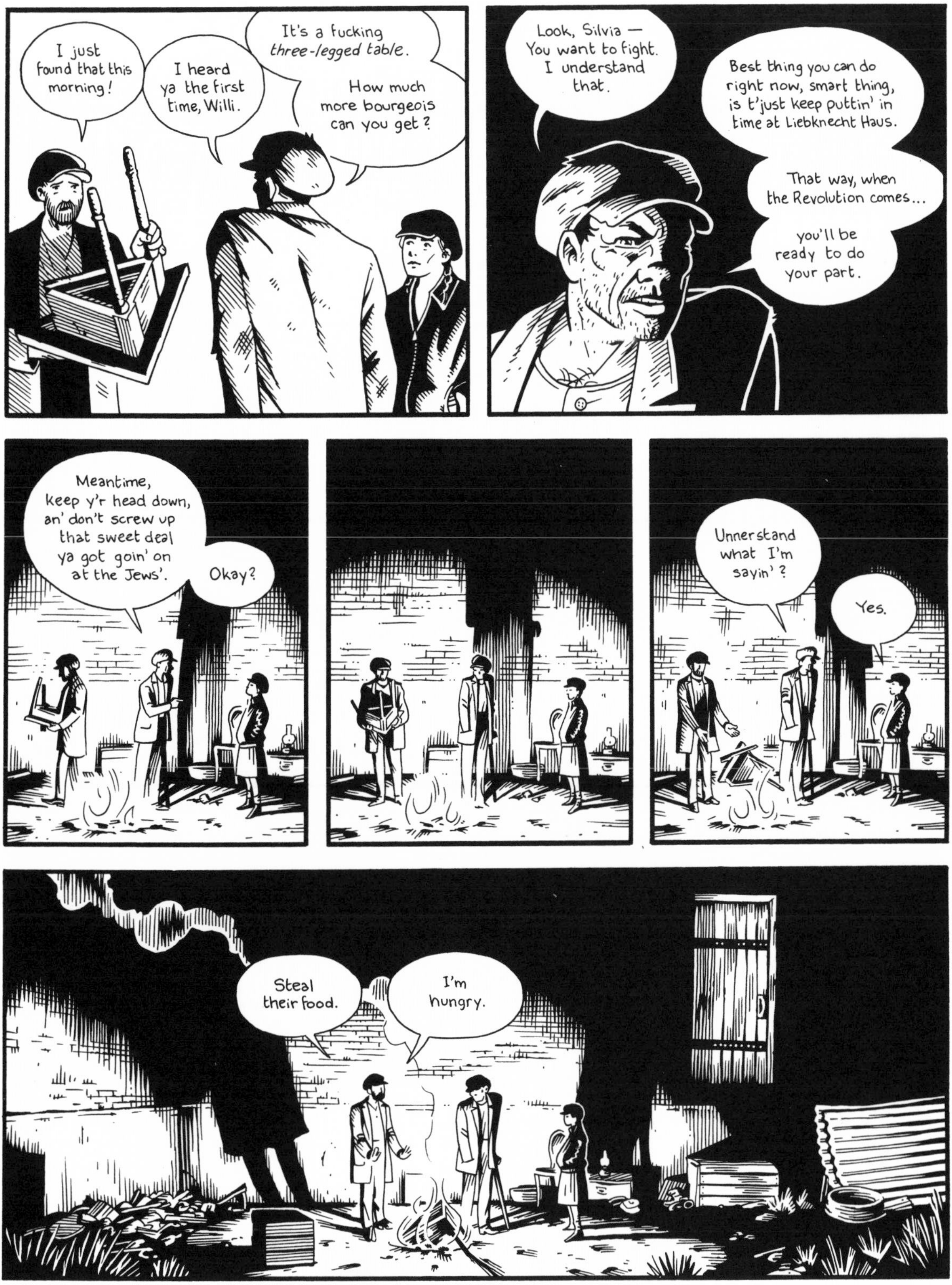
I just found that this morning!
I heard ya the first time, Willi.
It's a fucking *three-legged table*.
How much more bourgeois can you get?
Look, Silvia — You want to fight. I understand that.
Best thing you can do right now, smart thing, is t'just keep puttin' in time at Liebknecht Haus.
That way, when the Revolution comes...
you'll be ready to do your part.
Meantime, keep y'r head down, an' don't screw up that sweet deal ya got goin' on at the Jews'.
Okay?
Unnerstand what I'm sayin'?
Yes.
Steal their food.
I'm hungry.

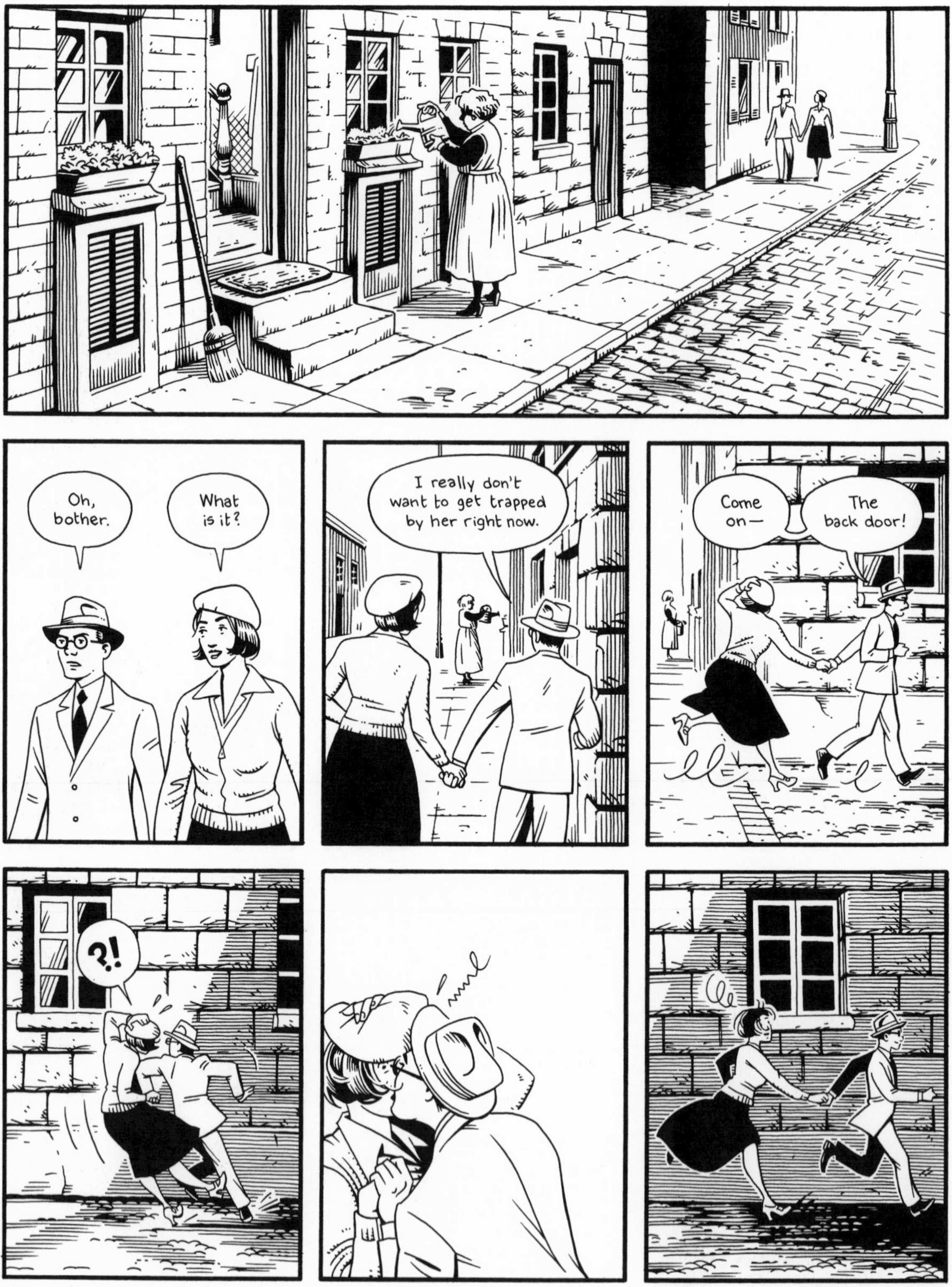
Oh, bother.
What is it?
I really don't want to get trapped by her right now.
Come on—
The back door!
?!

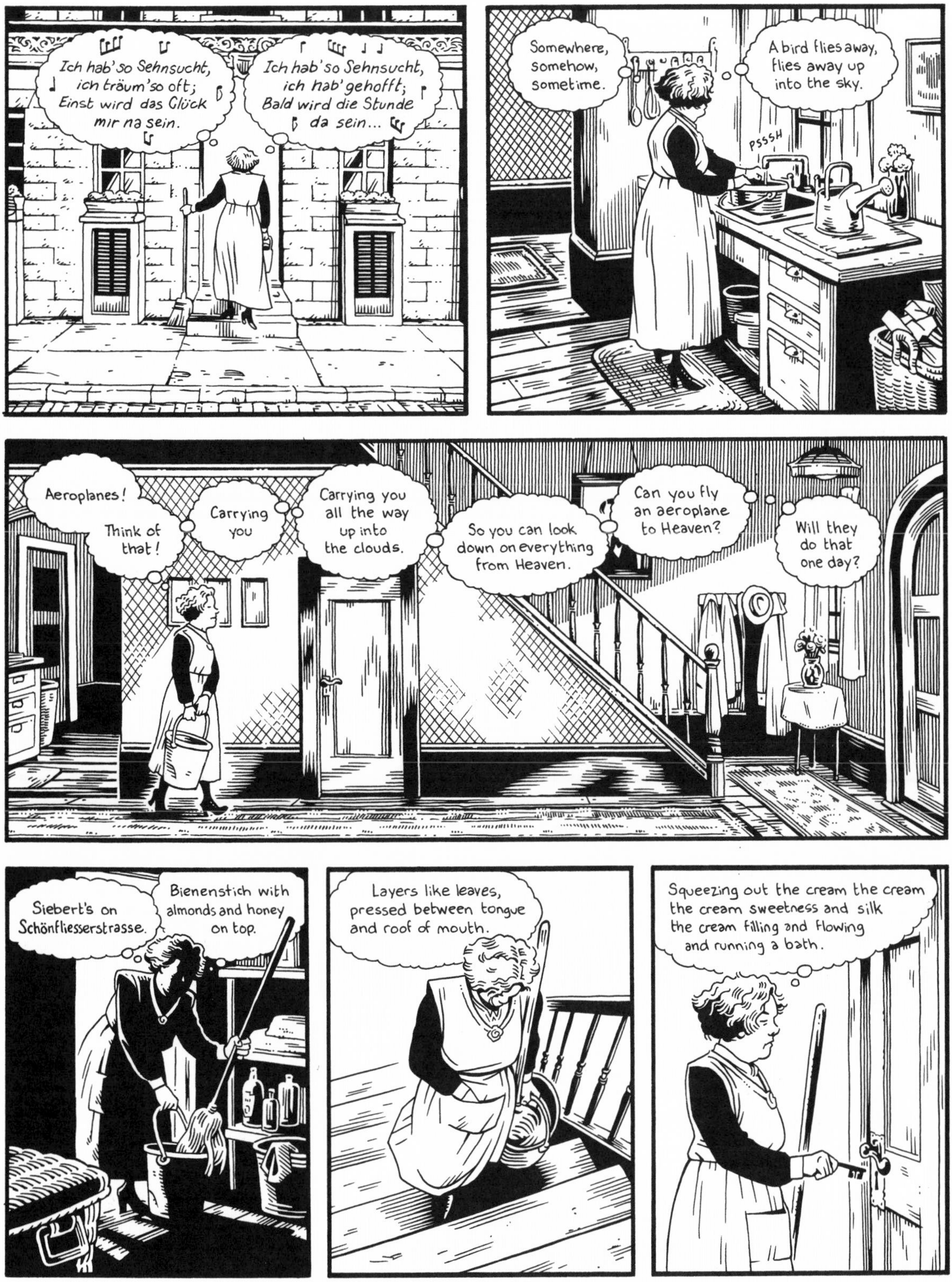
Ich hab' so Sehnsucht, ich träum' so oft; Einst wird das Glück mir na sein.
Ich hab' so Sehnsucht, ich hab' gehofft; Bald wird die Stunde da sein...
Somewhere, somehow, sometime.
A bird flies away, flies away up into the sky.
PSSSH
Aeroplanes!
Think of that!
Carrying you
Carrying you all the way up into the clouds.
So you can look down on everything from Heaven.
Can you fly an aeroplane to Heaven?
Will they do that one day?
Siebert's on Schönfliesserstrasse.
Bienenstich with almonds and honey on top.
Layers like leaves, pressed between tongue and roof of mouth.
Squeezing out the cream the cream the cream sweetness and silk the cream filling and flowing and running a bath.

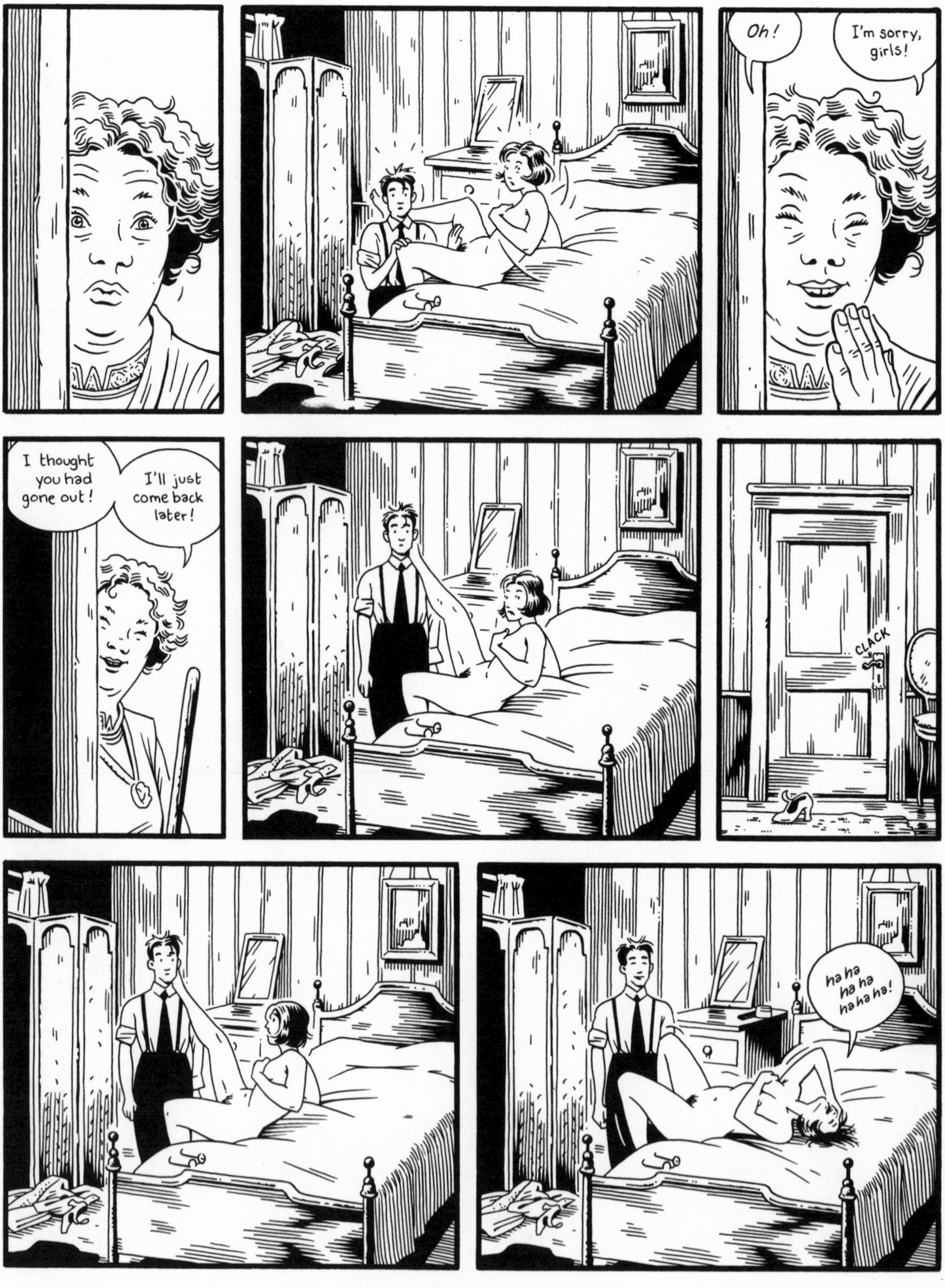
Oh!
I'm sorry, girls!
I thought you had gone out!
I'll just come back later!
CLACK
ha ha ha ha ha ha ha!

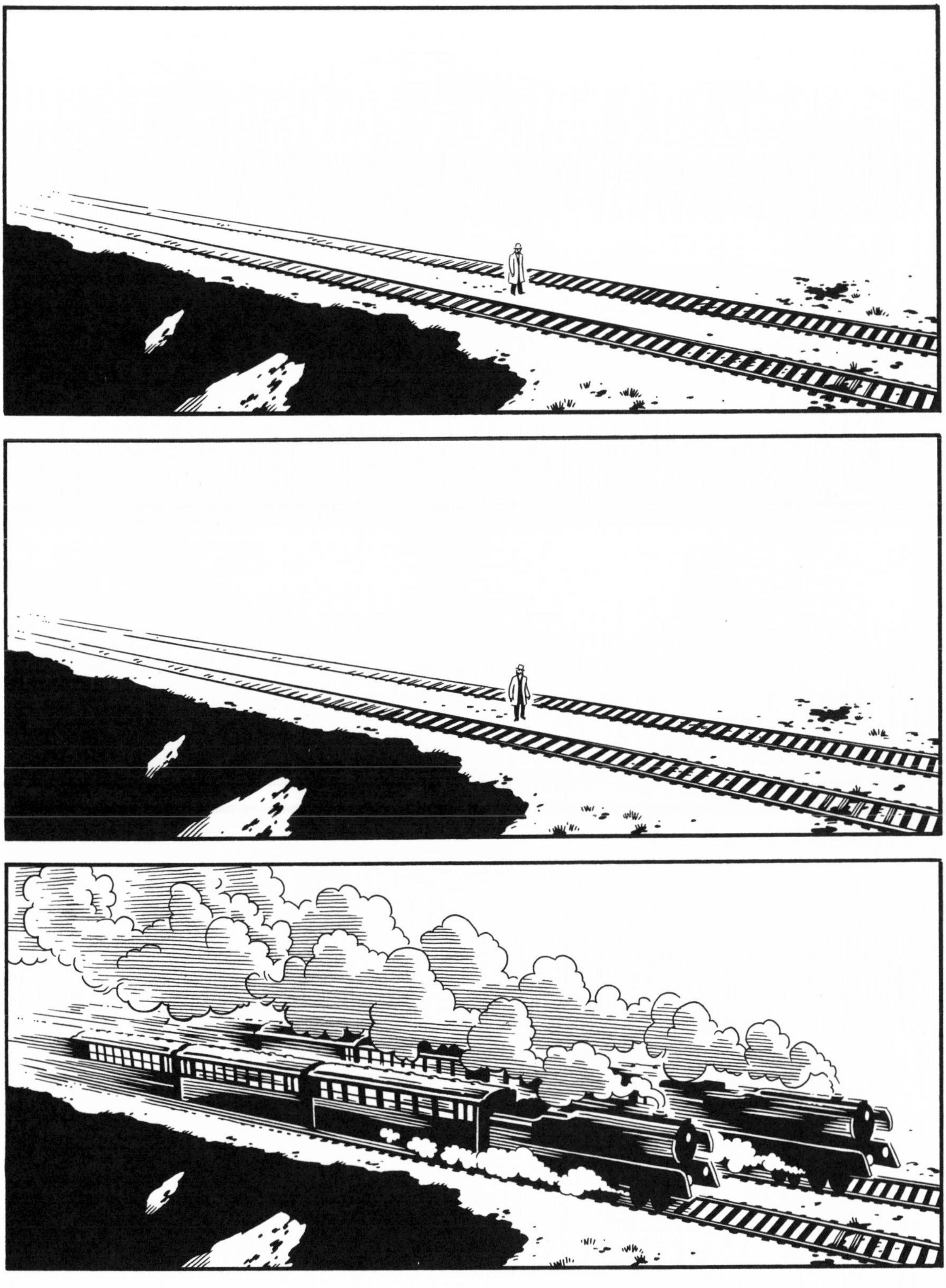

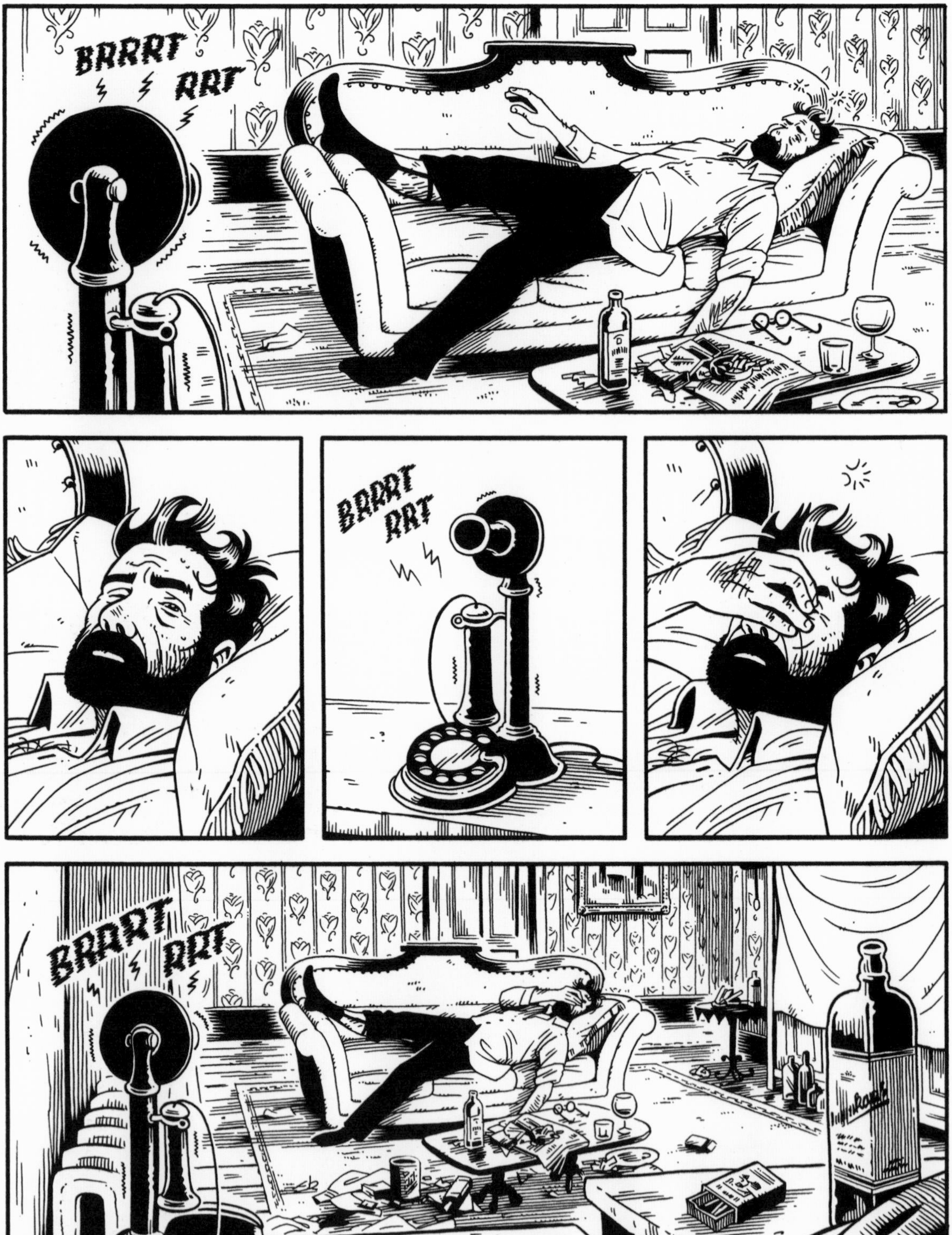
BRRRT RRT
BRRRT RRT
BRRRT RRT

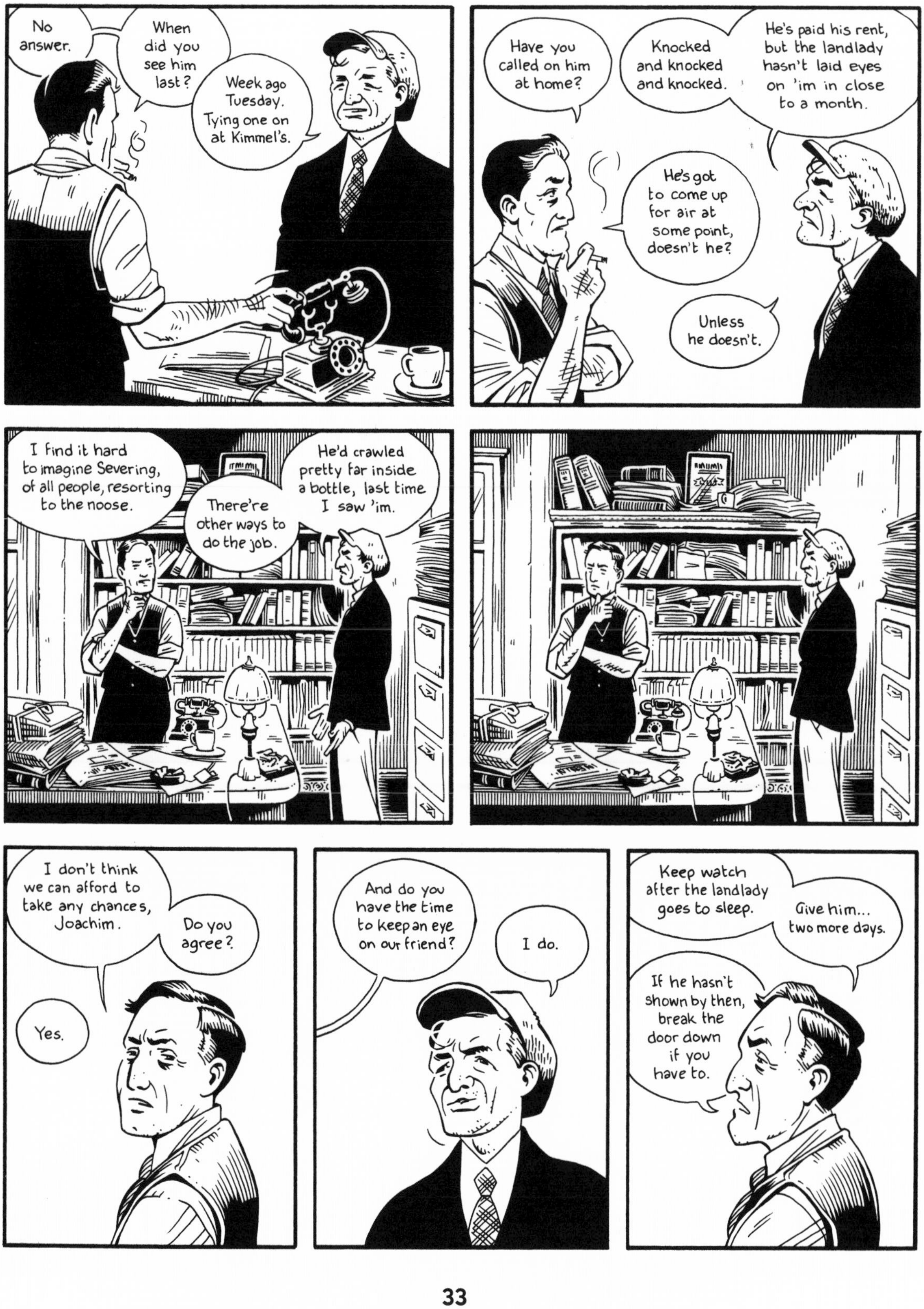
No answer.
When did you see him last?
Week ago Tuesday. Tying one on at Kimmel's.
Have you called on him at home?
Knocked and knocked and knocked.
He's paid his rent, but the landlady hasn't laid eyes on 'im in close to a month.
He's got to come up for air at some point, doesn't he?
Unless he doesn't.
I find it hard to imagine Severing, of all people, resorting to the noose.
There're other ways to do the job.
He'd crawled pretty far inside a bottle, last time I saw 'im.
I don't think we can afford to take any chances, Joachim.
Do you agree?
Yes.
And do you have the time to keep an eye on our friend?
I do.
Keep watch after the landlady goes to sleep.
Give him... two more days.
If he hasn't shown by then, break the door down if you have to.

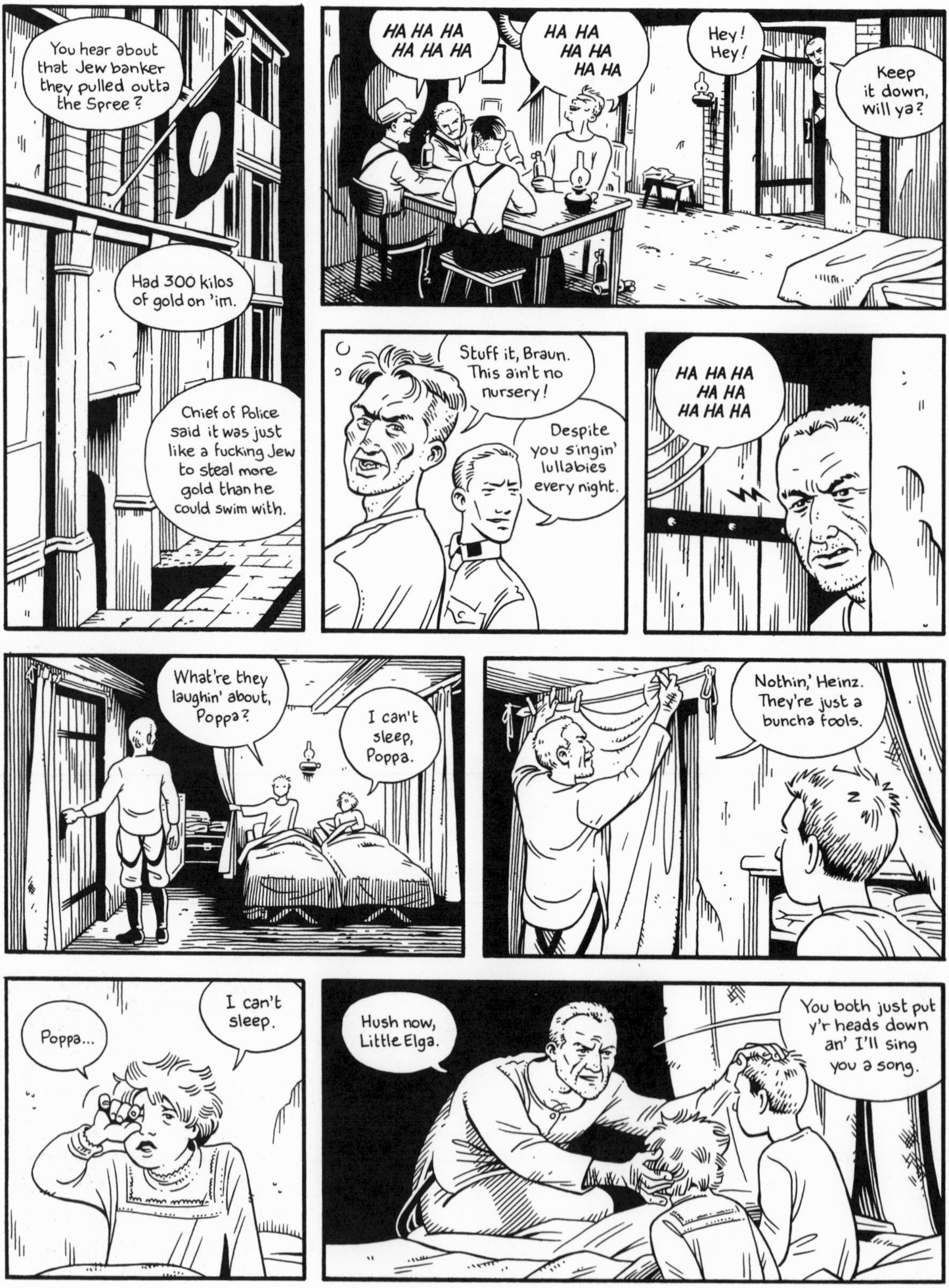
You hear about that Jew banker they pulled outta the Spree?
Had 300 kilos of gold on 'im.
Chief of Police said it was just like a fucking Jew to steal more gold than he could swim with.
HA HA HA HA HA HA
HA HA HA HA HA HA
Hey! Hey!
Keep it down, will ya?
Stuff it, Braun. This ain't no nursery!
Despite you singin' lullabies every night.
HA HA HA HA HA HA HA HA
What're they laughin' about, Poppa?
I can't sleep, Poppa.
Nothin', Heinz. They're just a buncha fools.
Poppa...
I can't sleep.
Hush now, Little Elga.
You both just put y'r heads down an' I'll sing you a song.

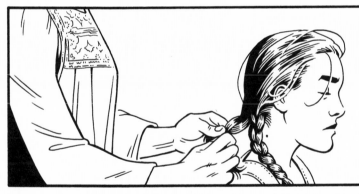

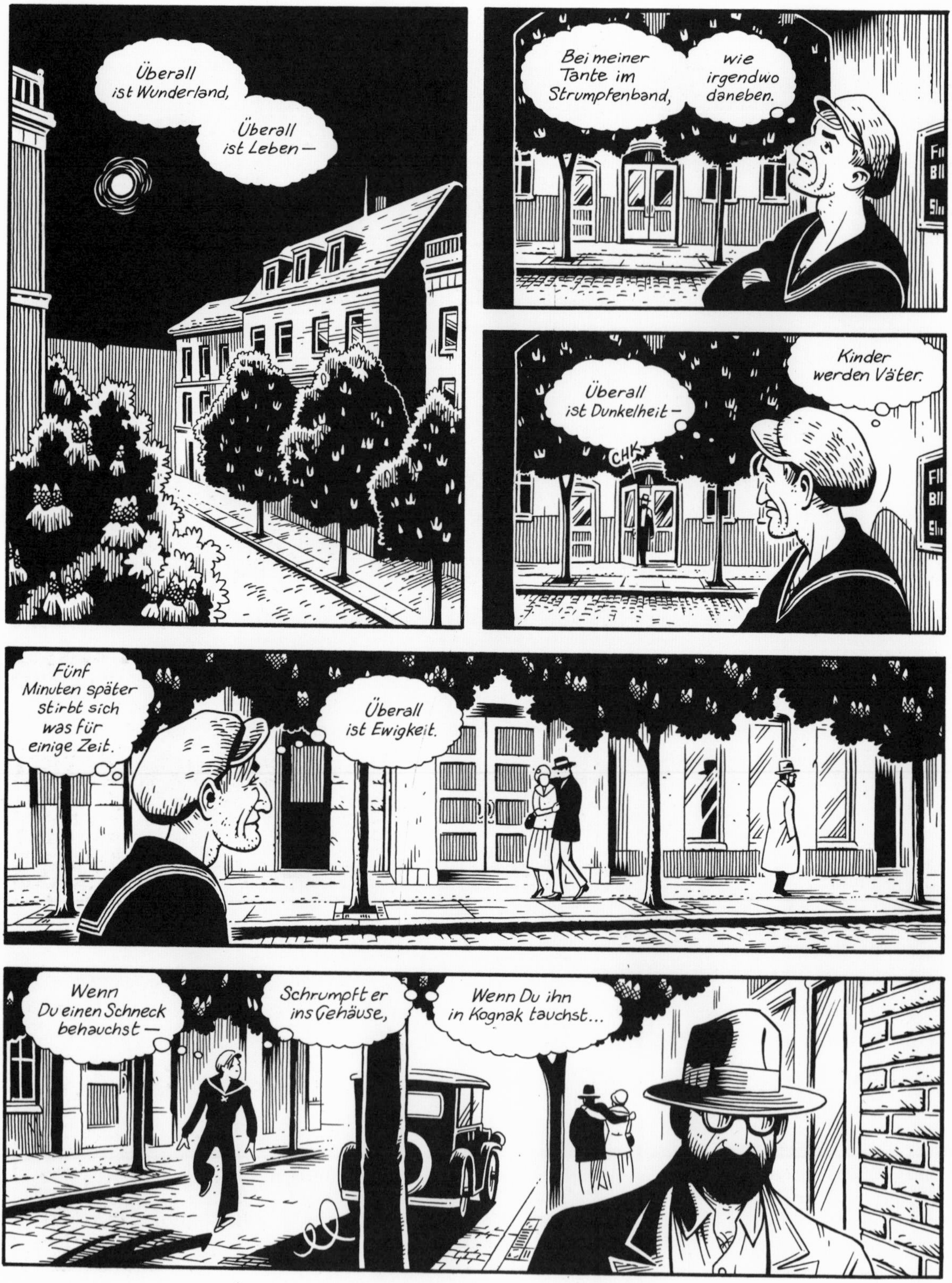
Überall ist Wunderland,
Überall ist Leben —
Bei meiner Tante im Strumpfenband,
wie irgendwo daneben.
Überall ist Dunkelheit —
Kinder werden Väter.
CHK
Fünf Minuten später stirbt sich was für einige Zeit.
Überall ist Ewigkeit.
Wenn Du einen Schneck behauchst —
Schrumpft er ins Gehäuse,
Wenn Du ihn in Kognak tauchst...

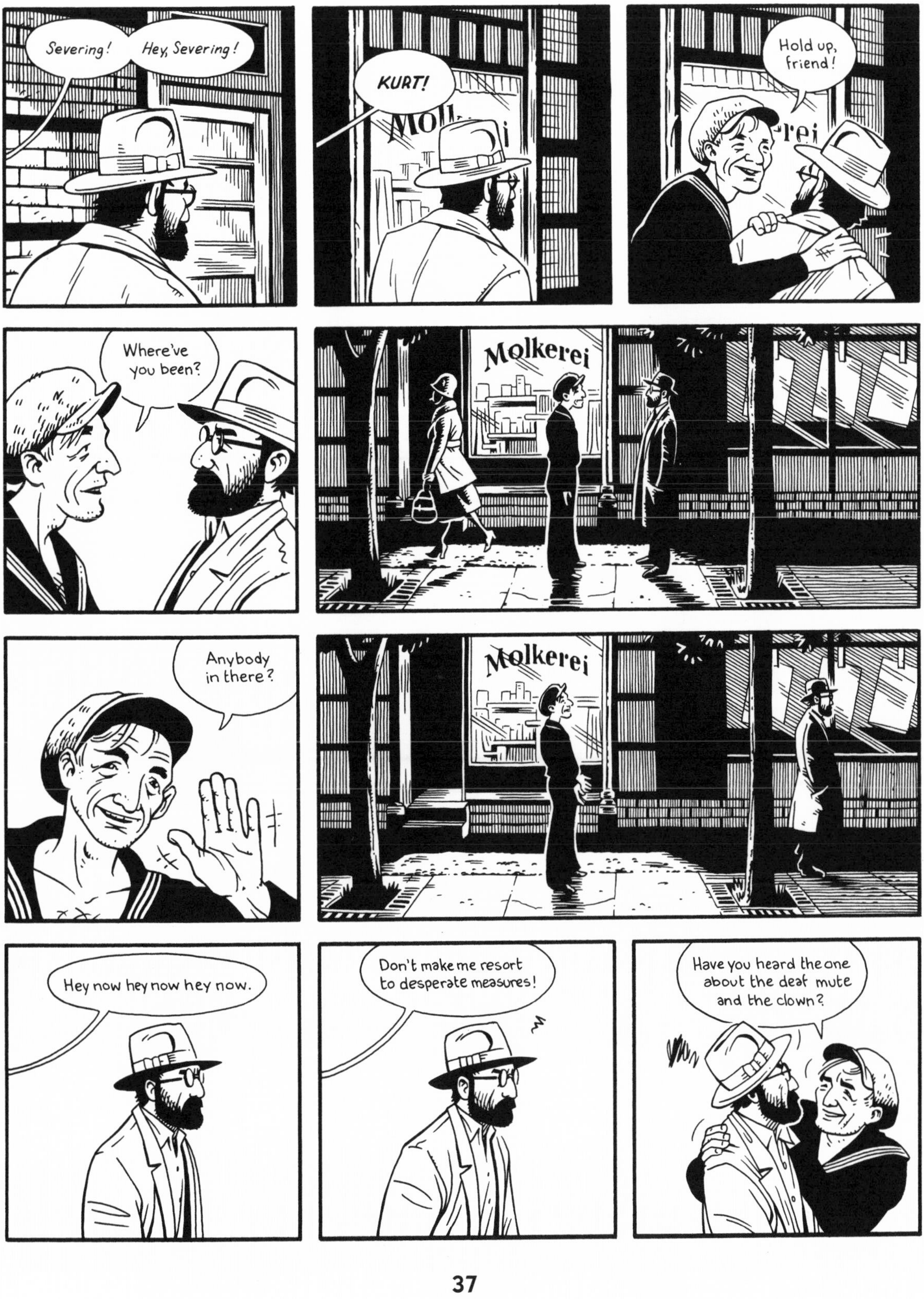
Severing!
Hey, Severing!
KURT!
Moll
Hold up, friend!
rei
Where've you been?
Molkerei
Anybody in there?
Molkerei
Hey now hey now hey now.
Don't make me resort to desperate measures!
Have you heard the one about the deaf mute and the clown?

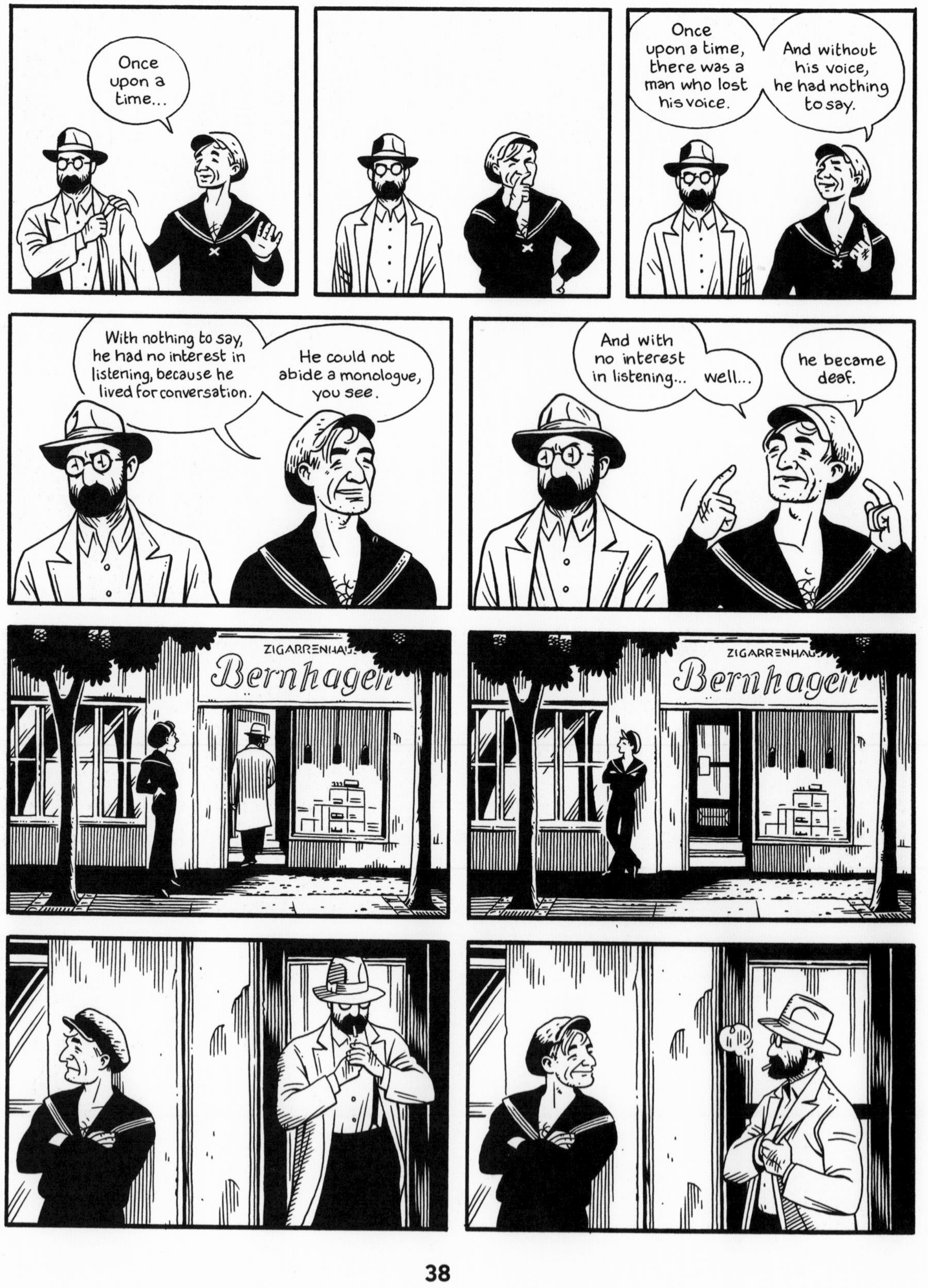

Once upon a time...
Once upon a time, there was a man who lost his voice.
And without his voice, he had nothing to say.
With nothing to say, he had no interest in listening, because he lived for conversation.
He could not abide a monologue, you see.
And with no interest in listening... well...
he became deaf.
ZIGARRENHAU
Bernhagen
ZIGARRENHAU
Bernhagen

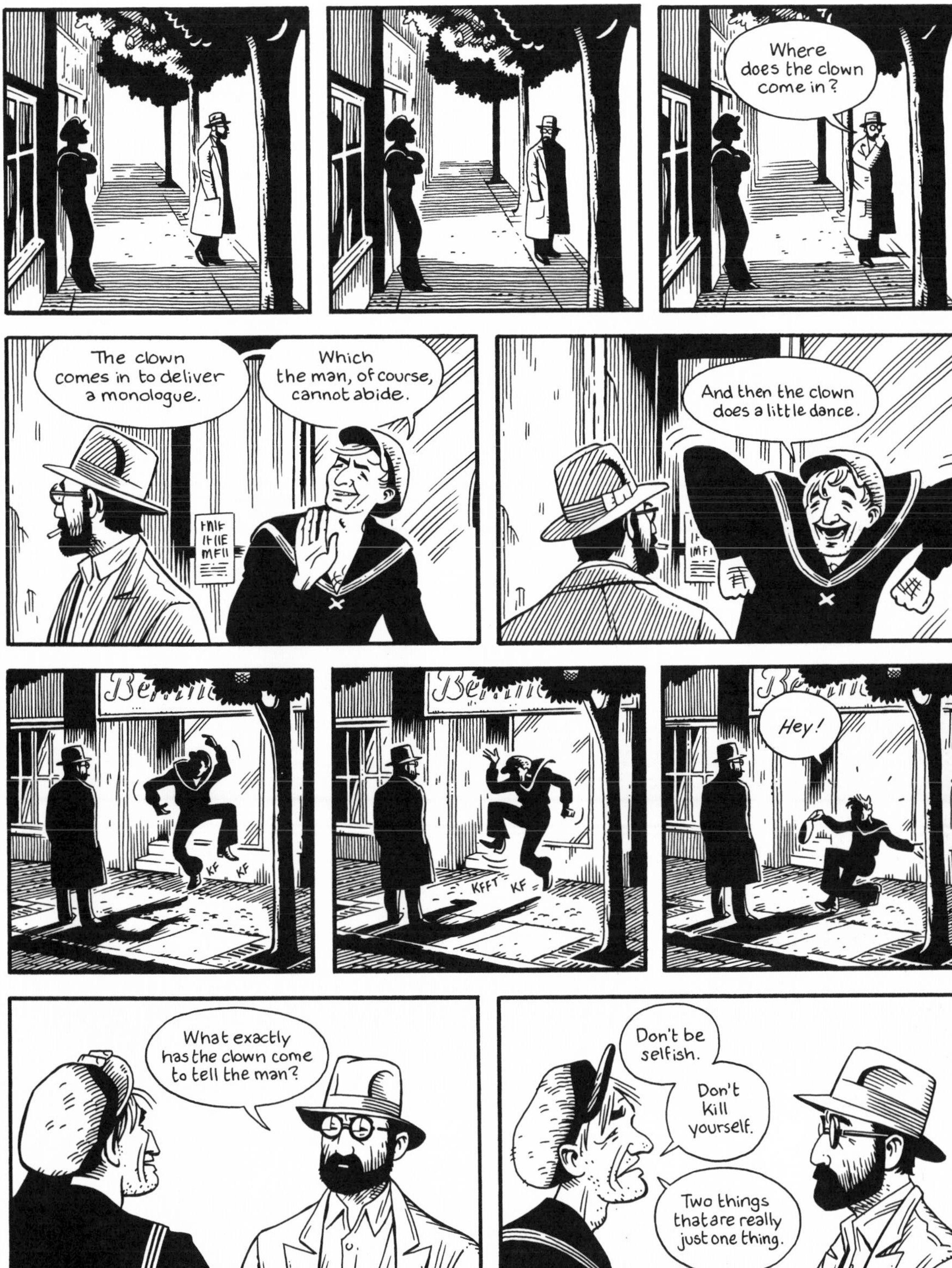
Where does the clown come in?
The clown comes in to deliver a monologue.
Which the man, of course, cannot abide.
And then the clown does a little dance.
KF
KF
KFFT
KF
Hey!
What exactly has the clown come to tell the man?
Don't be selfish.
Don't kill yourself.
Two things that are really just one thing.

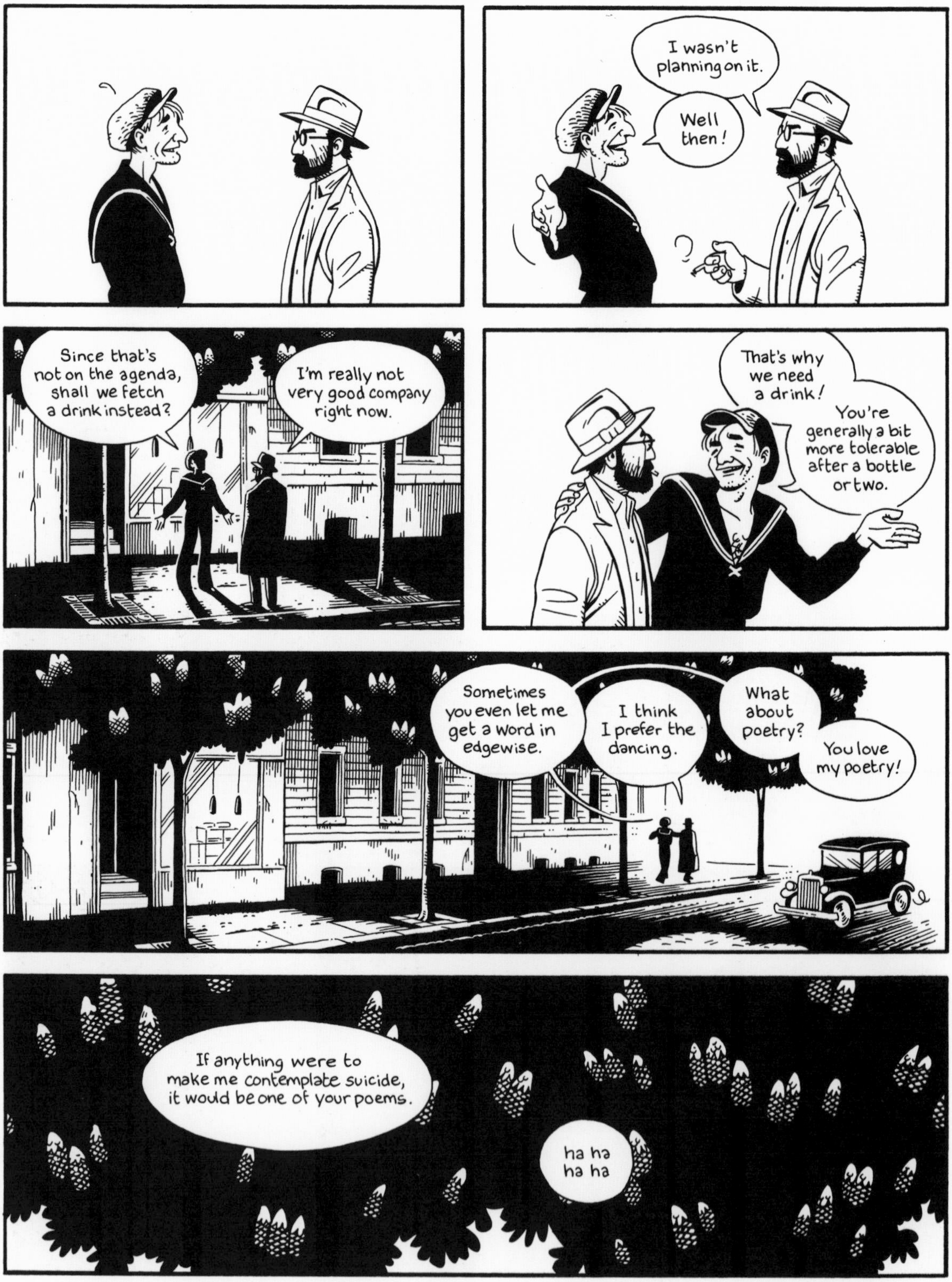
I wasn't planning on it.
Well then!
Since that's not on the agenda, shall we fetch a drink instead?
I'm really not very good company right now.
That's why we need a drink!
You're generally a bit more tolerable after a bottle or two.
Sometimes you even let me get a word in edgewise.
I think I prefer the dancing.
What about poetry?
You love my poetry!
If anything were to make me contemplate suicide, it would be one of your poems.
ha ha ha ha

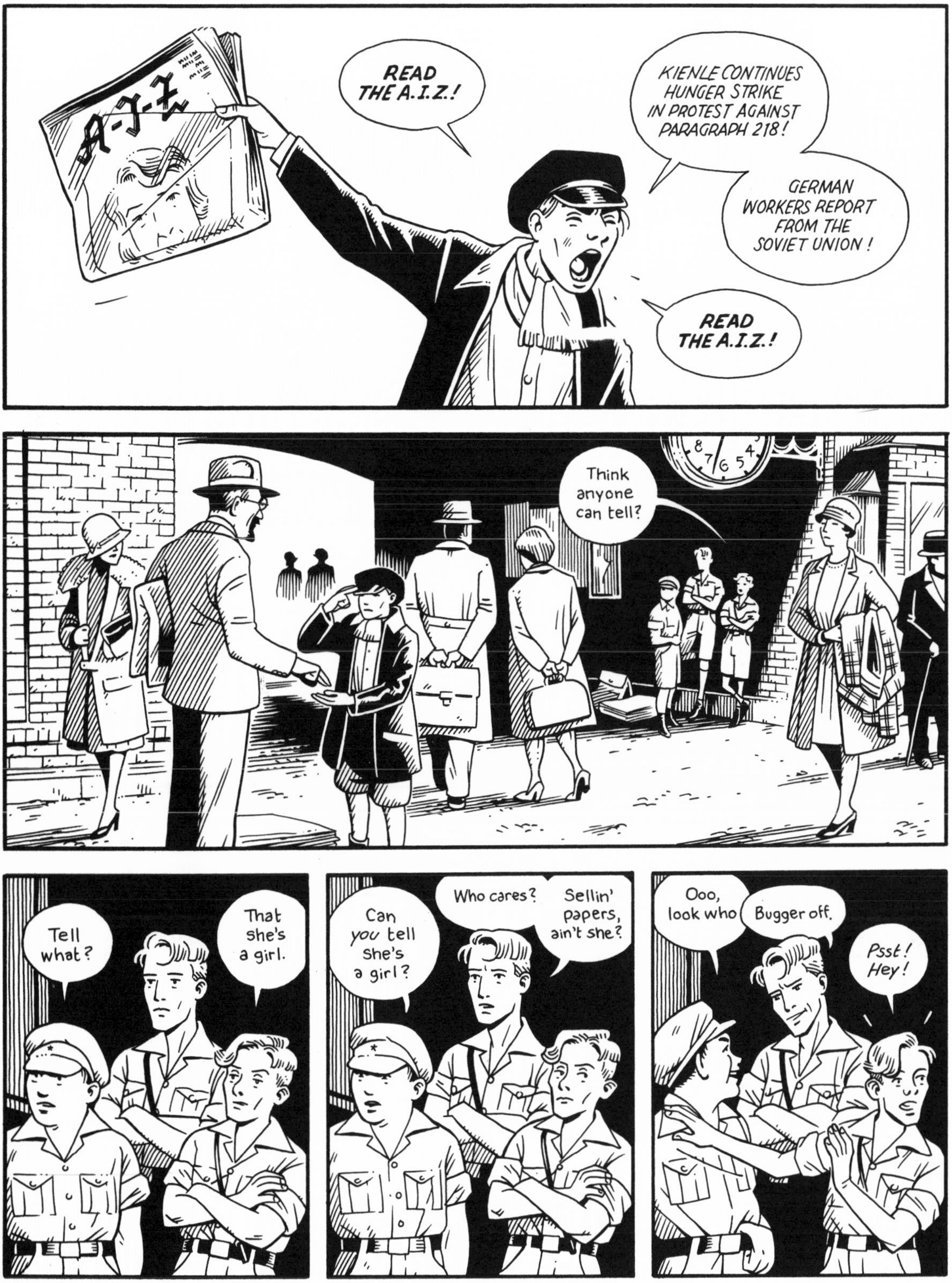

READ THE A.I.Z.!
KIENLE CONTINUES HUNGER STRIKE IN PROTEST AGAINST PARAGRAPH 218!
GERMAN WORKERS REPORT FROM THE SOVIET UNION!
READ THE A.I.Z.!
Think anyone can tell?
Tell what?
That she's a girl.
Can *you* tell she's a girl?
Who cares?
Sellin' papers, ain't she?
Ooo, look who
Bugger off.
Psst! Hey!

SHALOM
READ THE A.I.Z.!
A-I-Z
A-I-Z
HA HA HA HA HA HA HA
BRAUN!
Braun!
Are you all right?

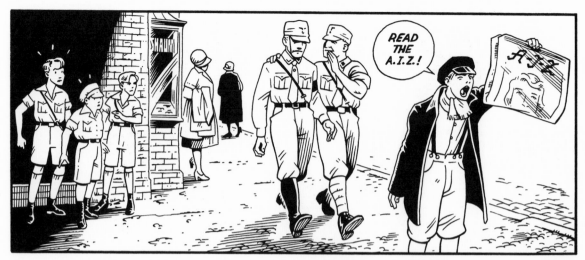

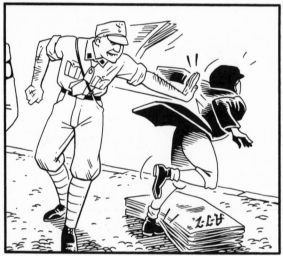

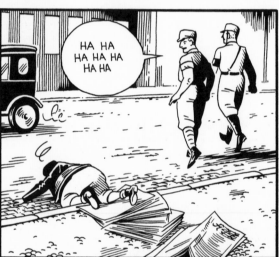

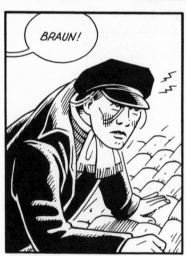

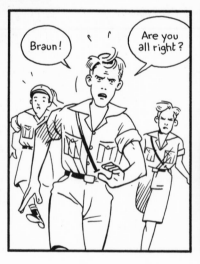

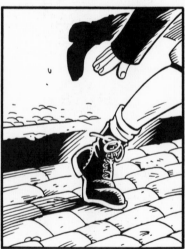

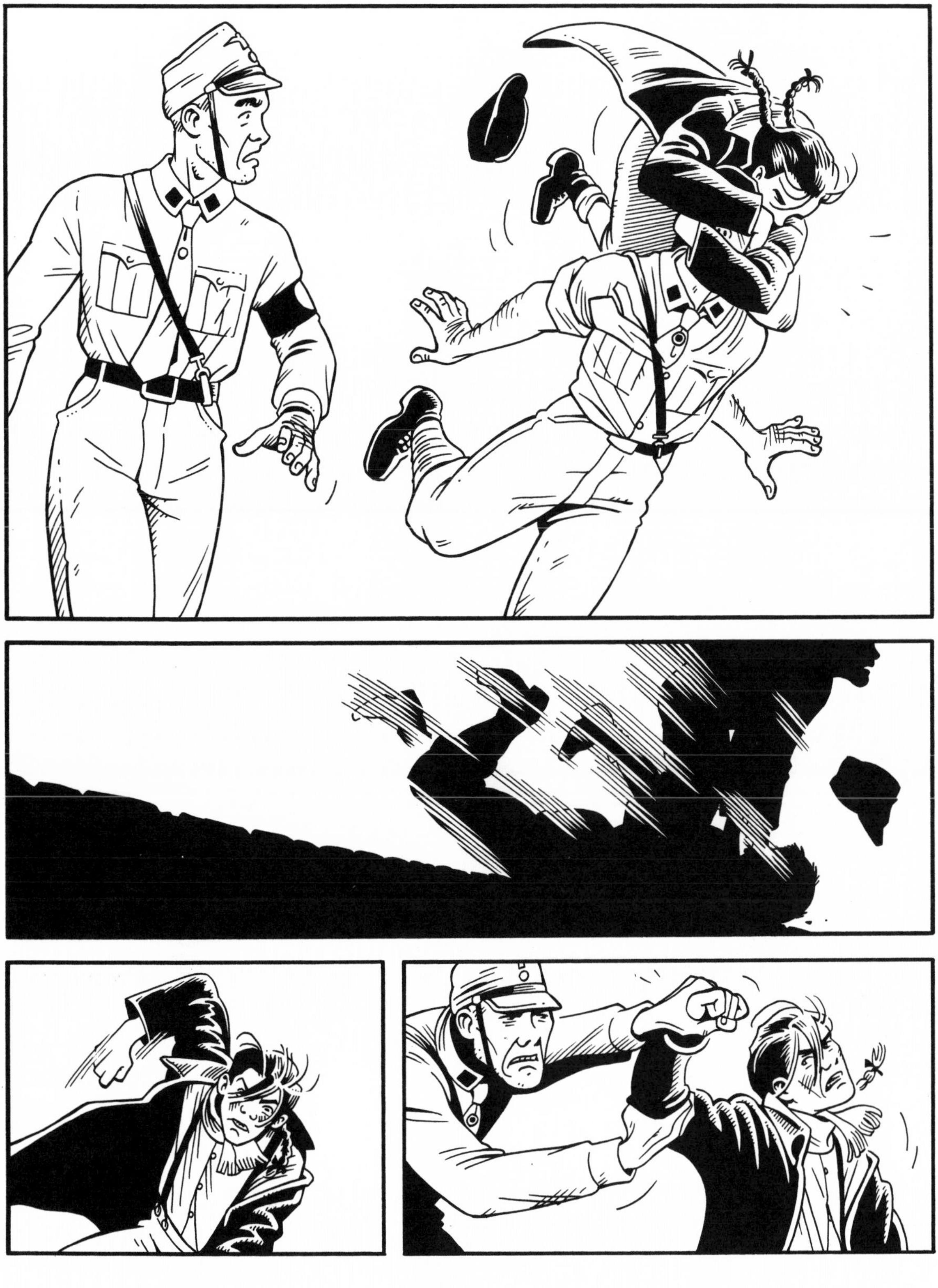

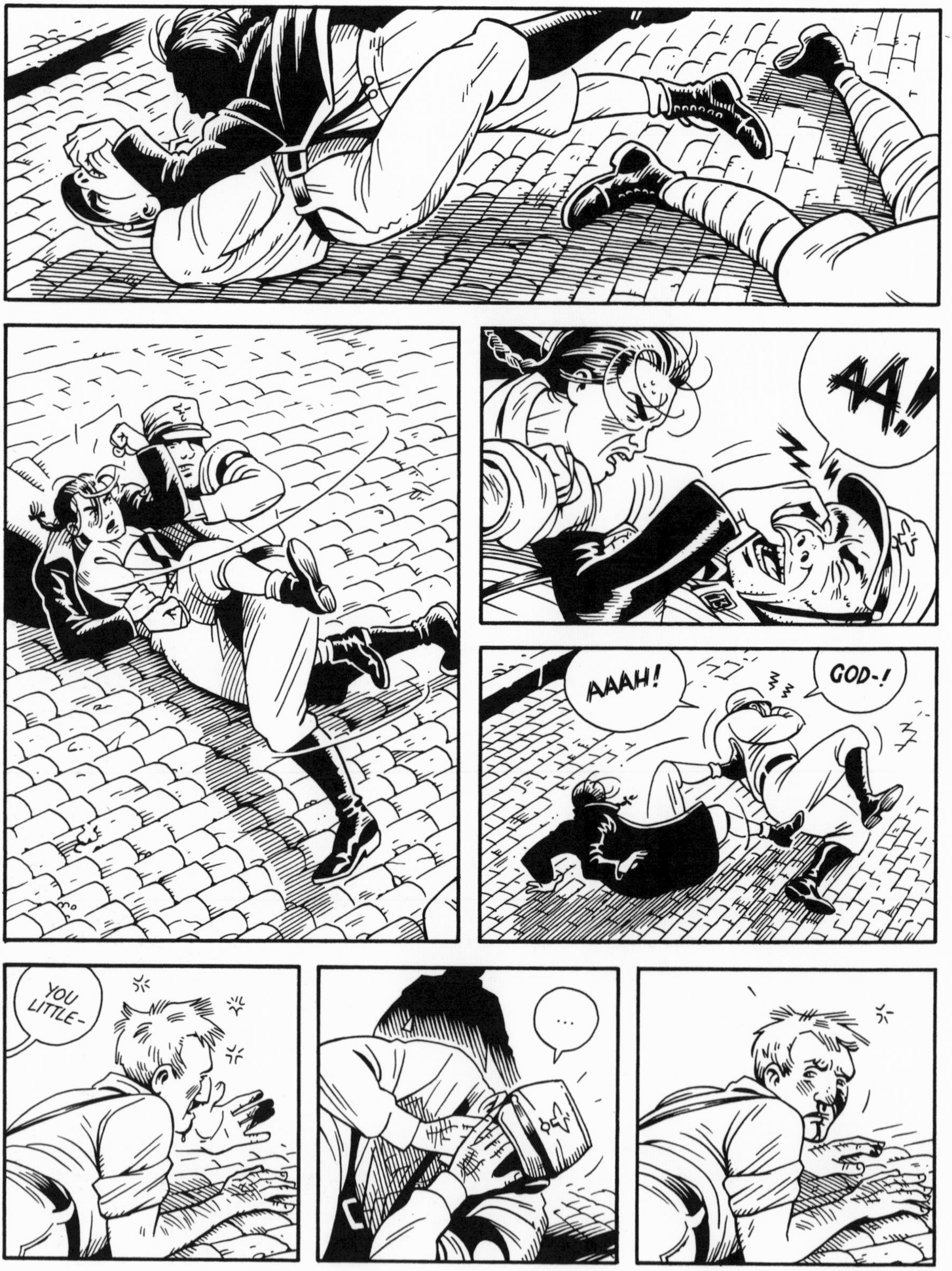
AA!
AAAH!
GOD-!
YOU LITTLE-
...

BRAUN!
BULLS!
RUN!
PHWEEEET!
ENK ENK!

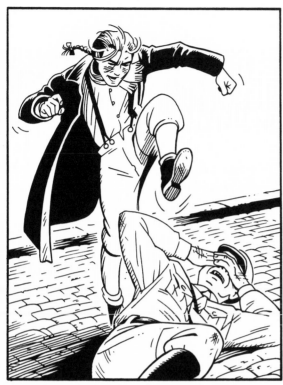

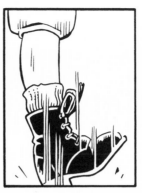

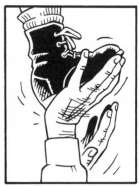

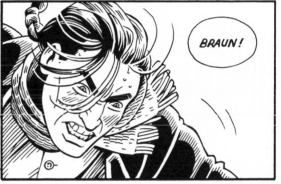

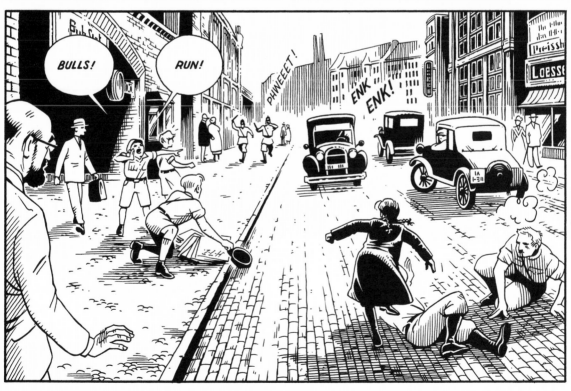

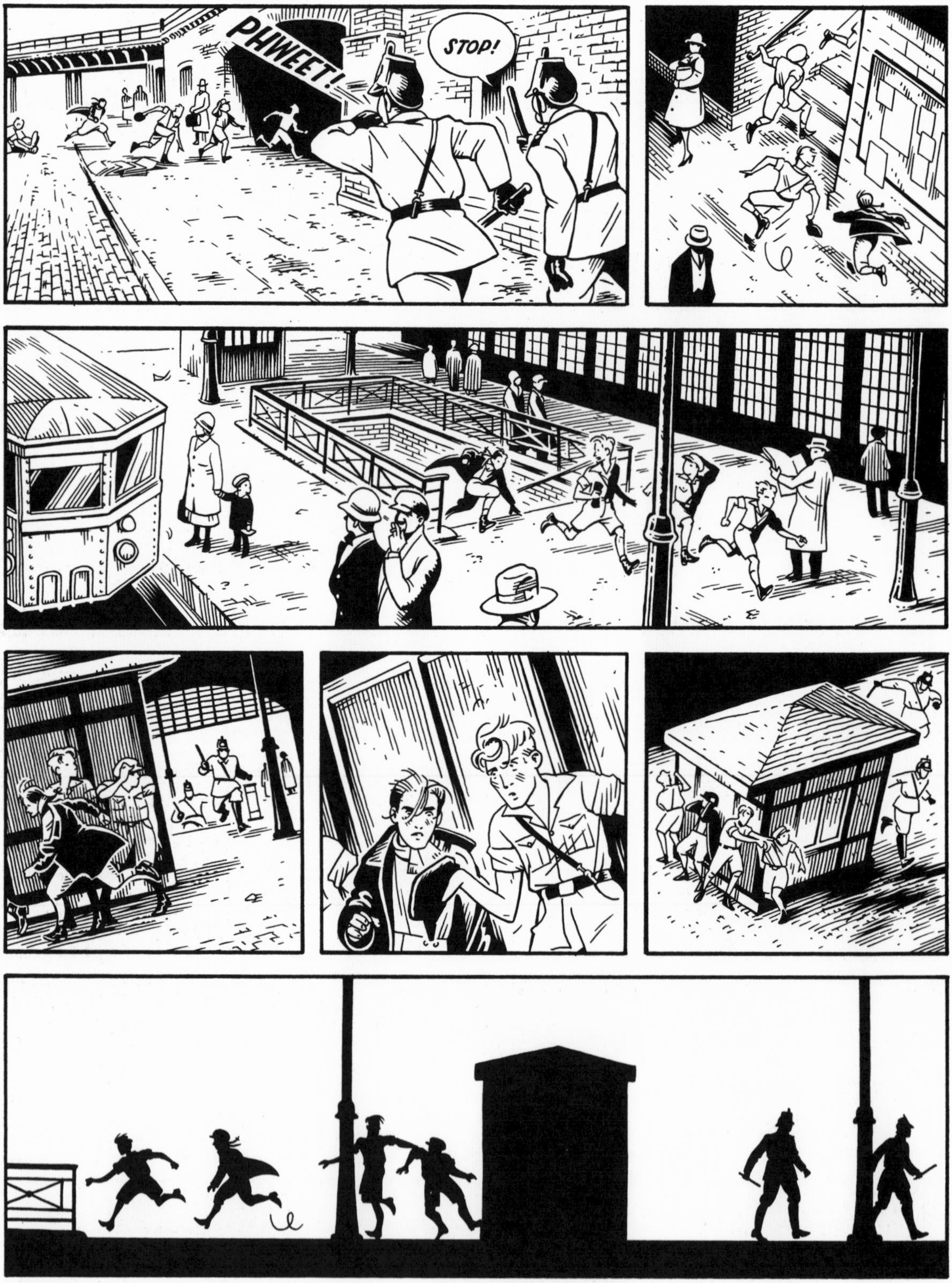
PHWEET!
STOP!

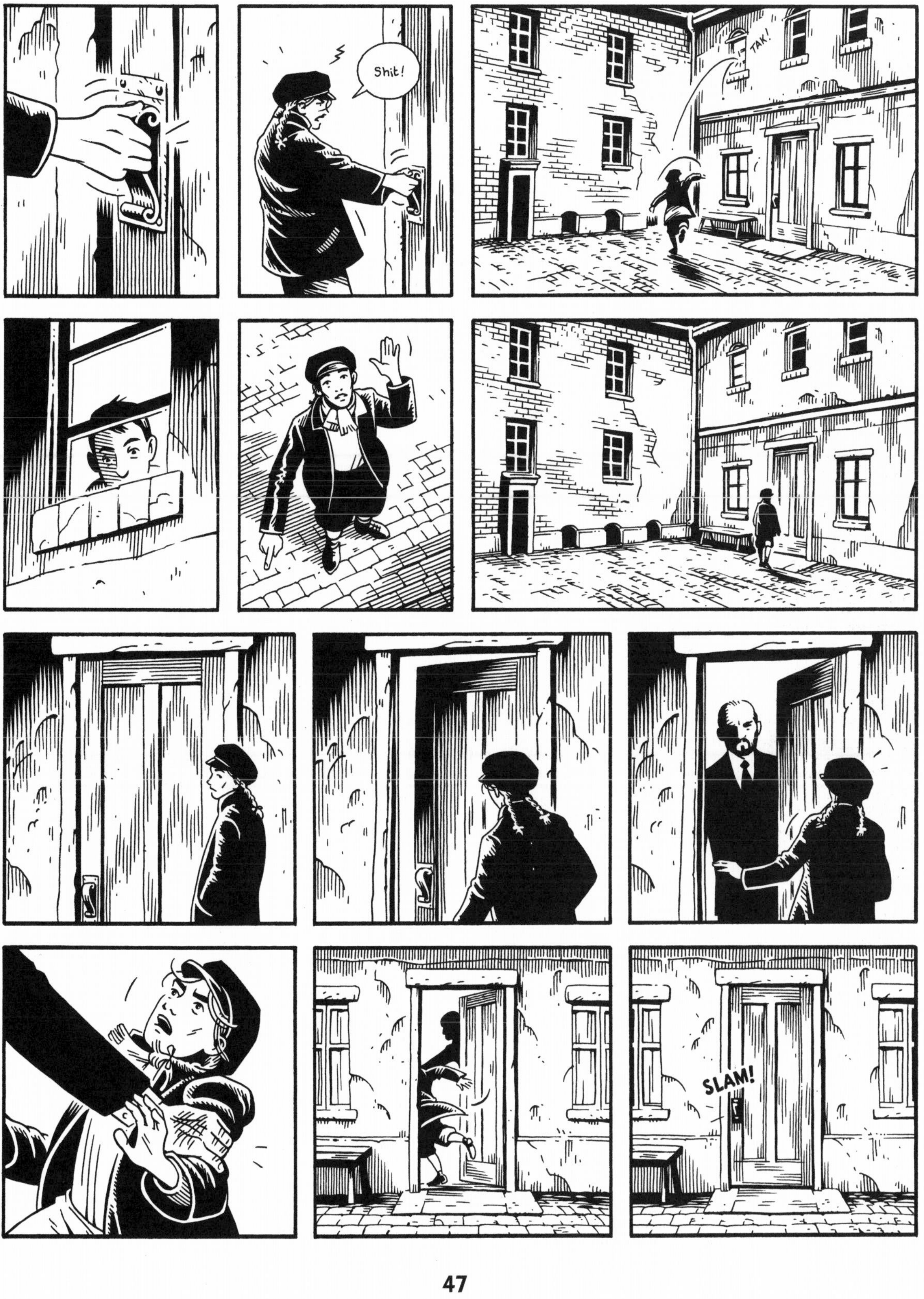
Shit!
TAK!
SLAM!

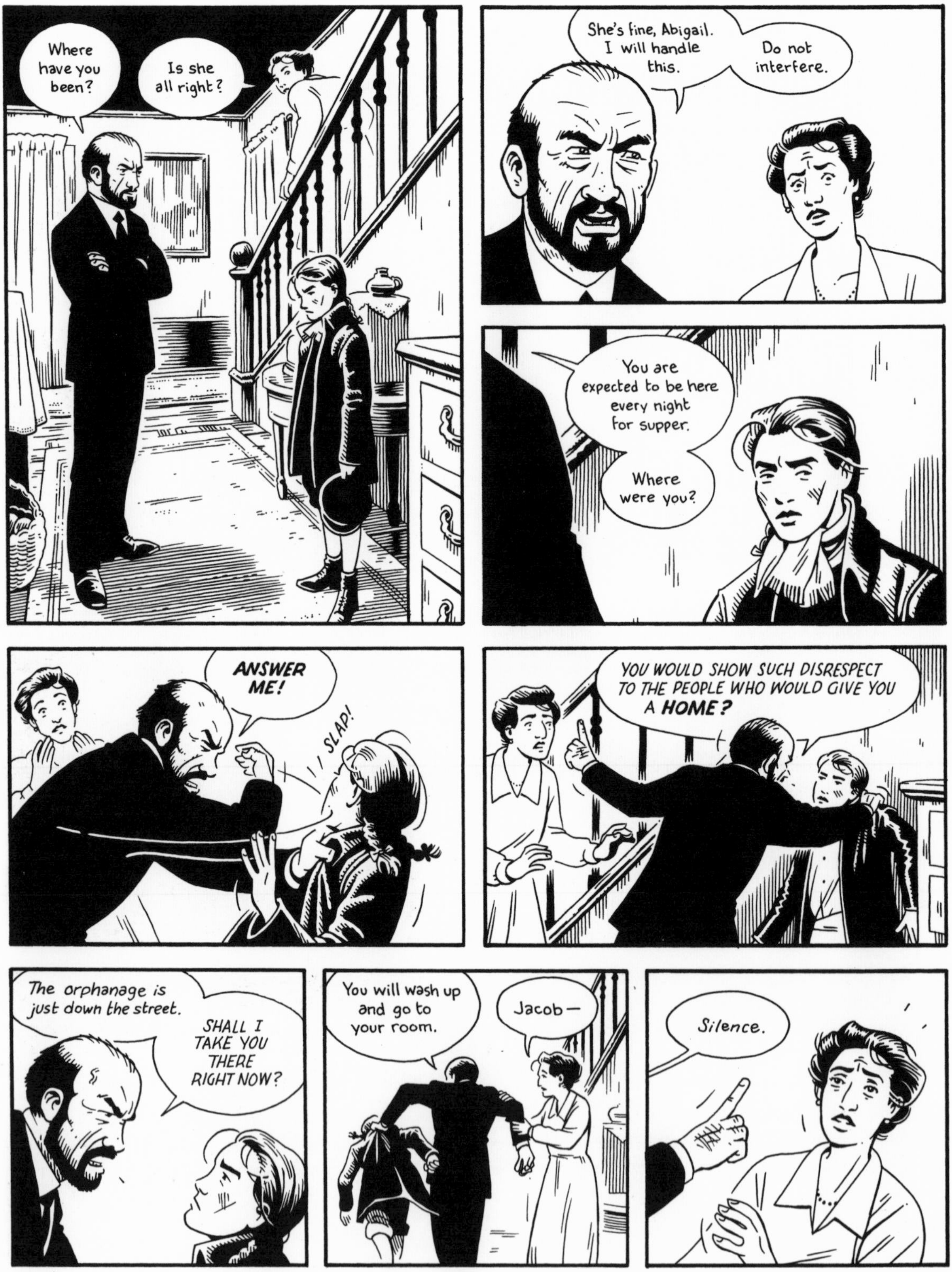
Where have you been?
Is she all right?
She's fine, Abigail. I will handle this.
Do not interfere.
You are expected to be here every night for supper.
Where were you?
ANSWER ME!
SLAP!
YOU WOULD SHOW SUCH DISRESPECT TO THE PEOPLE WHO WOULD GIVE YOU A HOME?
The orphanage is just down the street.
SHALL I TAKE YOU THERE RIGHT NOW?
You will wash up and go to your room.
Jacob—
Silence.

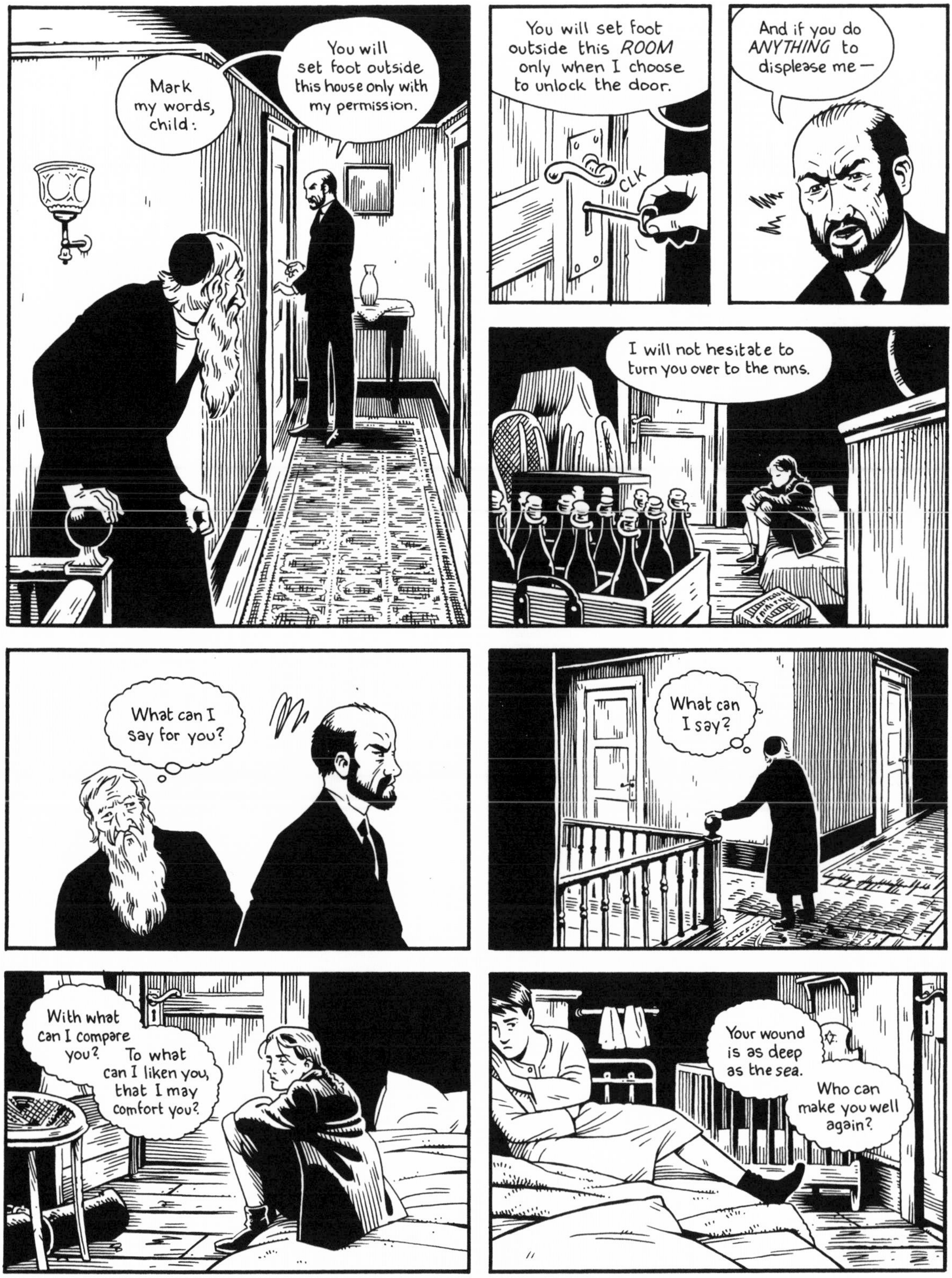

Mark my words, child:
You will set foot outside this house only with my permission.
You will set foot outside this ROOM only when I choose to unlock the door.
CLK
And if you do ANYTHING to displease me—
I will not hesitate to turn you over to the nuns.
What can I say for you?
What can I say?
With what can I compare you?
To what can I liken you, that I may comfort you?
Your wound is as deep as the sea.
Who can make you well again?

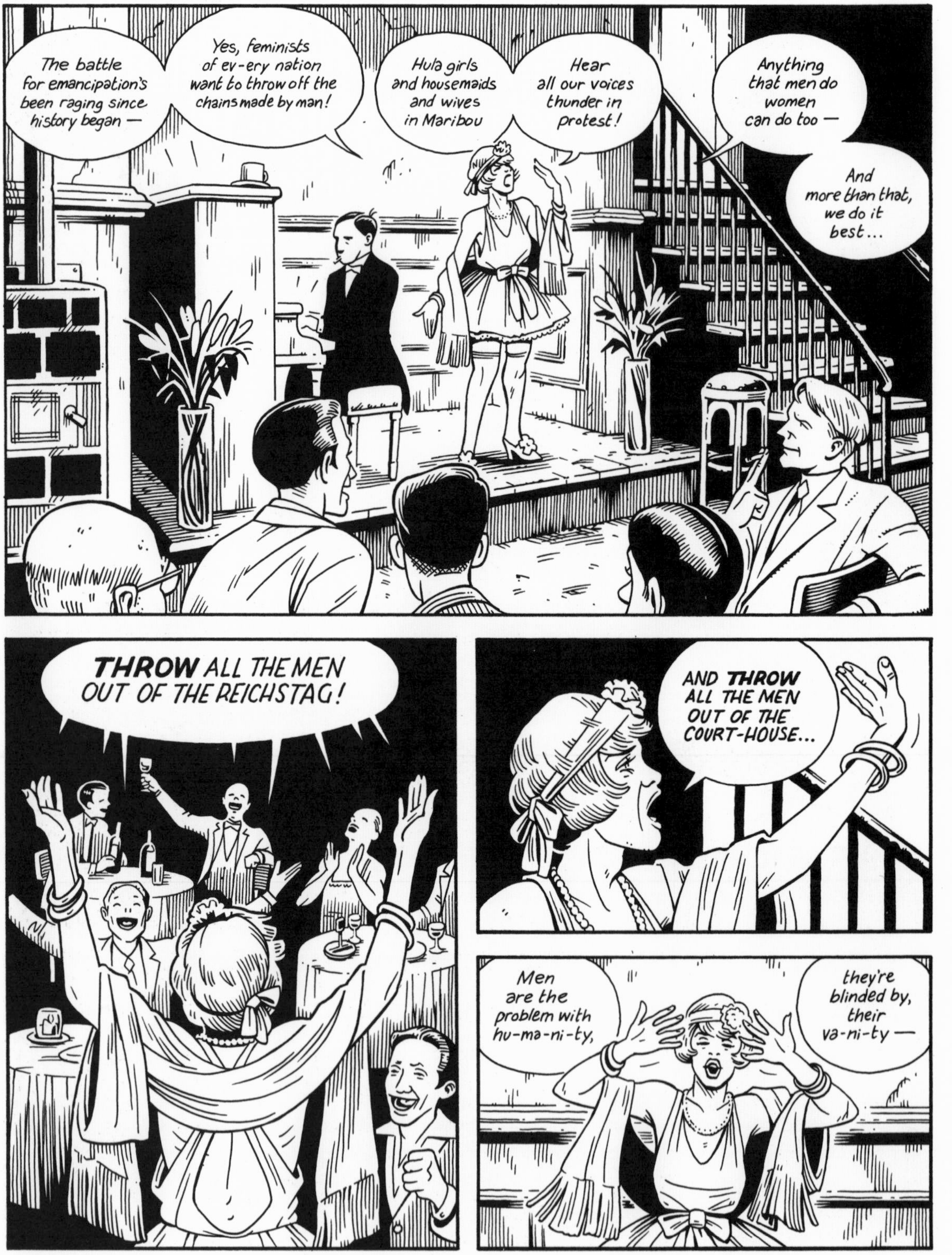
The battle for emancipation's been raging since history began —
Yes, feminists of ev-ery nation want to throw off the chains made by man!
Hula girls and housemaids and wives in Maribou
Hear all our voices thunder in protest!
Anything that men do women can do too —
And more than that, we do it best...
THROW ALL THE MEN OUT OF THE REICHSTAG!
AND THROW ALL THE MEN OUT OF THE COURT-HOUSE...
Men are the problem with hu-ma-ni-ty,
they're blinded by, their va-ni-ty —

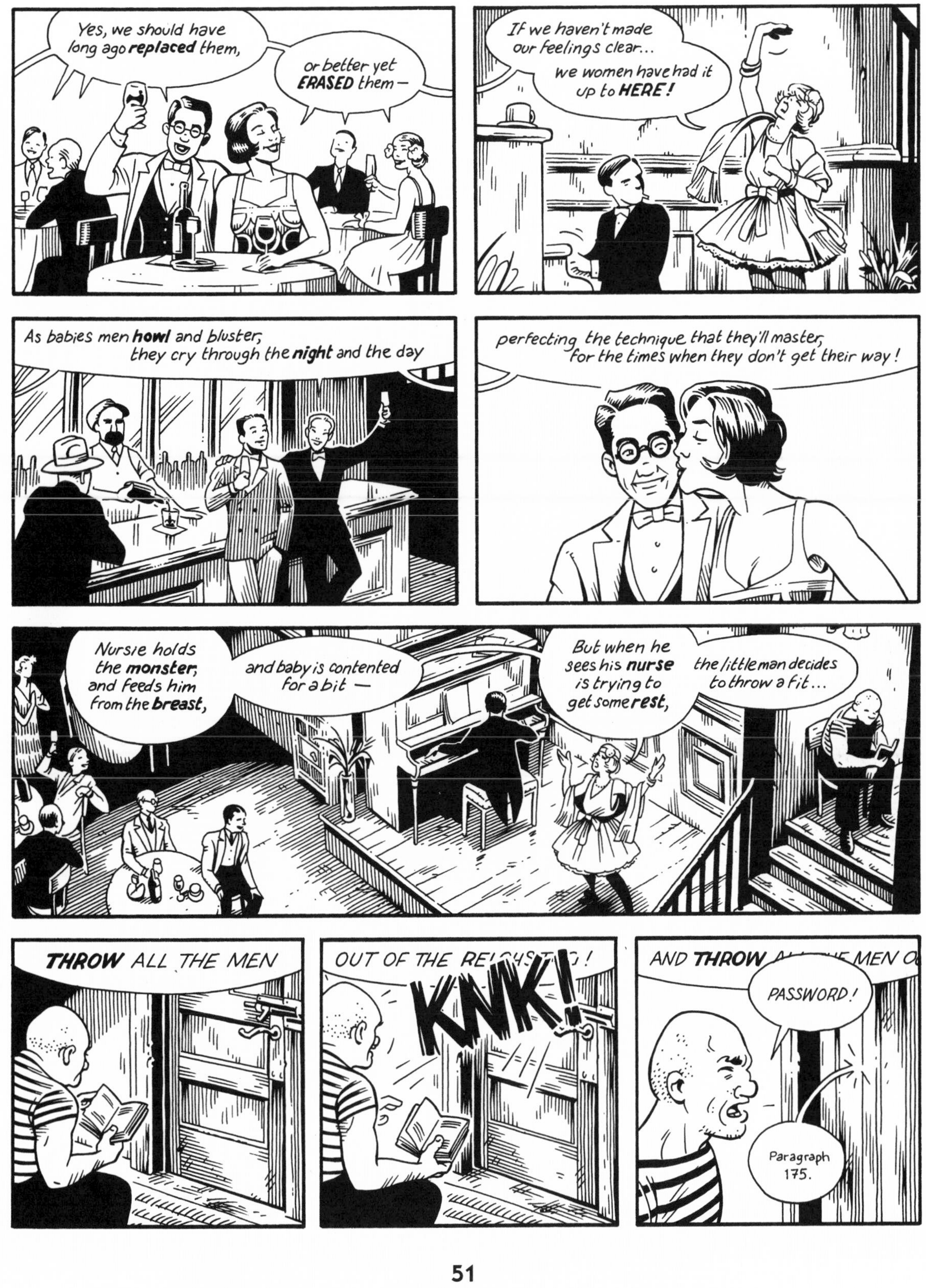
Yes, we should have long ago **replaced** them,
or better yet **ERASED** them —
If we haven't made our feelings clear...
we women have had it up to **HERE!**
As babies men **howl** and bluster, they cry through the **night** and the day
perfecting the technique that they'll master, for the times when they don't get their way!
Nursie holds the **monster**, and feeds him from the **breast**,
and baby is contented for a bit —
But when he sees his **nurse** is trying to get some **rest**,
the little man decides to throw a fit...
THROW ALL THE MEN
OUT OF THE
KNK!
AND **THROW**
MEN
PASSWORD!
Paragraph 175.

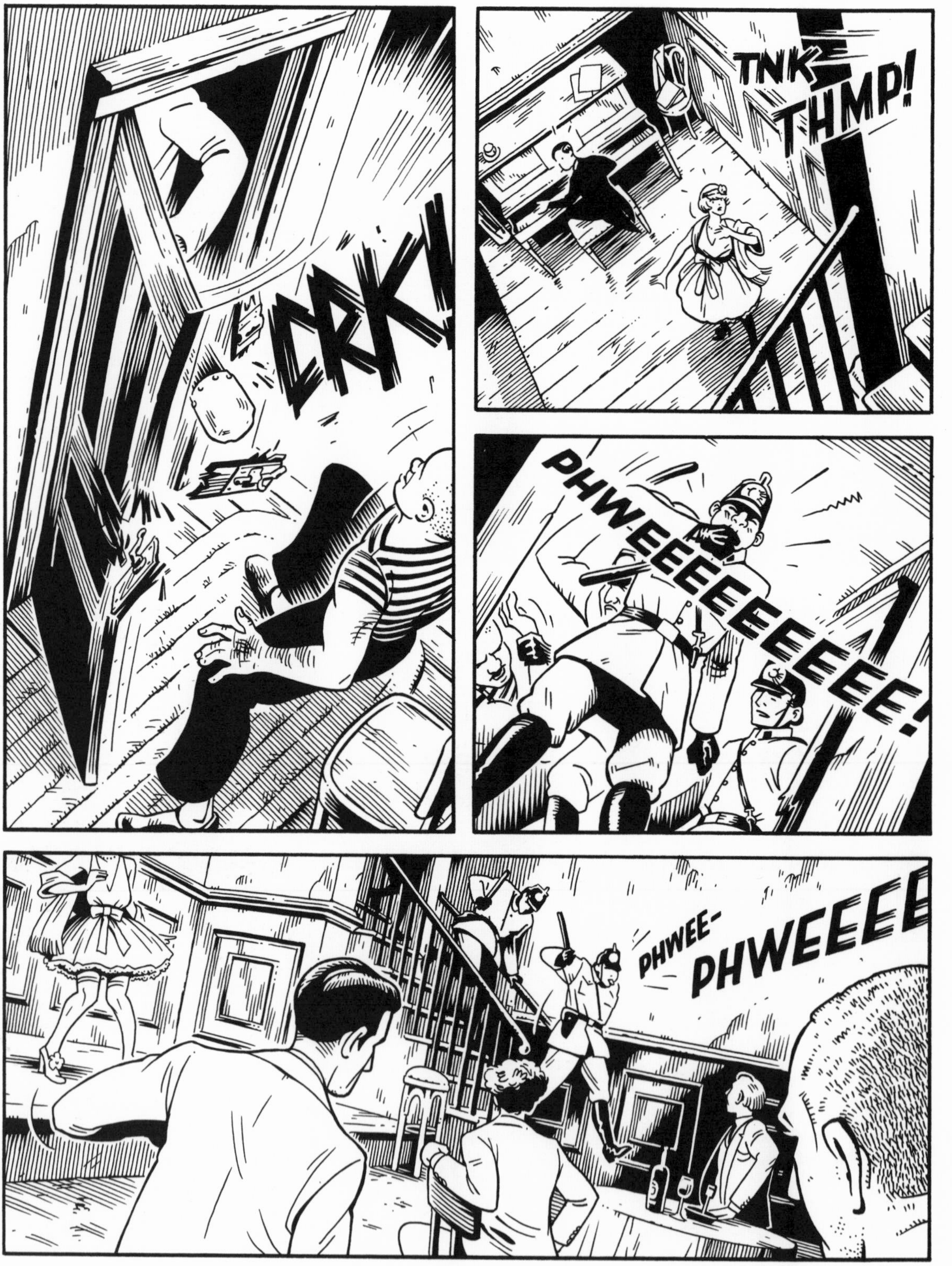
CRK!
TNK
THMP!
PHWEEEEEEEEEEEE!
PHWEE-
PHWEEEEE

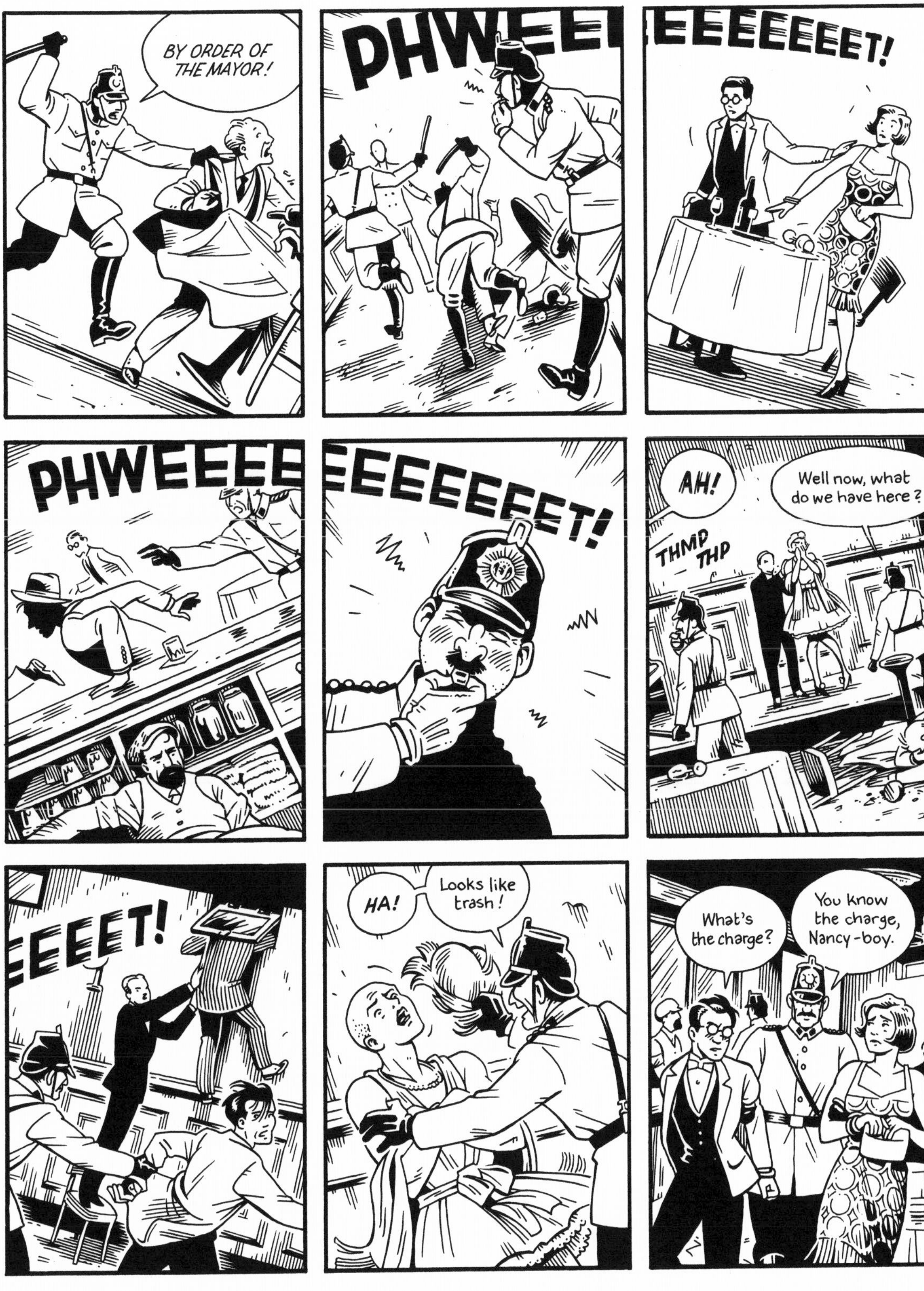
BY ORDER OF THE MAYOR!
PHWEEEEEEEEEEEET!
PHWEEEEEEEEEEEEET!
AH!
Well now, what do we have here?
THMP THP
EEEEET!
HA!
Looks like trash!
What's the charge?
You know the charge, Nancy-boy.

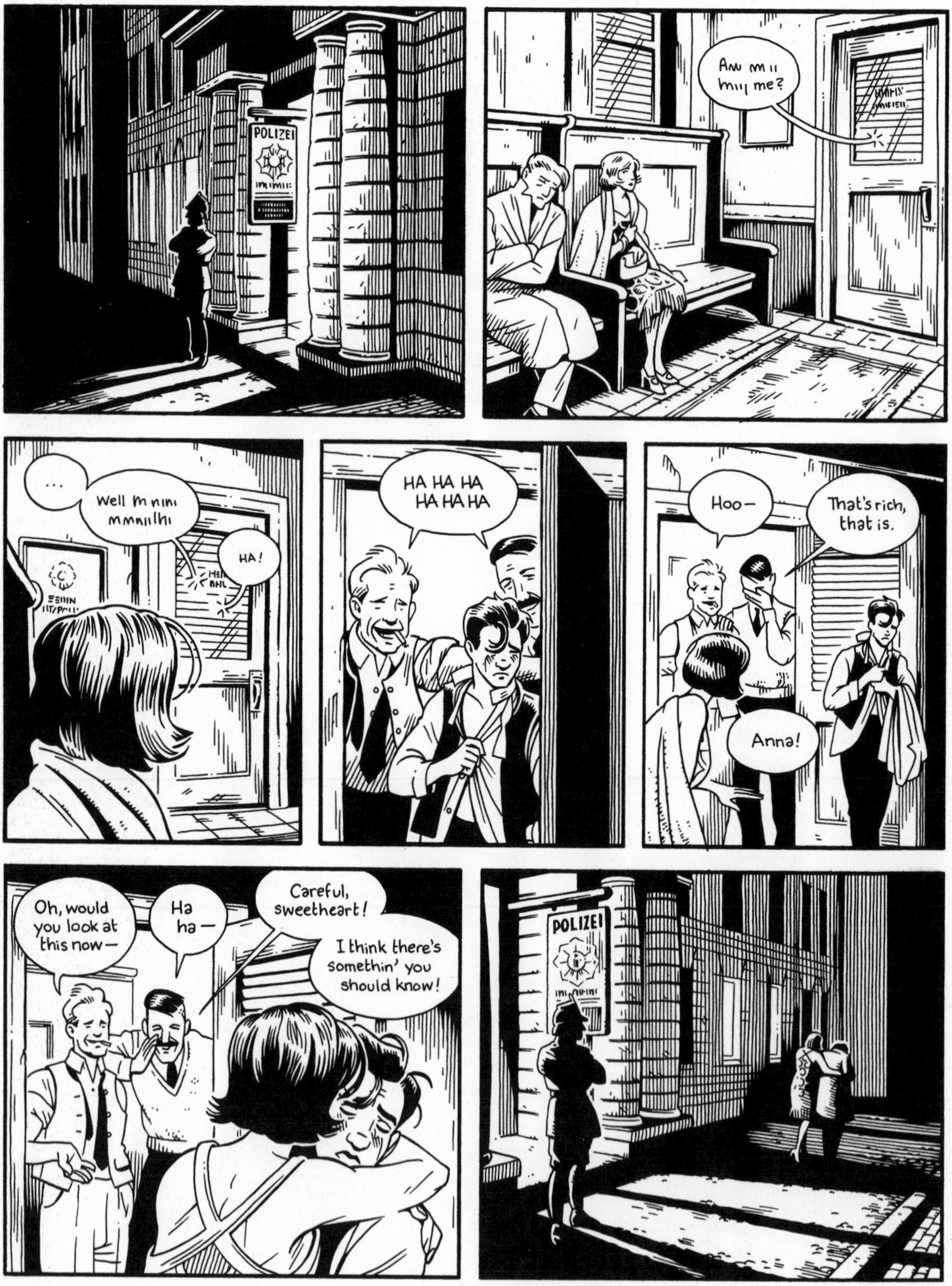

POLIZEI
Am m ıı
mıı| me?
...
Well m nını
mmnıılhı
HA!
HA HA HA
HA HA HA
Hoo—
That's rich,
that is.
Anna!
Oh, would
you look at
this now—
Ha
ha—
Careful,
sweetheart!
I think there's
somethin' you
should know!
POLIZEI

3

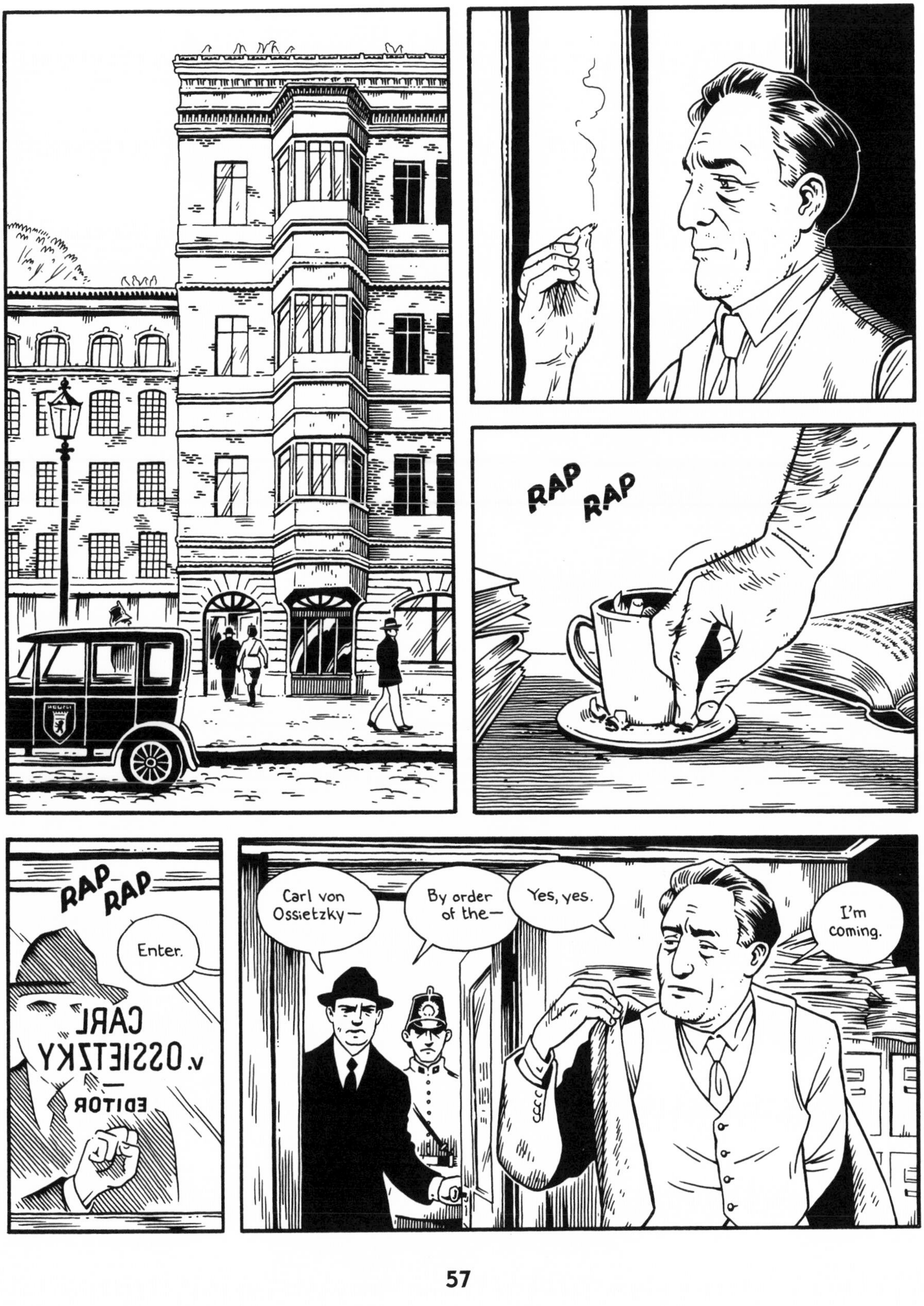

RAP
RAP
RAP
RAP
Enter.
CARL v. OSSIETZKY — EDITOR
Carl von Ossietzky—
By order of the—
Yes, yes.
I'm coming.

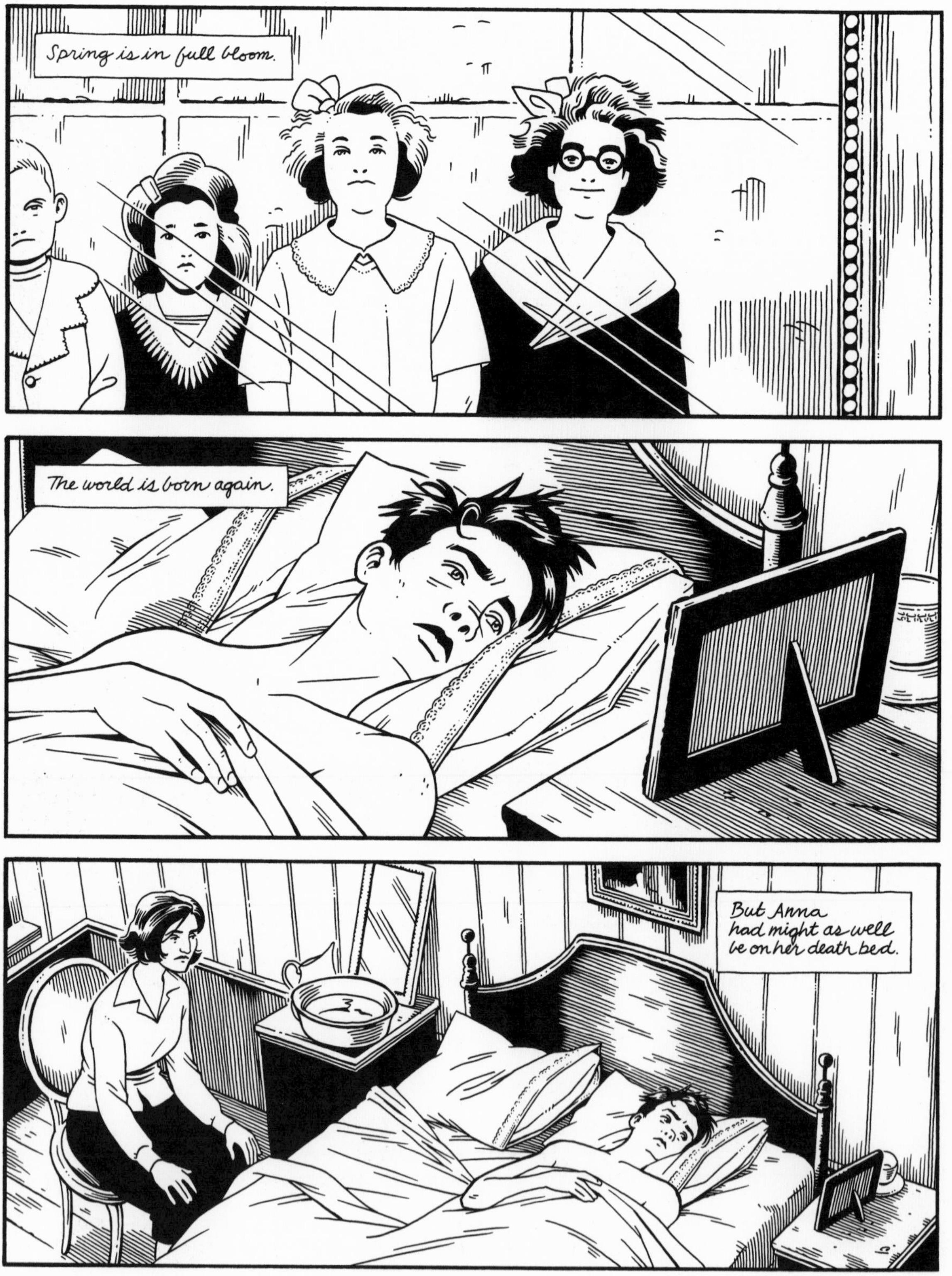
Spring is in full bloom.
The world is born again.
But Anna had might as well be on her death bed.

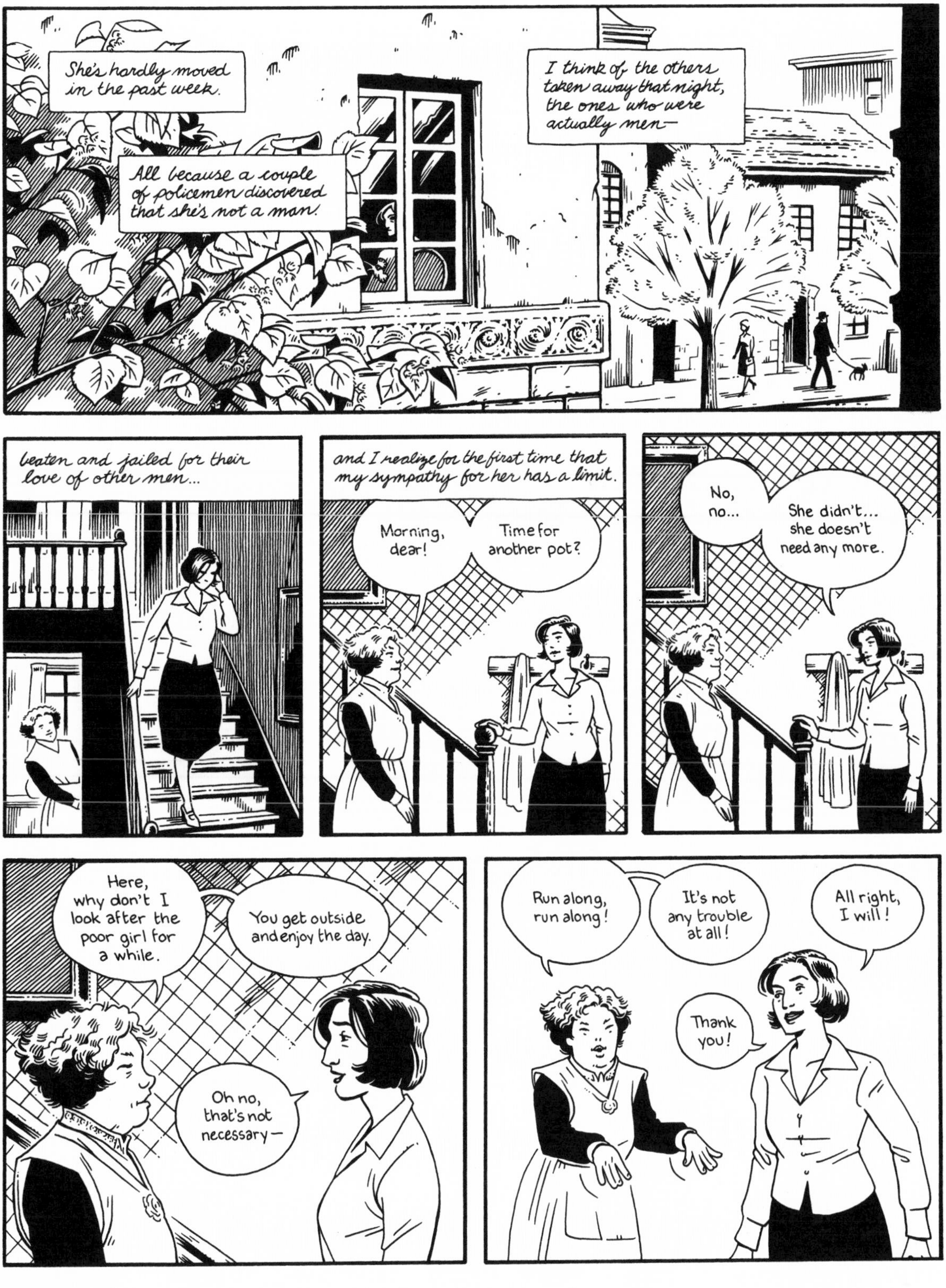

She's hardly moved in the past week.
All because a couple of policemen discovered that she's not a man.
I think of the others taken away that night, the ones who were actually men—
beaten and jailed for their love of other men...
and I realize for the first time that my sympathy for her has a limit.
Morning, dear!
Time for another pot?
No, no...
She didn't... she doesn't need any more.
Here, why don't I look after the poor girl for a while.
You get outside and enjoy the day.
Oh no, that's not necessary—
Run along, run along!
It's not any trouble at all!
All right, I will!
Thank you!

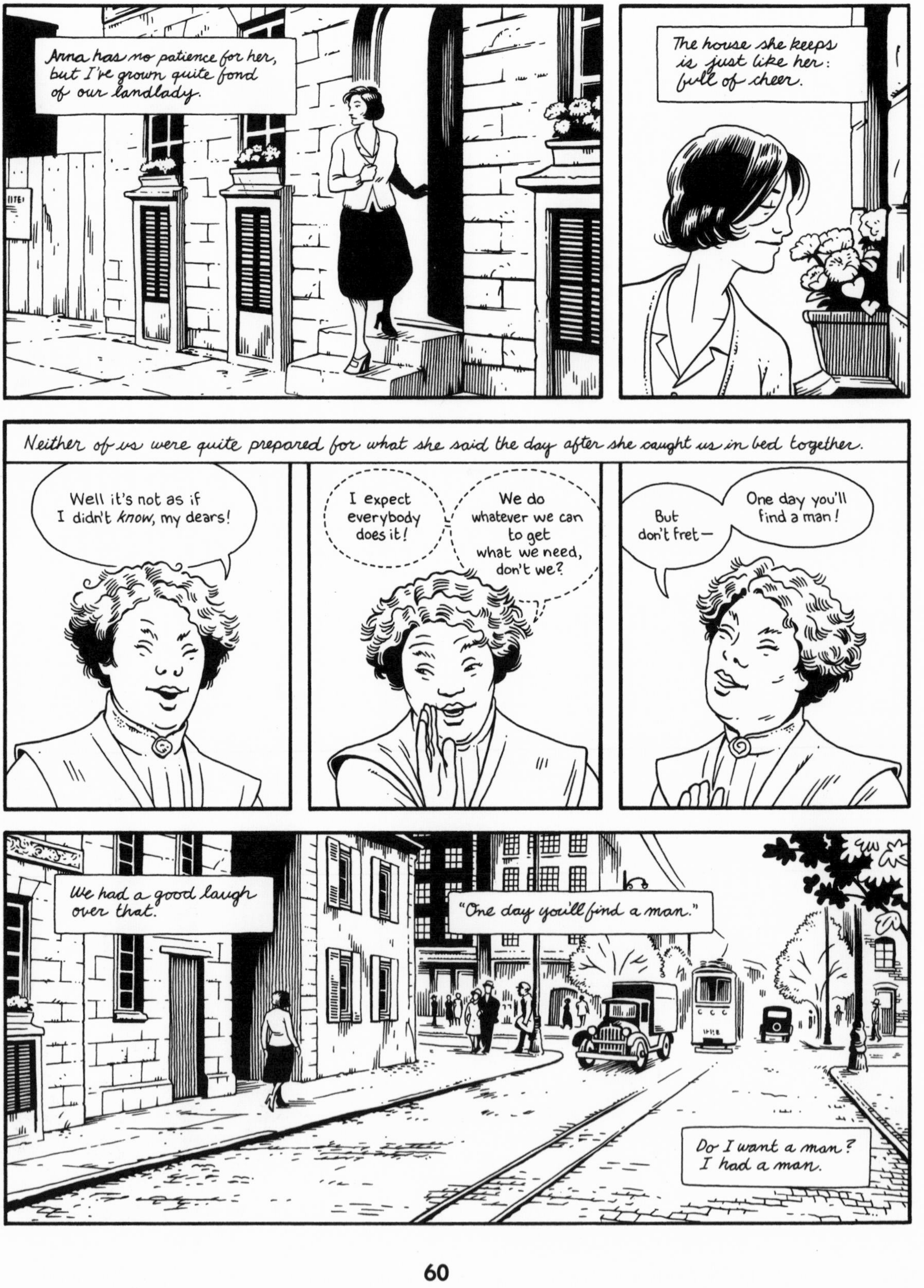

Anna has no patience for her, but I've grown quite fond of our landlady.
The house she keeps is just like her: full of cheer.
Neither of us were quite prepared for what she said the day after she caught us in bed together.
Well it's not as if I didn't *know*, my dears!
I expect everybody does it!
We do whatever we can to get what we need, don't we?
But don't fret—
One day you'll find a man!
We had a good laugh over that.
"One day you'll find a man."
Do I want a man? I had a man.

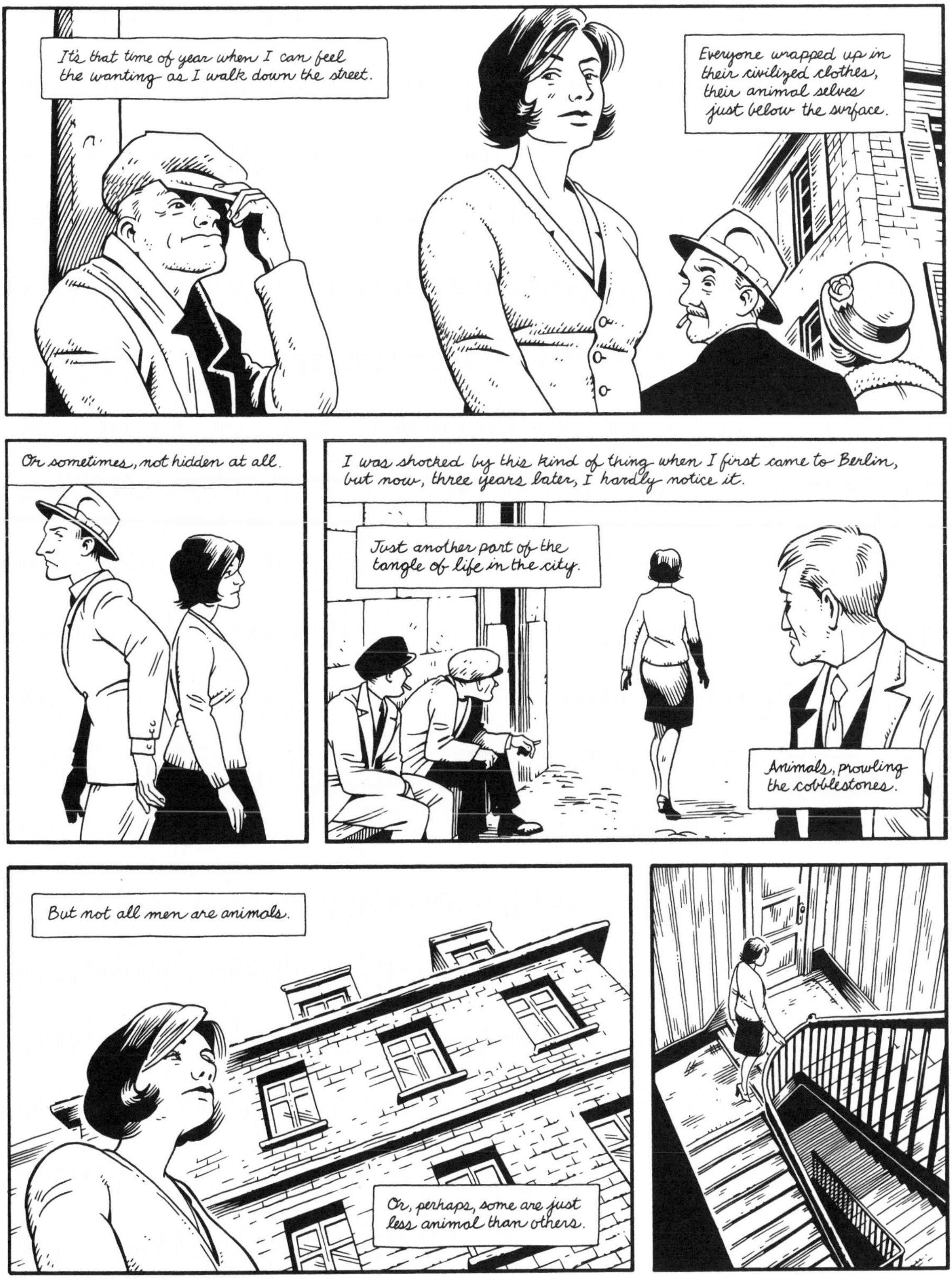
It's that time of year when I can feel the wanting as I walk down the street.
Everyone wrapped up in their civilized clothes, their animal selves just below the surface.
Or sometimes, not hidden at all.
I was shocked by this kind of thing when I first came to Berlin, but now, three years later, I hardly notice it.
Just another part of the tangle of life in the city.
Animals, prowling the cobblestones.
But not all men are animals.
Or, perhaps, some are just less animal than others.

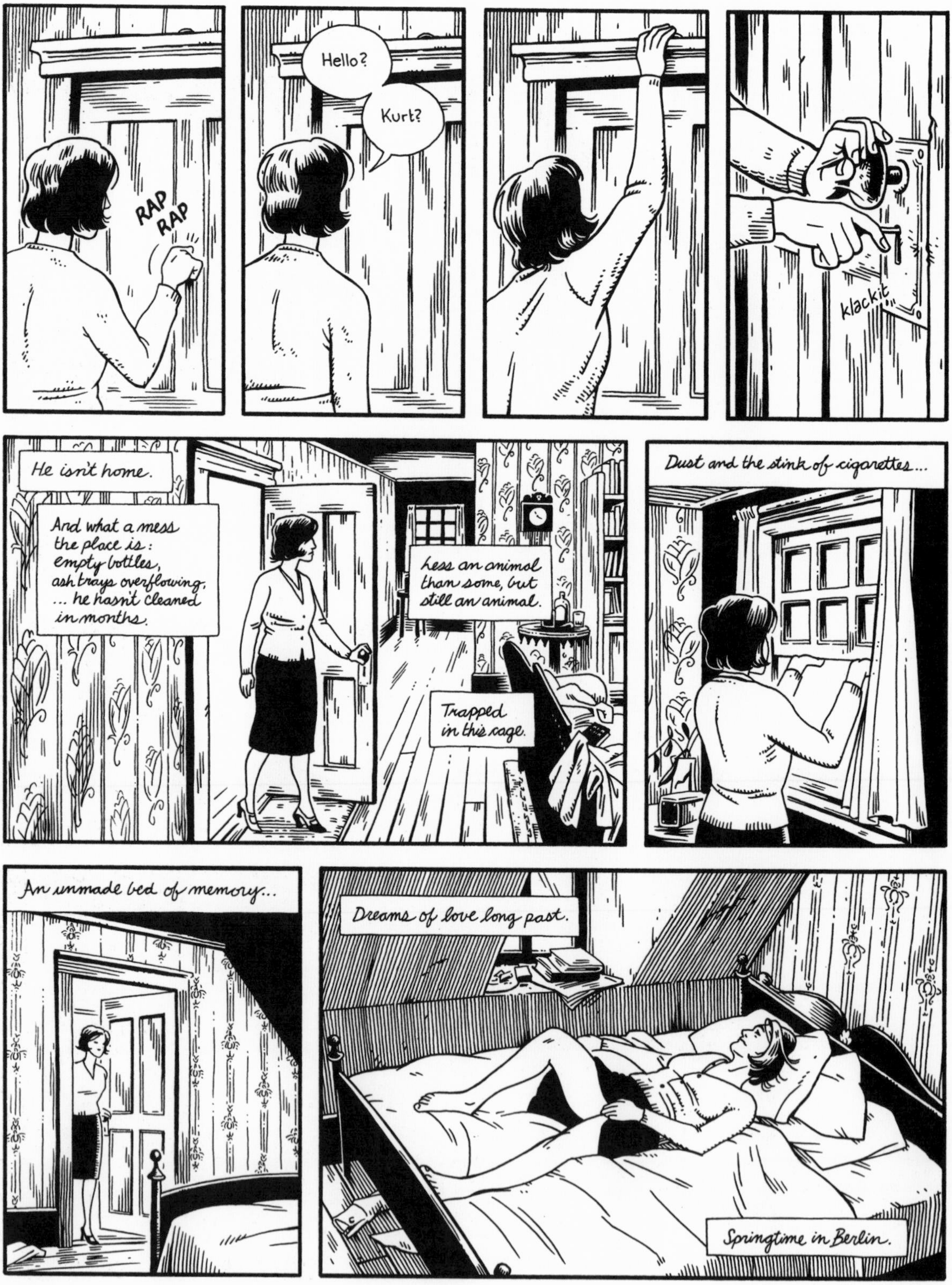
RAP RAP
Hello?
Kurt?
klackit
He isn't home.
And what a mess the place is: empty bottles, ash trays overflowing, ... he hasn't cleaned in months.
Less an animal than some, but still an animal.
Trapped in this cage.
Dust and the stink of cigarettes...
An unmade bed of memory...
Dreams of love long past.
Springtime in Berlin.

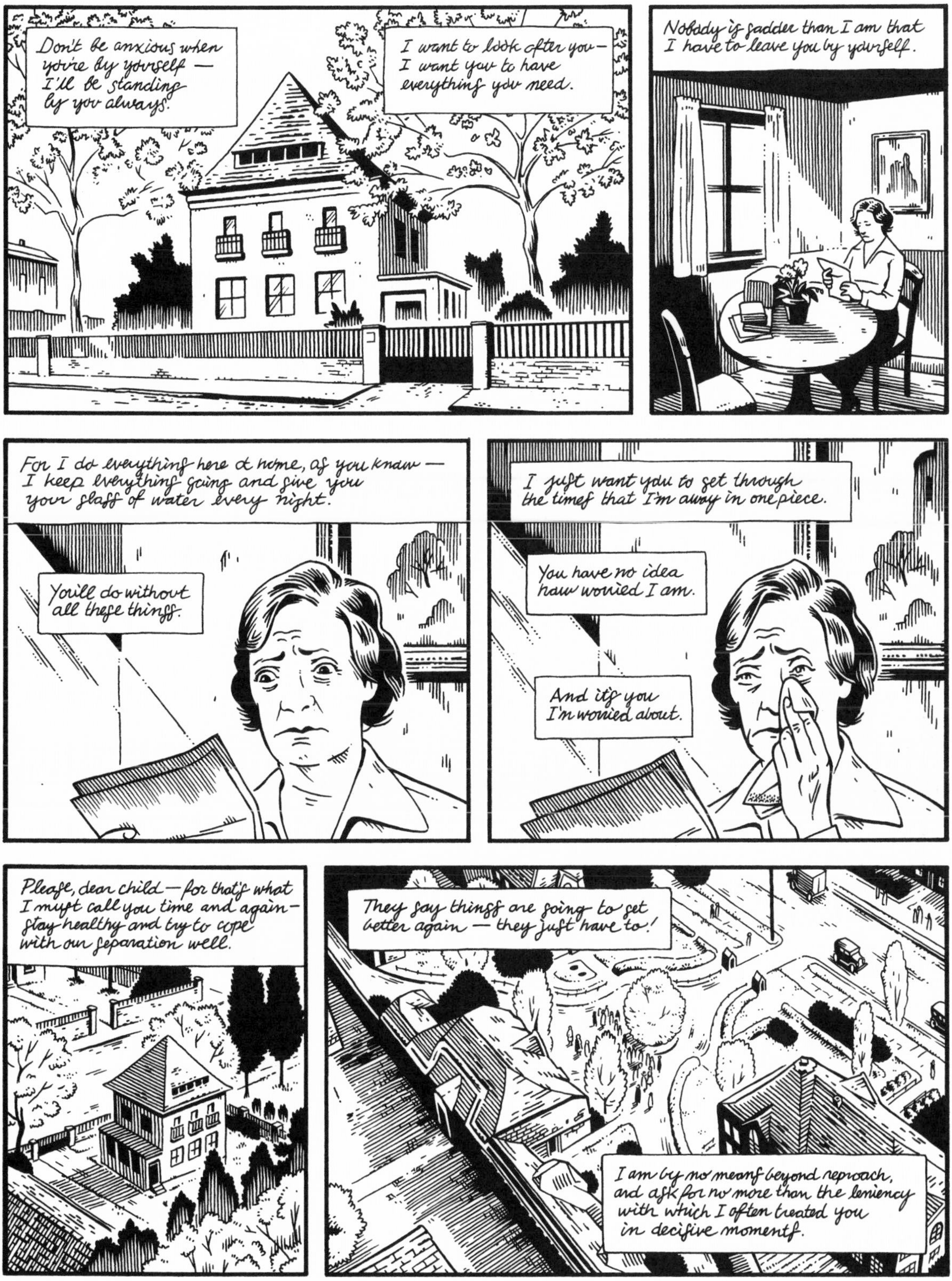
Don't be anxious when you're by yourself — I'll be standing by you always.
I want to look after you — I want you to have everything you need.
Nobody is sadder than I am that I have to leave you by yourself.
For I do everything here at home, as you know — I keep everything going and give you your glass of water every night.
You'll do without all these things.
I just want you to get through the times that I'm away in one piece.
You have no idea how worried I am.
And it's you I'm worried about.
Please, dear child — for that's what I must call you time and again — stay healthy and try to cope with our separation well.
They say things are going to get better again — they just have to!
I am by no means beyond reproach, and ask for no more than the leniency with which I often treated you in decisive moments.

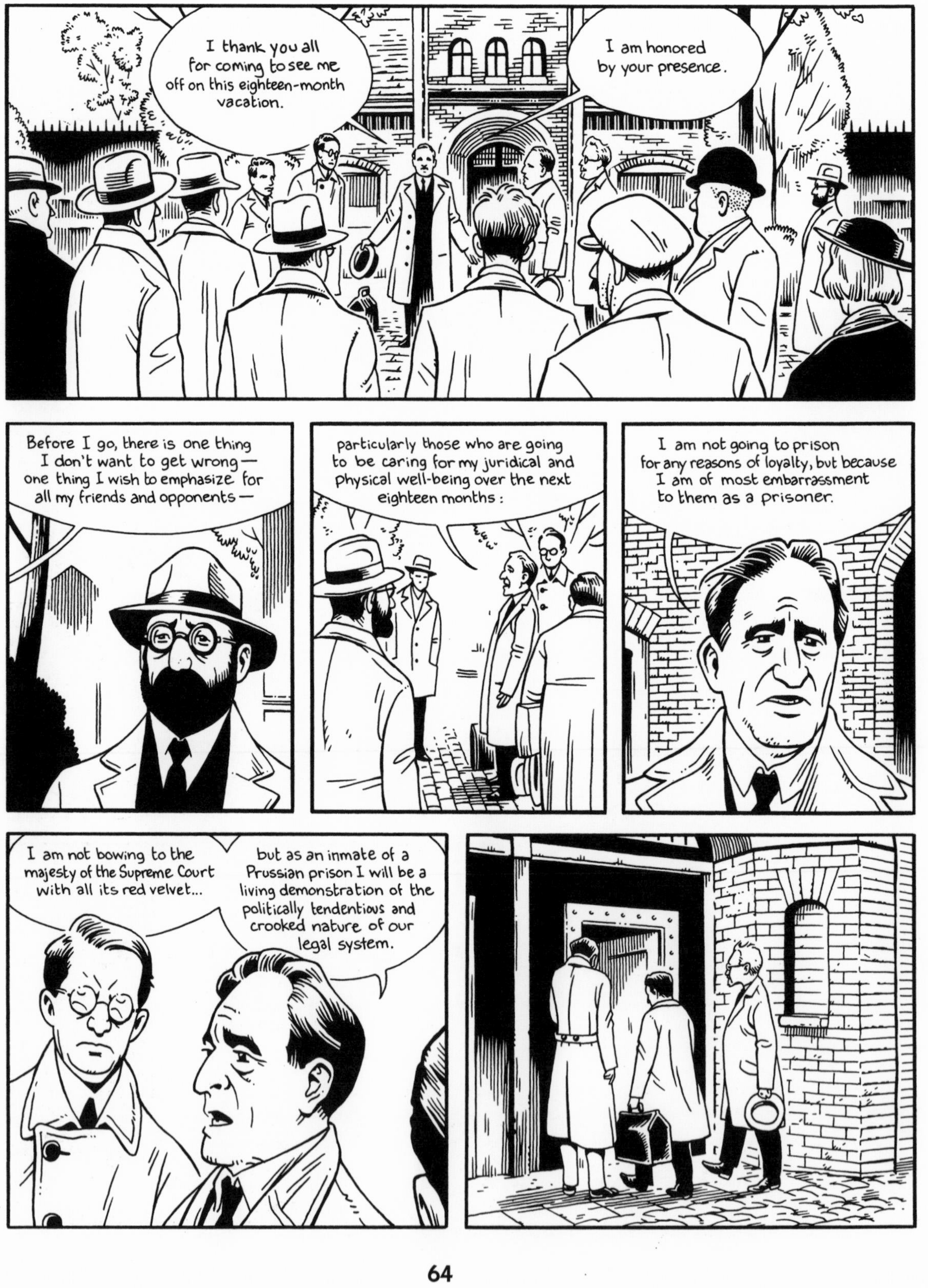
I thank you all for coming to see me off on this eighteen-month vacation.
I am honored by your presence.
Before I go, there is one thing I don't want to get wrong — one thing I wish to emphasize for all my friends and opponents —
particularly those who are going to be caring for my juridical and physical well-being over the next eighteen months :
I am not going to prison for any reasons of loyalty, but because I am of most embarrassment to them as a prisoner.
I am not bowing to the majesty of the Supreme Court with all its red velvet...
but as an inmate of a Prussian prison I will be a living demonstration of the politically tendentious and crooked nature of our legal system.

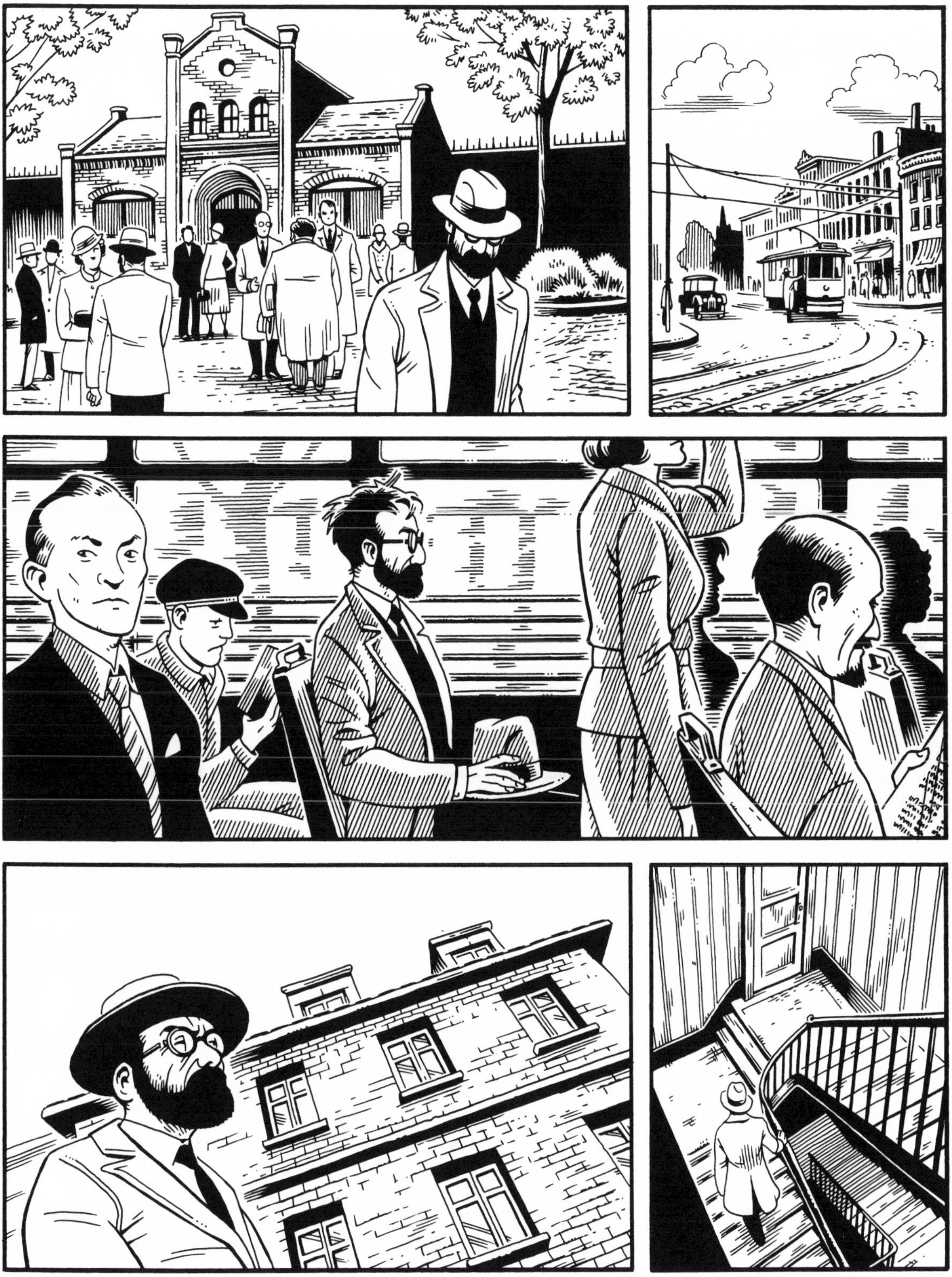

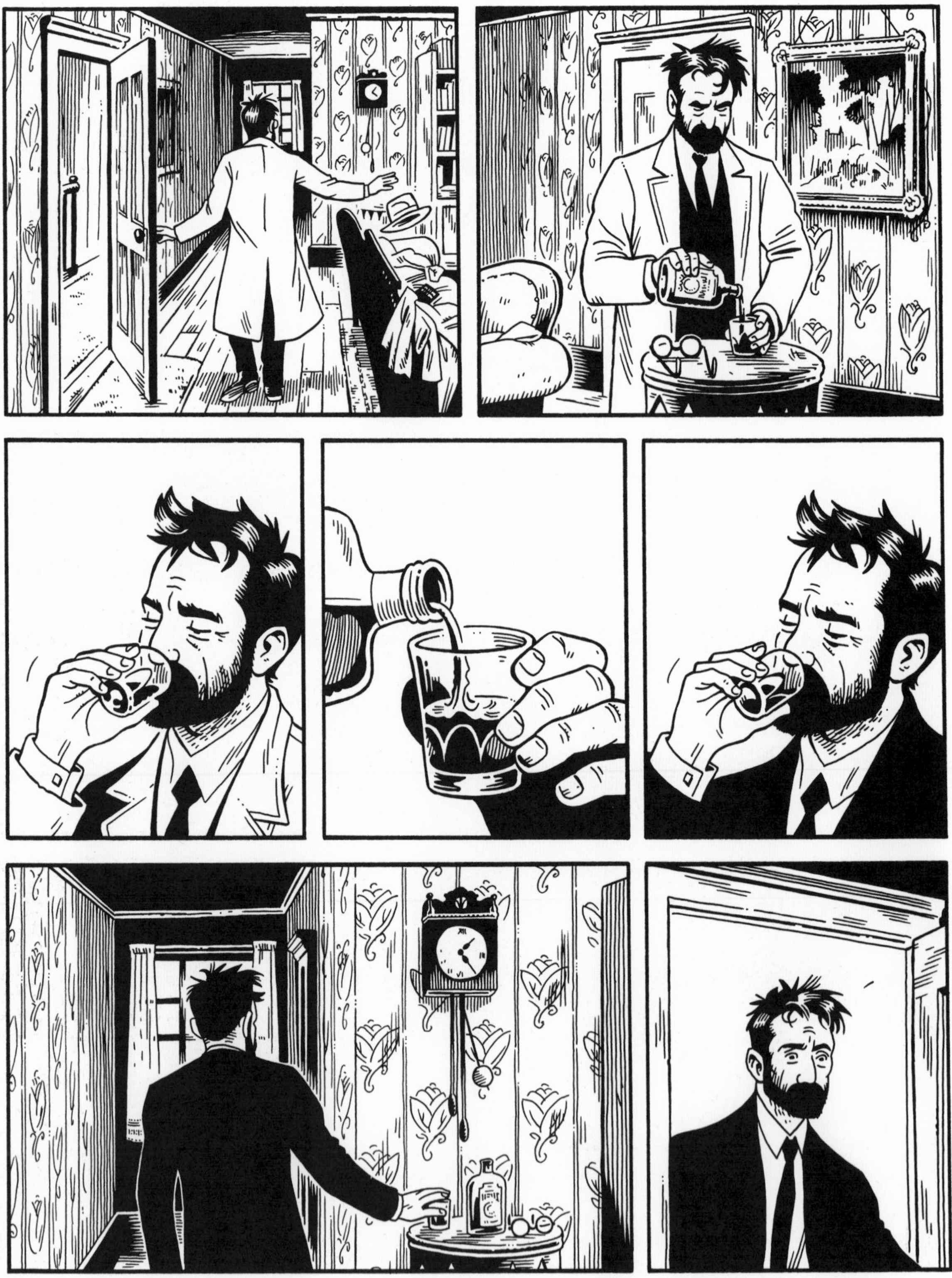

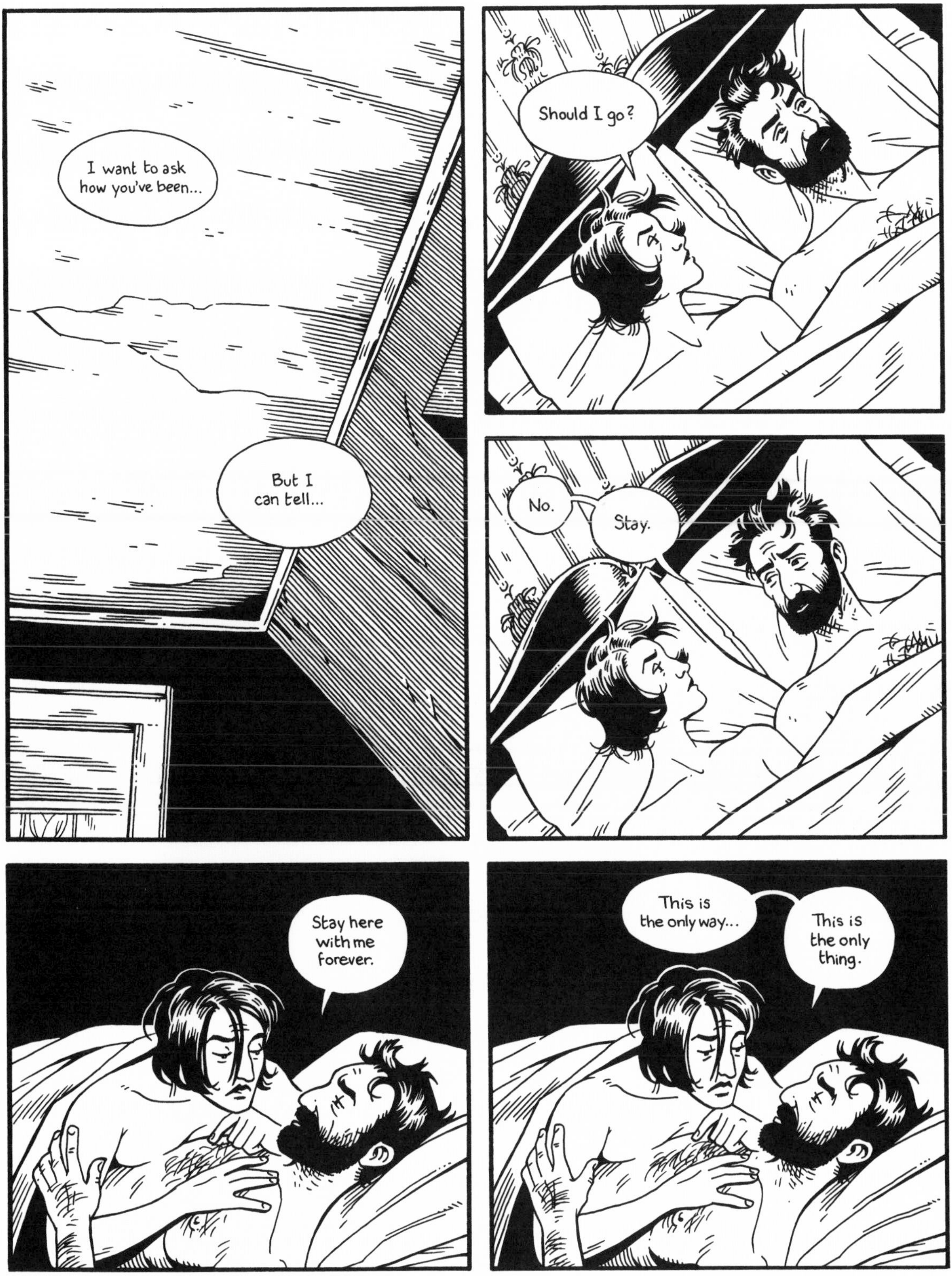
I want to ask how you've been...
But I can tell...
Should I go?
No.
Stay.
Stay here with me forever.
This is the only way...
This is the only thing.

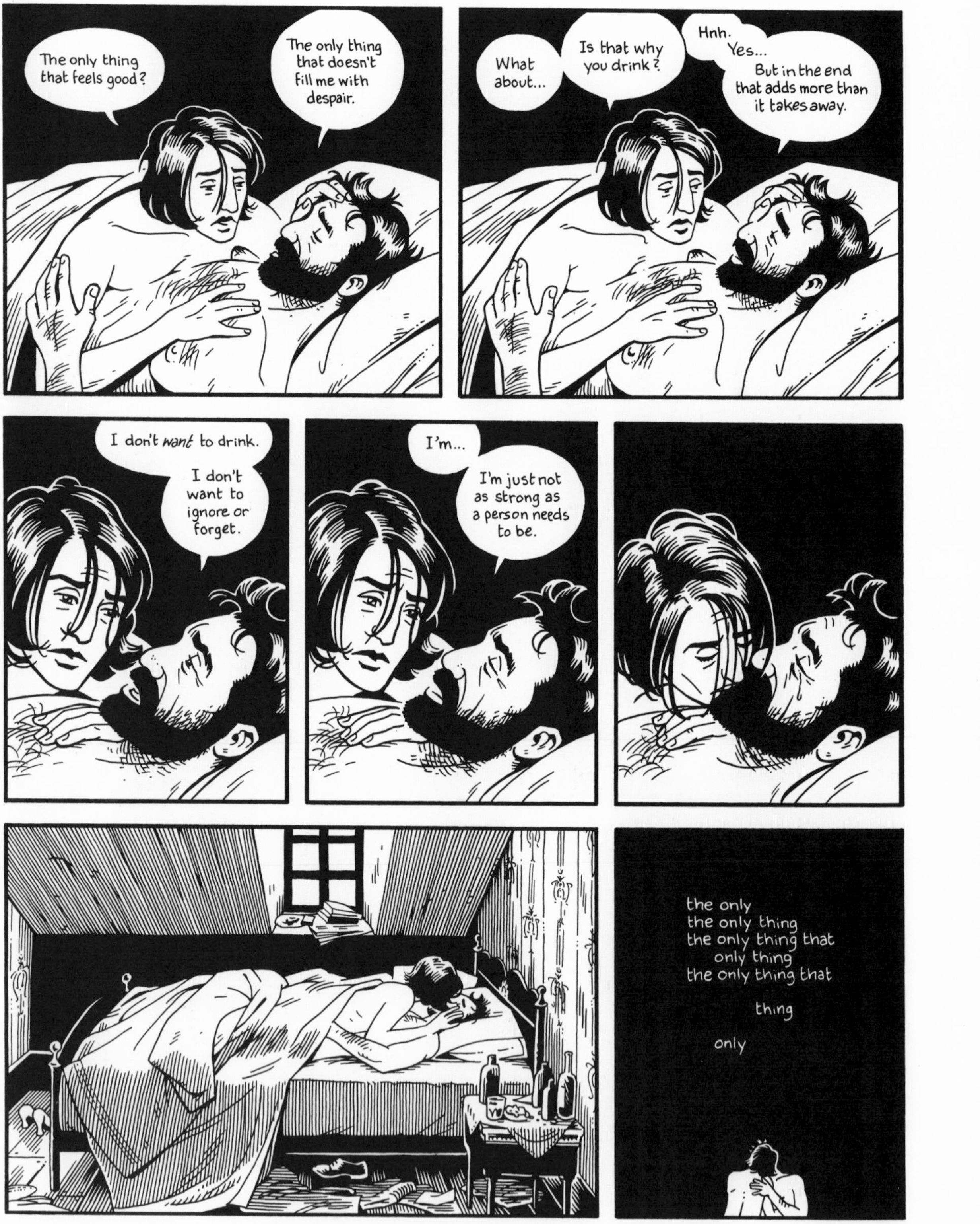
The only thing that feels good?
The only thing that doesn't fill me with despair.
What about...
Is that why you drink?
Hnh.
Yes...
But in the end that adds more than it takes away.
I don't *want* to drink.
I don't want to ignore or forget.
I'm...
I'm just not as strong as a person needs to be.
the only
the only thing
the only thing that
only thing
the only thing that
thing
only

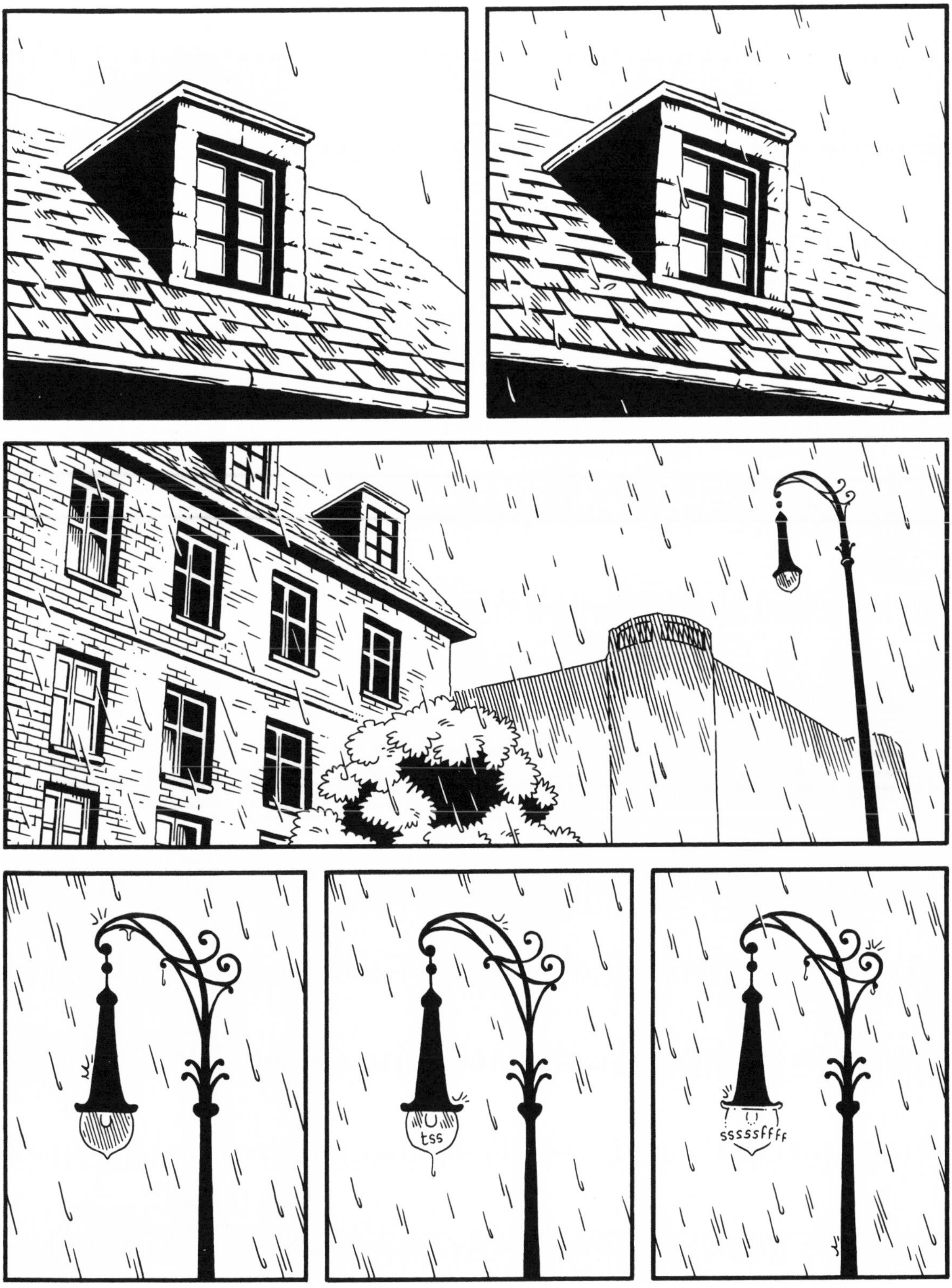
tss
ssssssffff

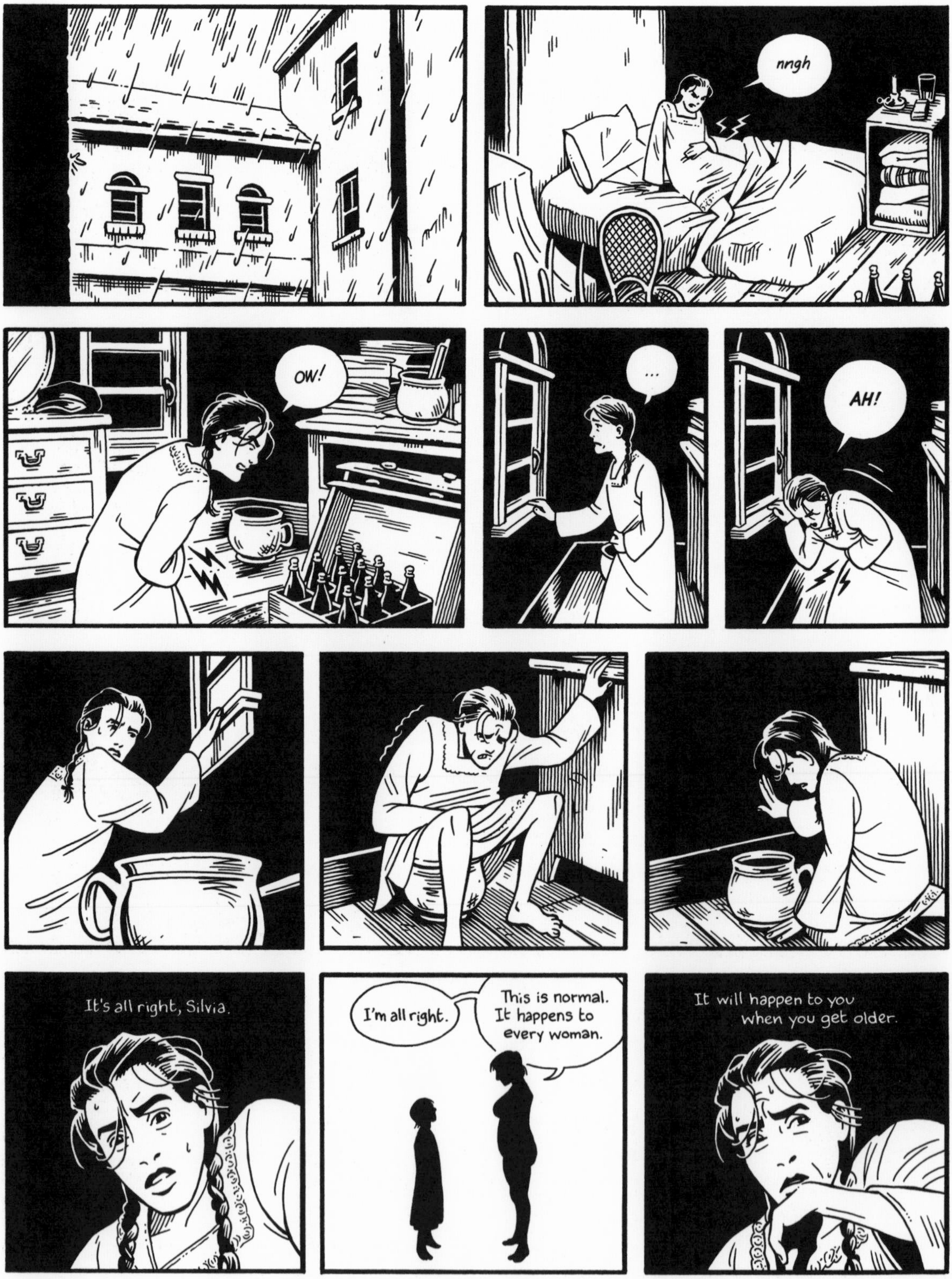
nngh
OW!
...
AH!
It's all right, Silvia.
I'm all right.
This is normal. It happens to every woman.
It will happen to you when you get older.

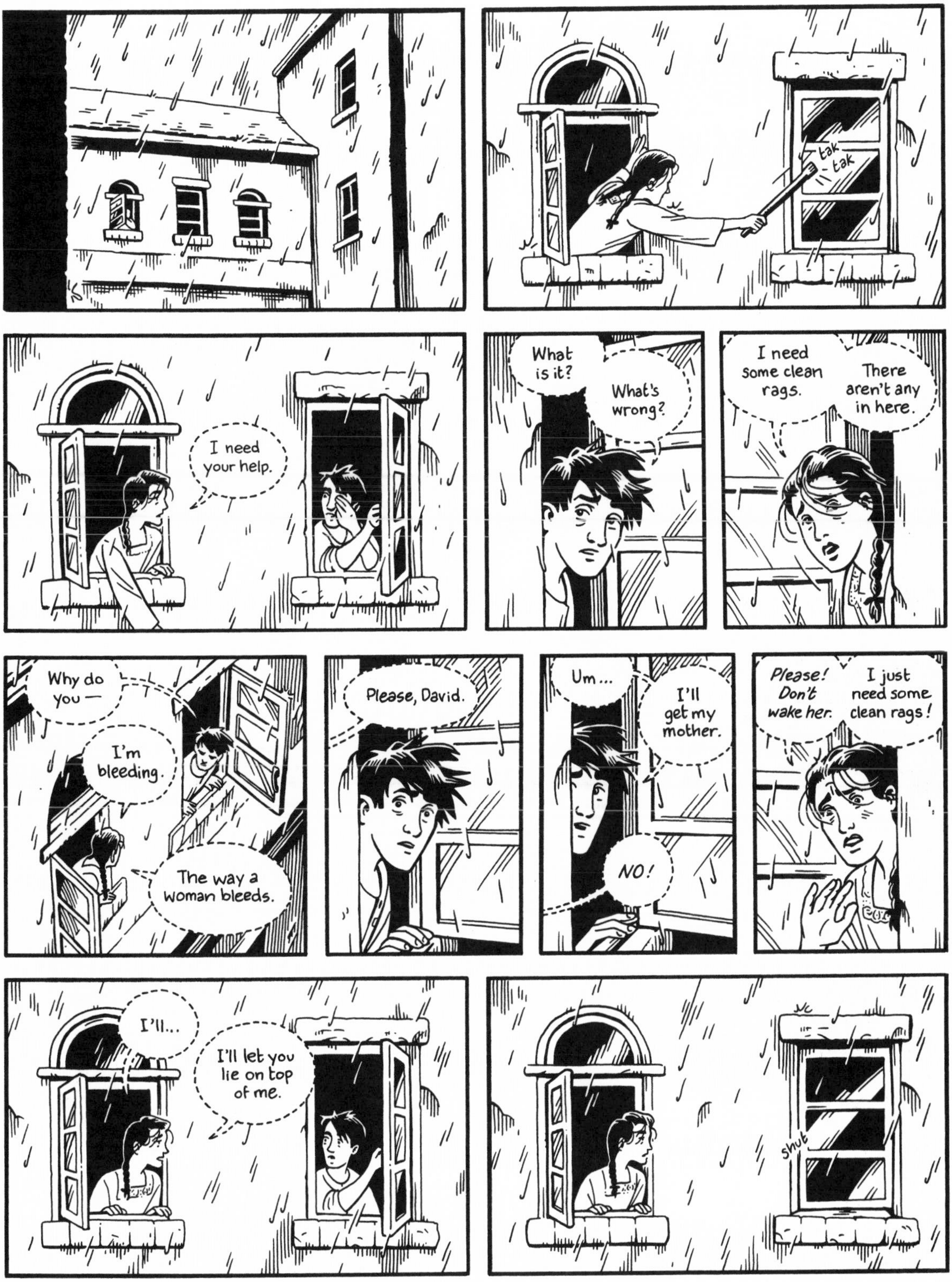
tak
tak
What is it?
What's wrong?
I need some clean rags.
There aren't any in here.
I need your help.
Why do you —
I'm bleeding.
The way a woman bleeds.
Please, David.
Um...
I'll get my mother.
NO!
Please! Don't wake her.
I just need some clean rags!
I'll...
I'll let you lie on top of me.
shut

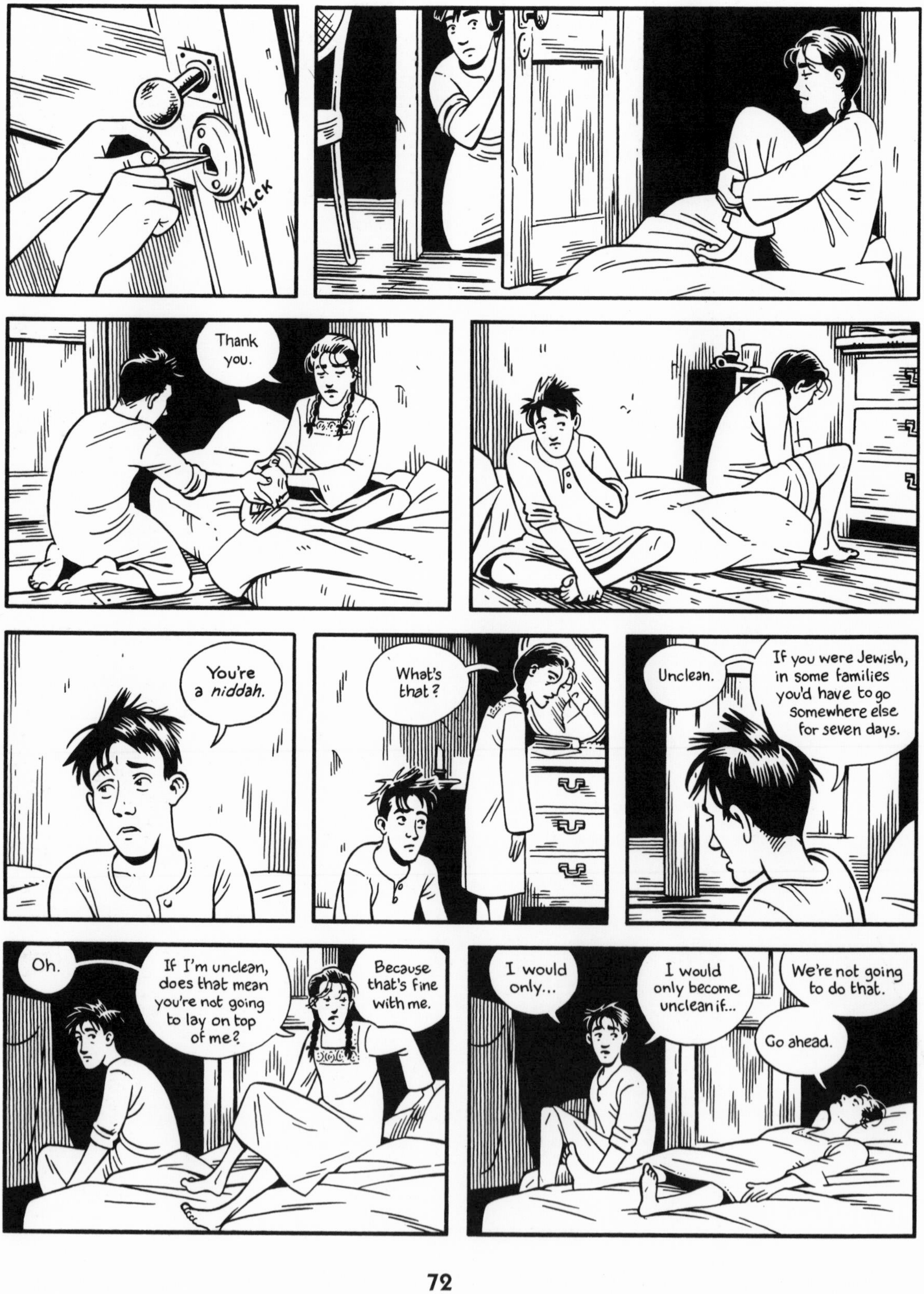
KLCK
Thank you.
You're a *niddah*.
What's that?
Unclean.
If you were Jewish, in some families you'd have to go somewhere else for seven days.
Oh.
If I'm unclean, does that mean you're not going to lay on top of me?
Because that's fine with me.
I would only...
I would only become unclean if...
We're not going to do that.
Go ahead.

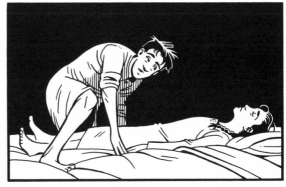

Your mother is excited about your birthday.

She says that you will become a man.

Is that when they cut off part of your...

No no no — that happened already!

When I was born!

Oh.

They didn't cut off very much.

I — only — it was only a little bit.

Oh.

May I put my hands on your chest?

I suppose.

There's not much to hold on to, you know.

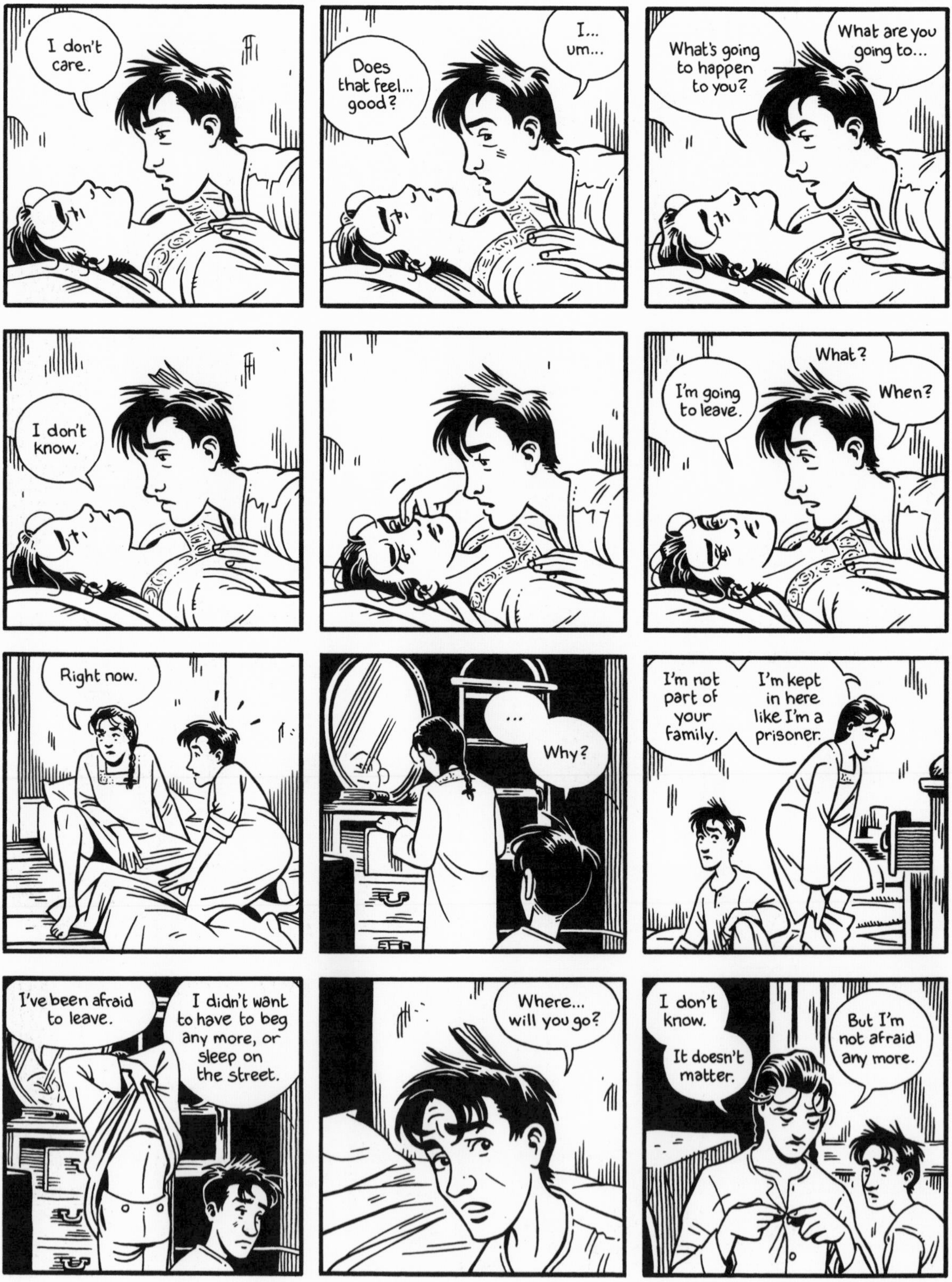
I don't care.
I... um...
Does that feel... good?
What's going to happen to you?
What are you going to...
I don't know.
I'm going to leave.
What?
When?
Right now.
...
Why?
I'm not part of your family.
I'm kept in here like I'm a prisoner.
I've been afraid to leave.
I didn't want to have to beg any more, or sleep on the street.
Where... will you go?
I don't know.
It doesn't matter.
But I'm not afraid any more.

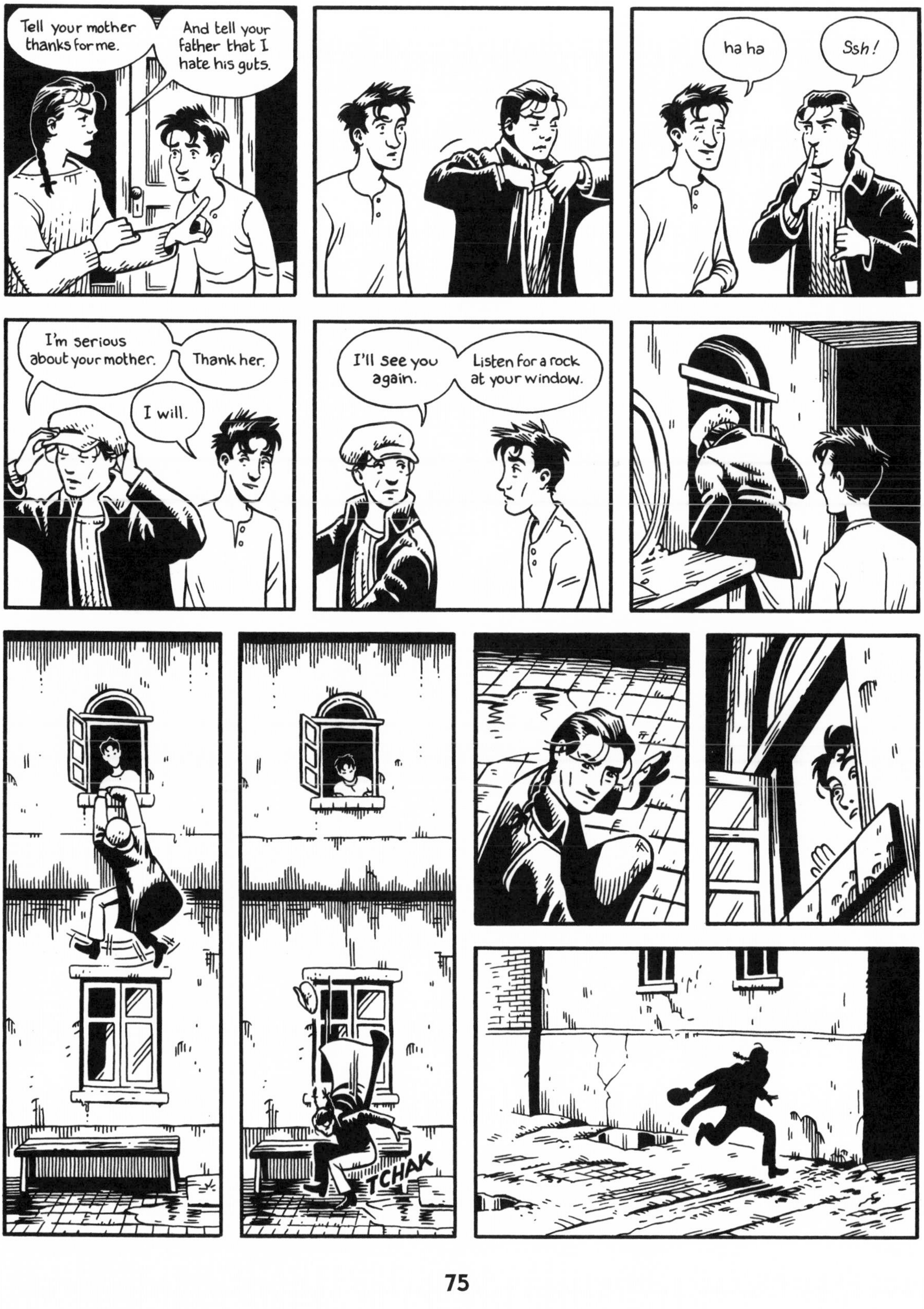
Tell your mother thanks for me.
And tell your father that I hate his guts.
ha ha
Ssh!
I'm serious about your mother.
Thank her.
I will.
I'll see you again.
Listen for a rock at your window.
TCHAK

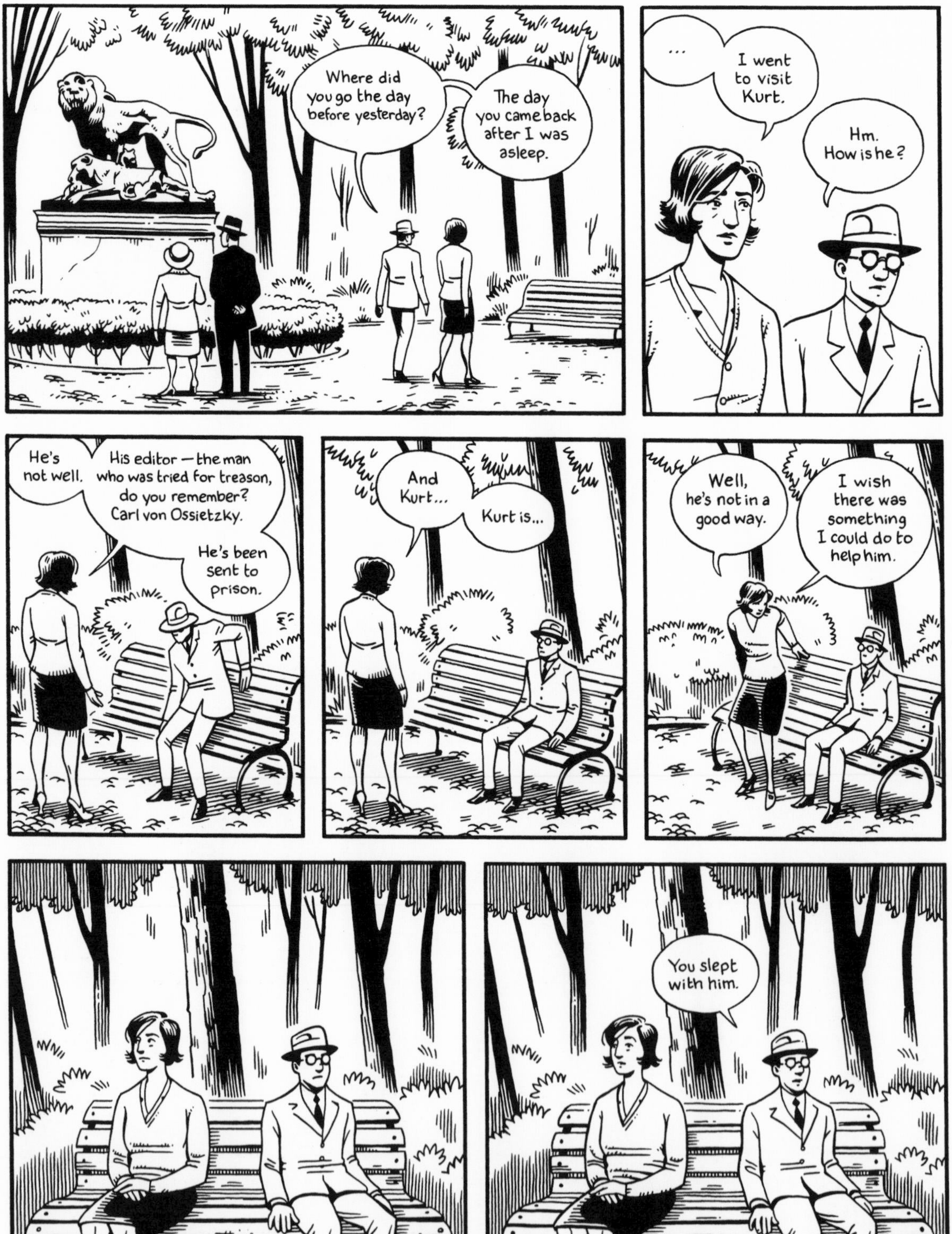
Where did you go the day before yesterday?
The day you came back after I was asleep.
...
I went to visit Kurt.
Hm. How is he?
He's not well.
His editor — the man who was tried for treason, do you remember? Carl von Ossietzky.
He's been sent to prison.
And Kurt...
Kurt is...
Well, he's not in a good way.
I wish there was something I could do to help him.
You slept with him.

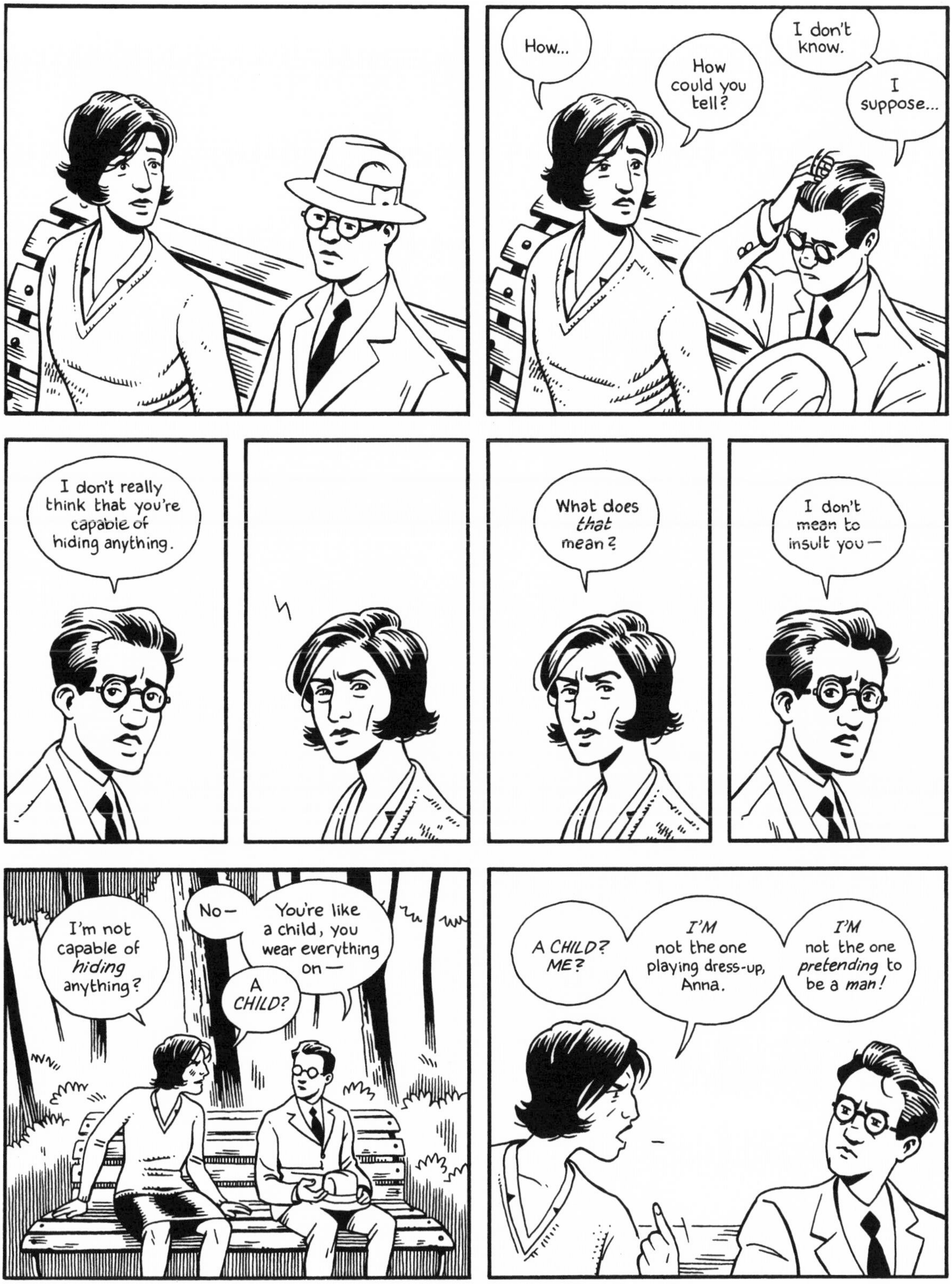
How...
How could you tell?
I don't know.
I suppose...
I don't really think that you're capable of hiding anything.
What does *that* mean?
I don't mean to insult you—
I'm not capable of *hiding* anything?
No—
You're like a child, you wear everything on—
A *CHILD?*
A *CHILD? ME?*
I'M not the one playing dress-up, Anna.
I'M not the one *pretending* to be a *man!*

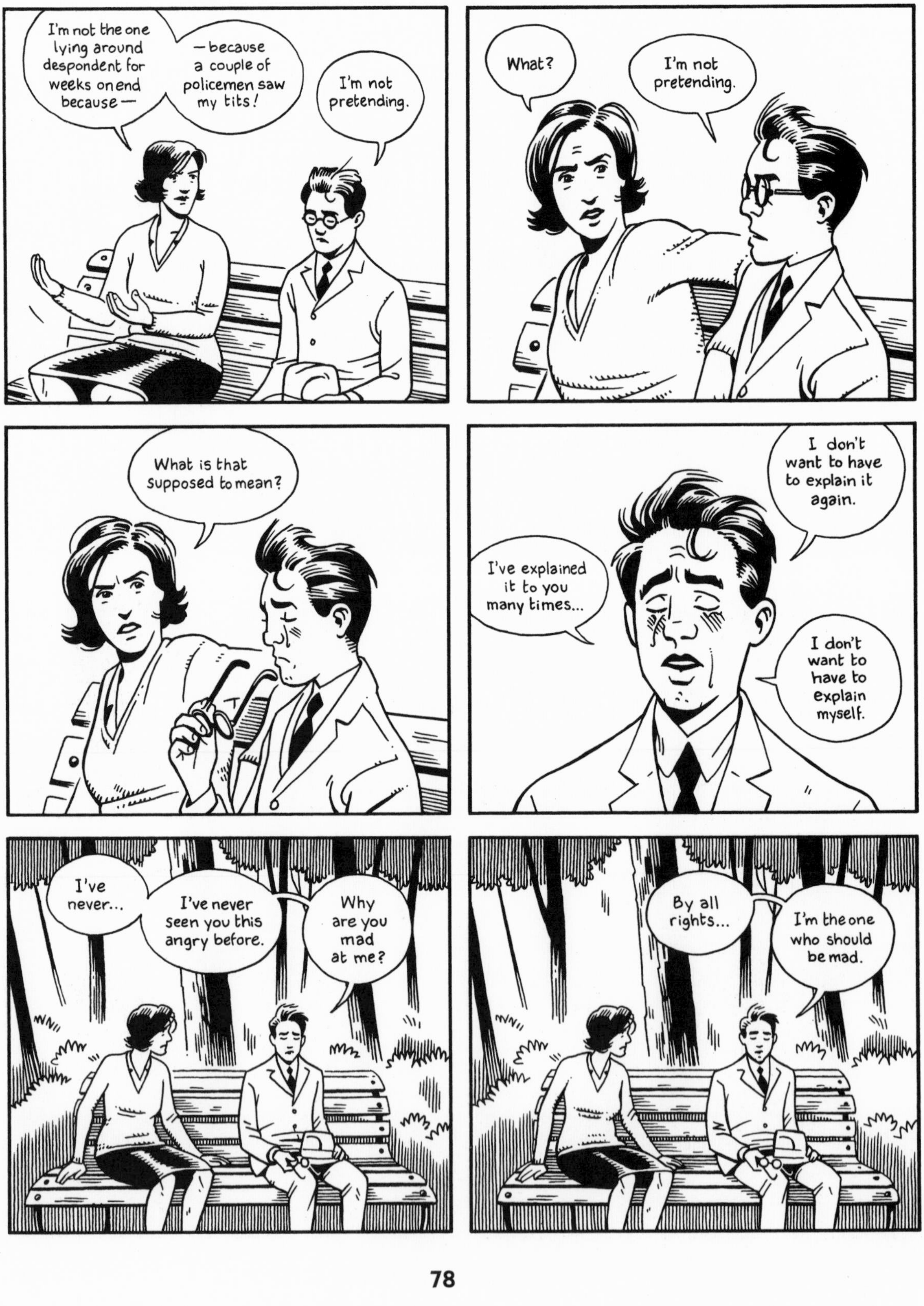
I'm not the one lying around despondent for weeks on end because—
—because a couple of policemen saw my tits!
I'm not pretending.
What?
I'm not pretending.
What is that supposed to mean?
I've explained it to you many times...
I don't want to have to explain it again.
I don't want to have to explain myself.
I've never...
I've never seen you this angry before.
Why are you mad at me?
By all rights...
I'm the one who should be mad.

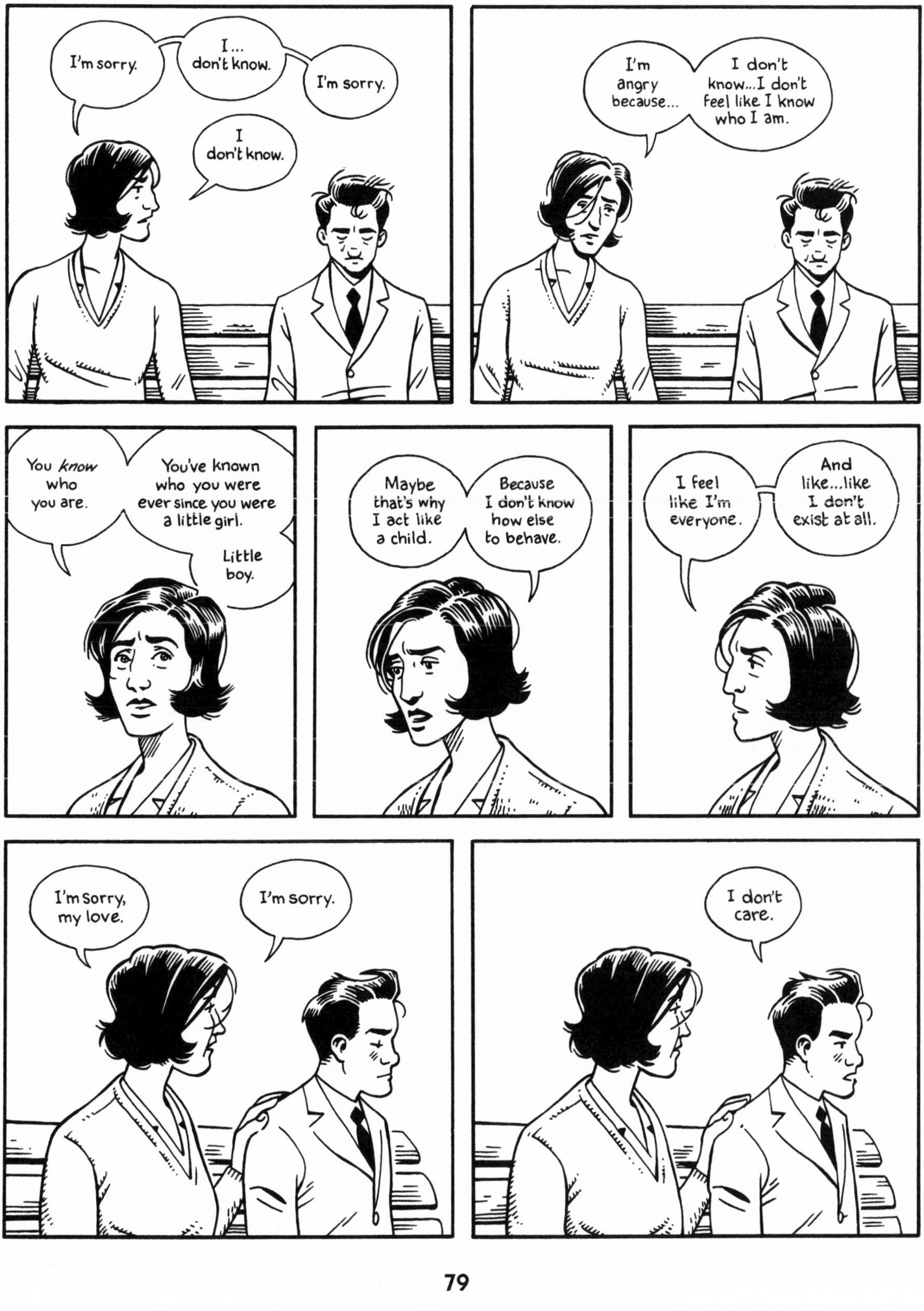
I'm sorry.
I... don't know.
I'm sorry.
I don't know.
I'm angry because...
I don't know...I don't feel like I know who I am.
You *know* who you are.
You've known who you were ever since you were a little girl.
Little boy.
Maybe that's why I act like a child.
Because I don't know how else to behave.
I feel like I'm everyone.
And like...like I don't exist at all.
I'm sorry, my love.
I'm sorry.
I don't care.

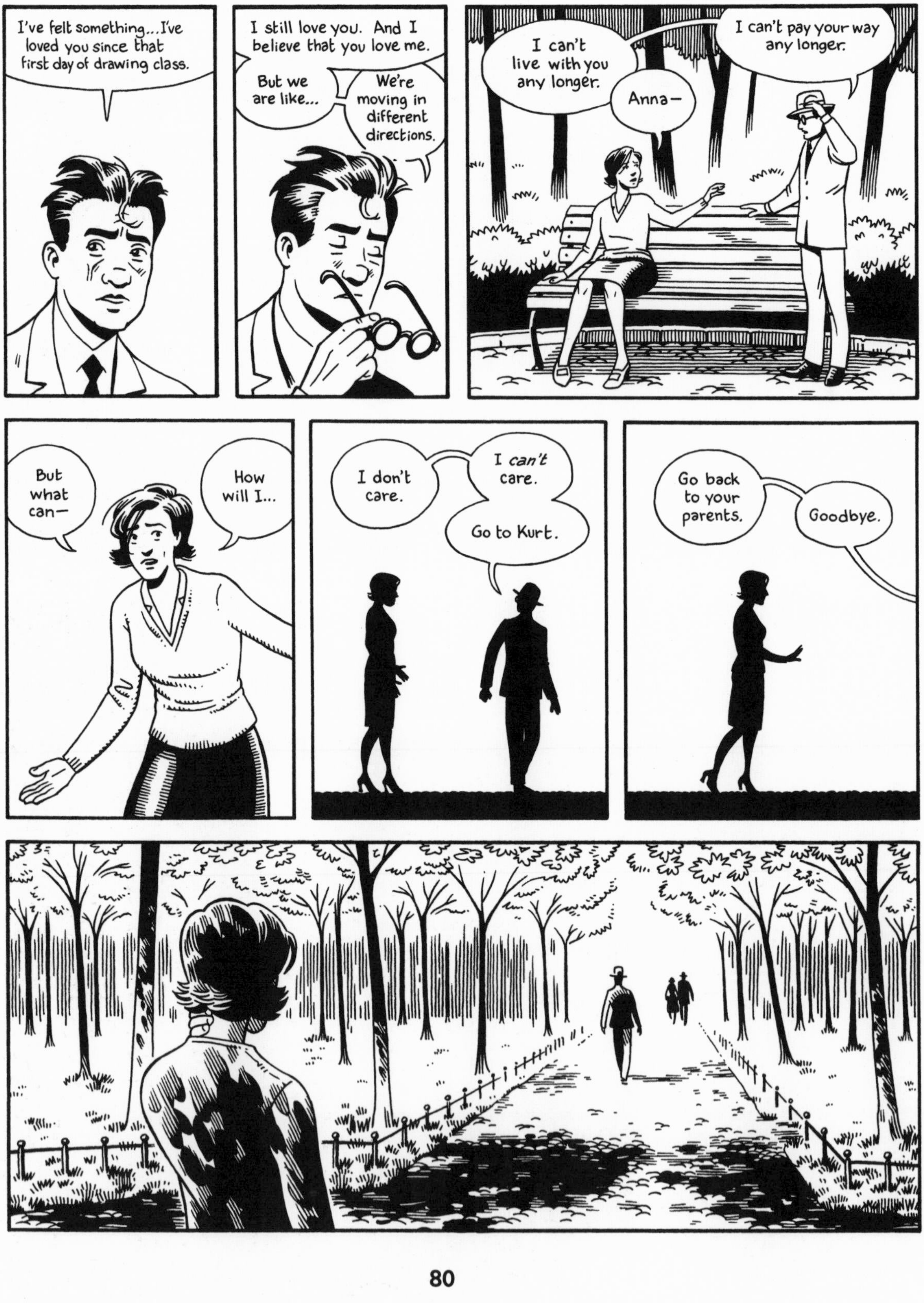
I've felt something... I've loved you since that first day of drawing class.
I still love you. And I believe that you love me.
But we are like...
We're moving in different directions.
I can't live with you any longer.
Anna—
I can't pay your way any longer.
But what can—
How will I...
I don't care.
I *can't* care.
Go to Kurt.
Go back to your parents.
Goodbye.

4

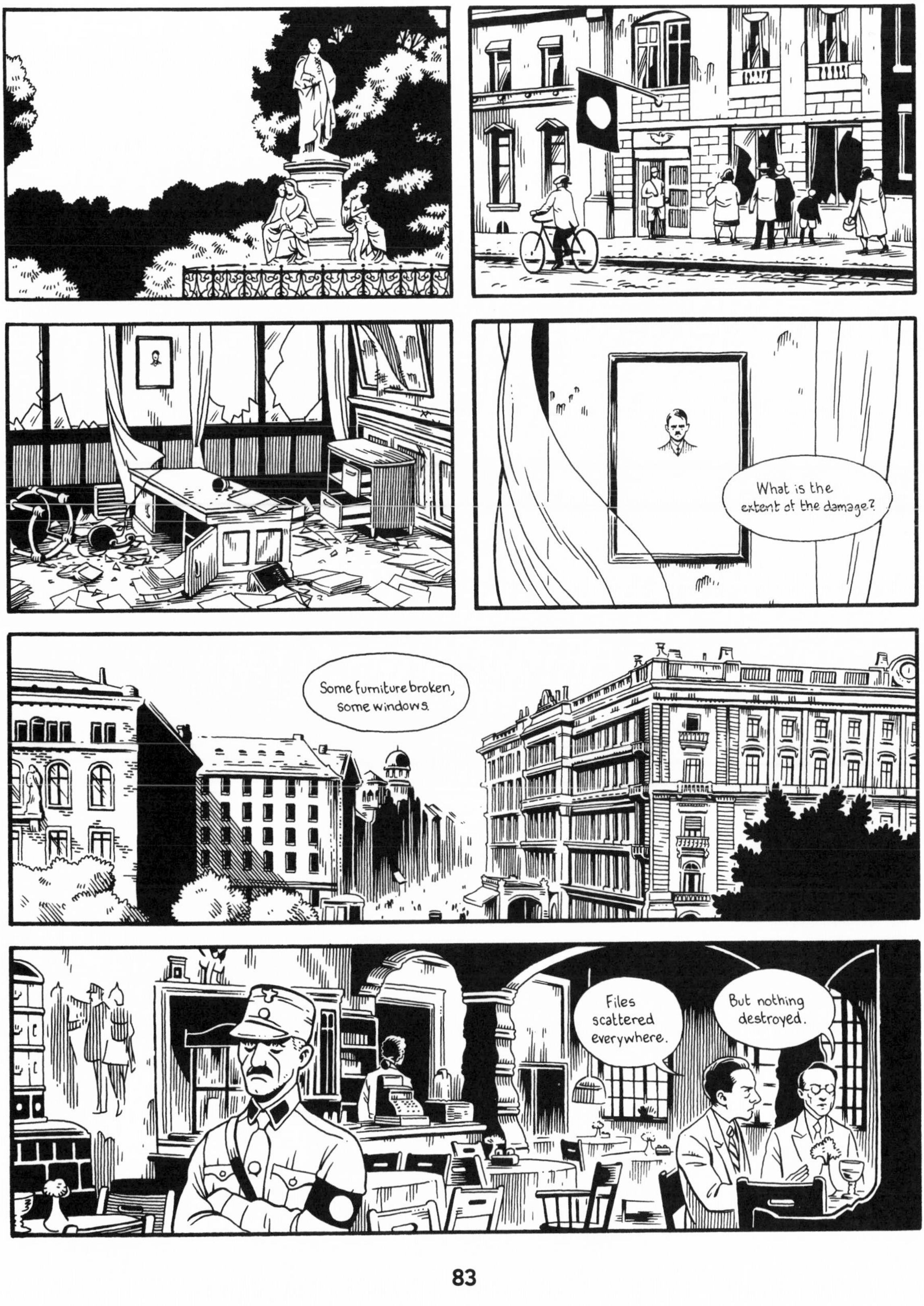
What is the extent of the damage?
Some furniture broken, some windows.
Files scattered everywhere.
But nothing destroyed.

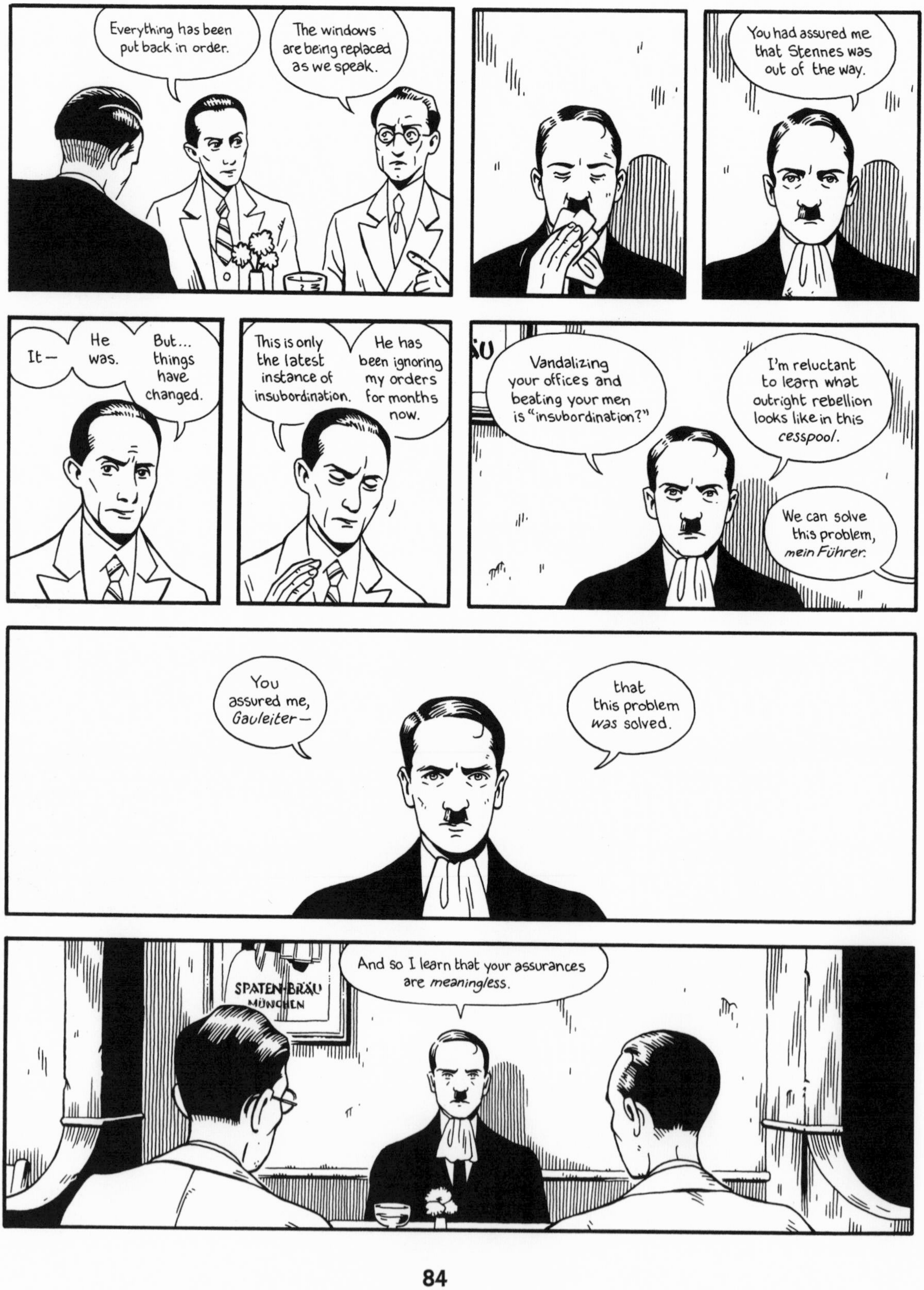
Everything has been put back in order.
The windows are being replaced as we speak.
You had assured me that Stennes was out of the way.
It—
He was.
But... things have changed.
This is only the latest instance of insubordination.
He has been ignoring my orders for months now.
ÄU
Vandalizing your offices and beating your men is "insubordination?"
I'm reluctant to learn what outright rebellion looks like in this *cesspool*.
We can solve this problem, *mein Führer*.
You assured me, *Gauleiter*—
that this problem *was* solved.
SPATEN-BRÄU
MÜNCHEN
And so I learn that your assurances are *meaningless*.

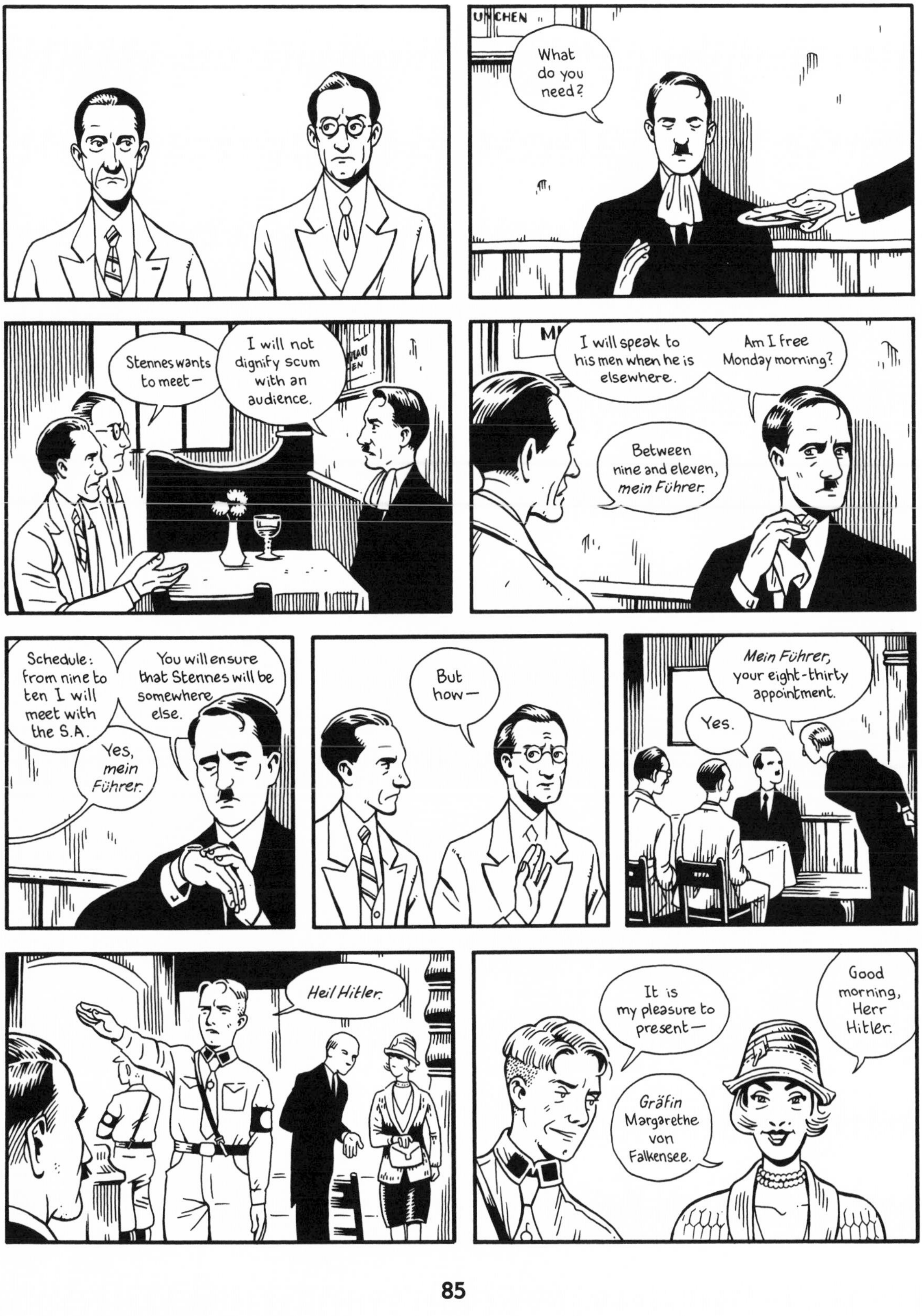
UNCHEN
What do you need?
Stennes wants to meet—
I will not dignify scum with an audience.
I will speak to his men when he is elsewhere.
Am I free Monday morning?
Between nine and eleven, *mein Führer.*
Schedule: from nine to ten I will meet with the S.A.
You will ensure that Stennes will be somewhere else.
Yes, *mein Führer.*
But how—
Mein Führer, your eight-thirty appointment.
Yes.
Heil Hitler.
It is my pleasure to present—
Good morning, Herr Hitler.
Gräfin Margarethe von Falkensee.

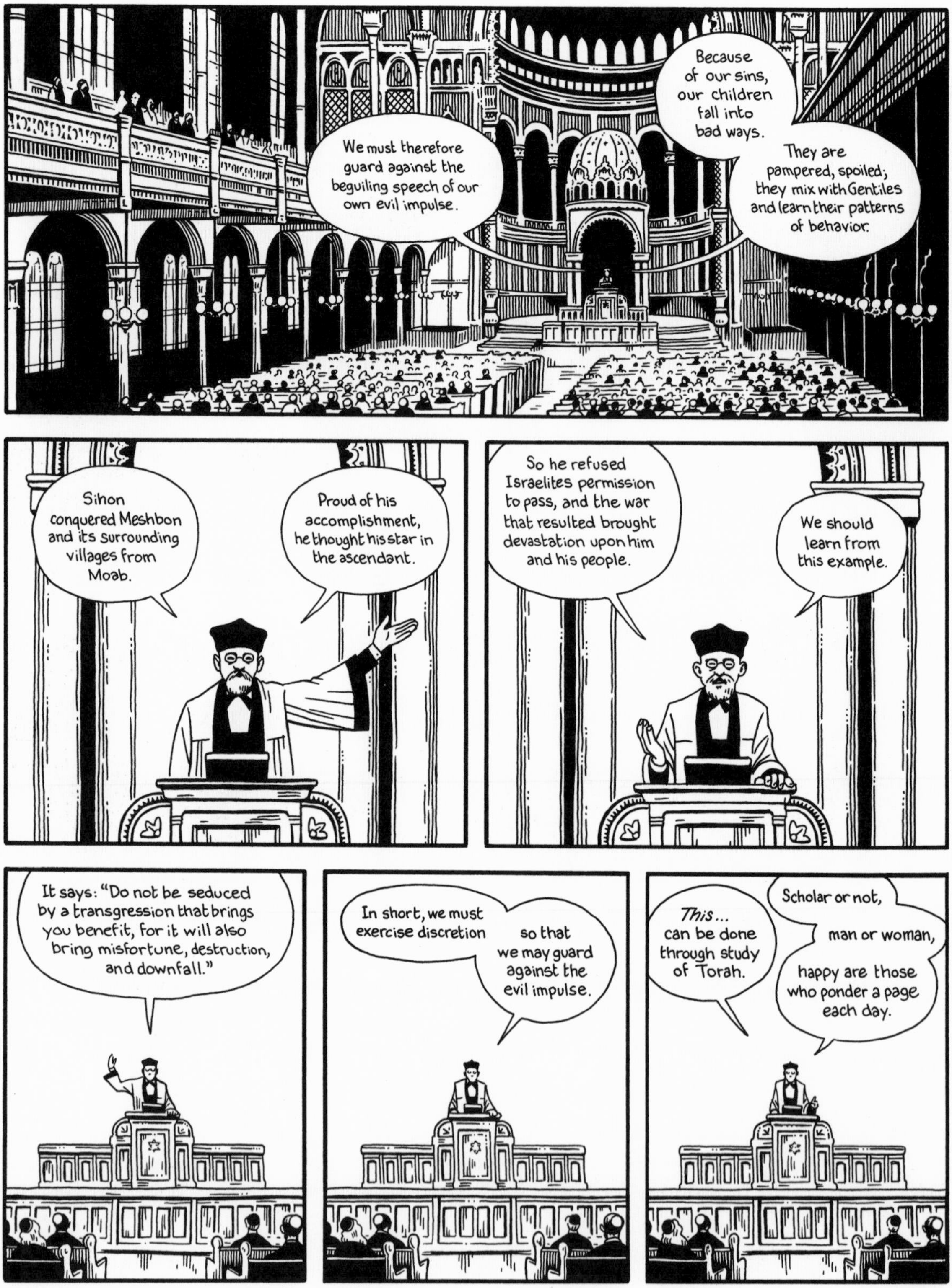
We must therefore guard against the beguiling speech of our own evil impulse.
Because of our sins, our children fall into bad ways.
They are pampered, spoiled; they mix with Gentiles and learn their patterns of behavior.
Sihon conquered Meshbon and its surrounding villages from Moab.
Proud of his accomplishment, he thought his star in the ascendant.
So he refused Israelites permission to pass, and the war that resulted brought devastation upon him and his people.
We should learn from this example.
It says: "Do not be seduced by a transgression that brings you benefit, for it will also bring misfortune, destruction, and downfall."
In short, we must exercise discretion
so that we may guard against the evil impulse.
This... can be done through study of Torah.
Scholar or not,
man or woman,
happy are those who ponder a page each day.

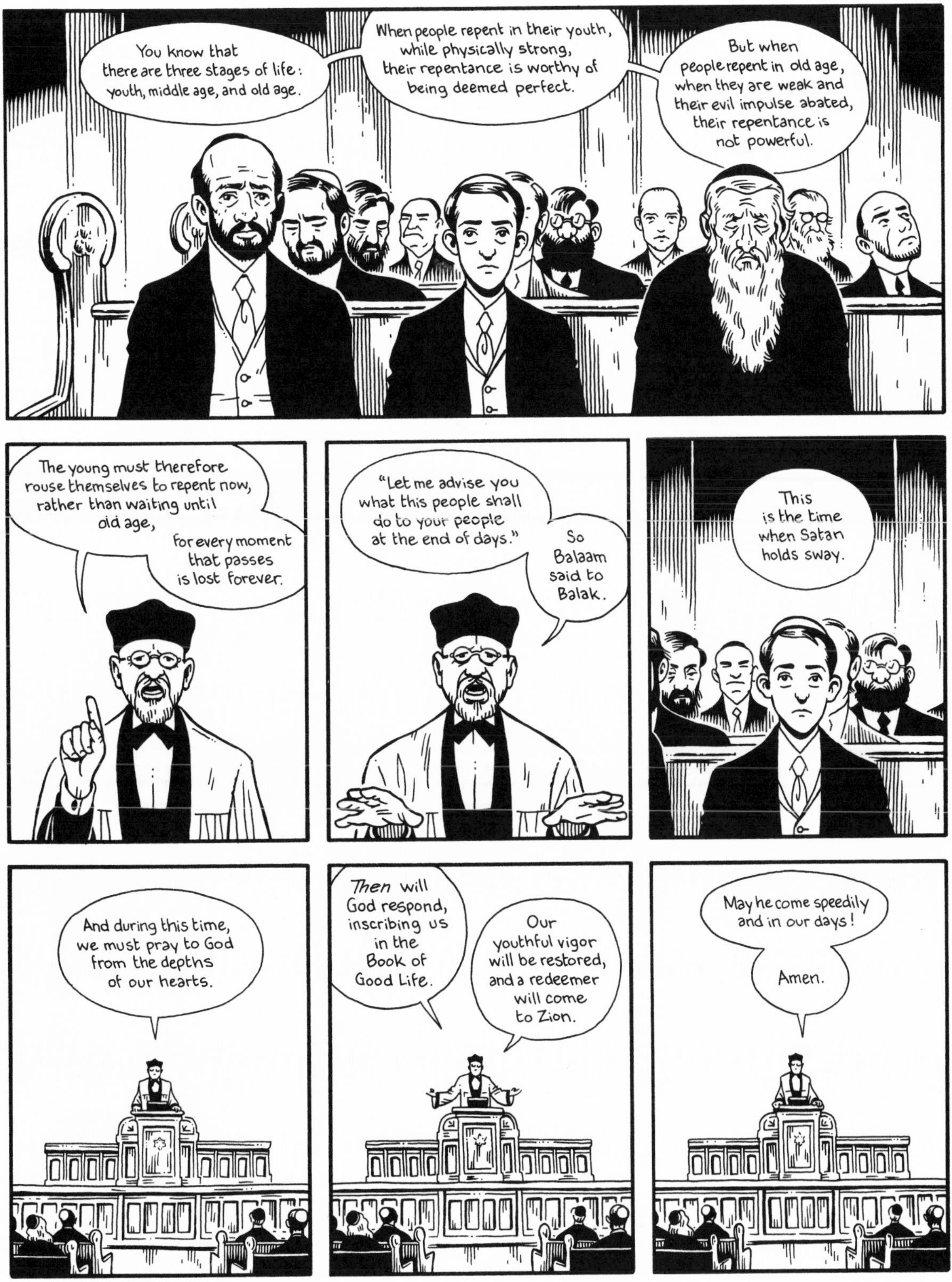
You know that there are three stages of life: youth, middle age, and old age.
When people repent in their youth, while physically strong, their repentance is worthy of being deemed perfect.
But when people repent in old age, when they are weak and their evil impulse abated, their repentance is not powerful.
The young must therefore rouse themselves to repent now, rather than waiting until old age,
for every moment that passes is lost forever.
"Let me advise you what this people shall do to your people at the end of days."
So Balaam said to Balak.
This is the time when Satan holds sway.
And during this time, we must pray to God from the depths of our hearts.
Then will God respond, inscribing us in the Book of Good Life.
Our youthful vigor will be restored, and a redeemer will come to Zion.
May he come speedily and in our days!
Amen.

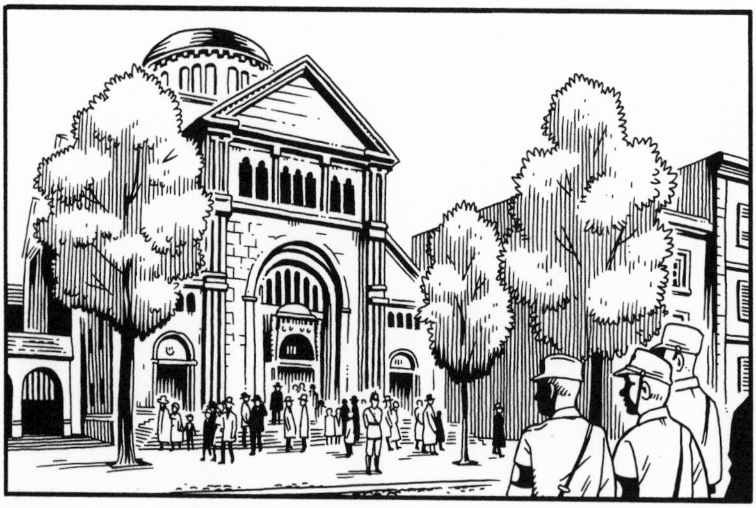

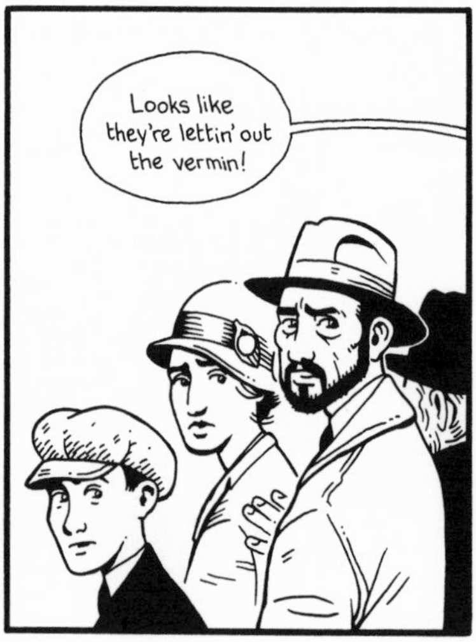
Looks like they're lettin' out the vermin!

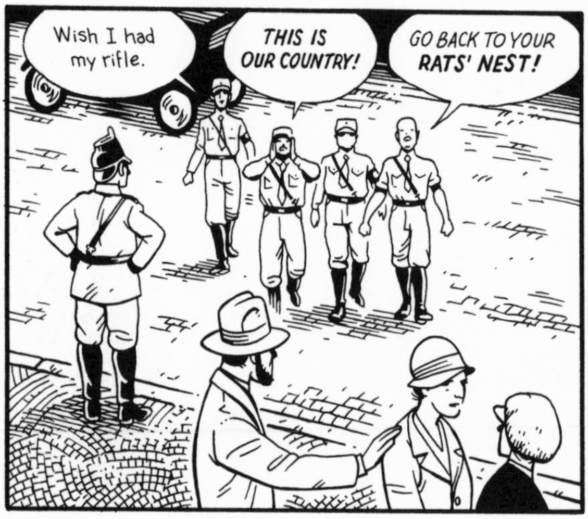
Wish I had my rifle.
THIS IS OUR COUNTRY!
GO BACK TO YOUR RATS' NEST!

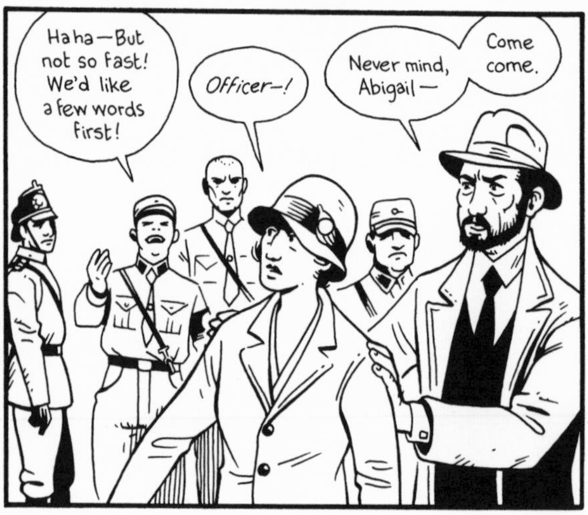
Ha ha—But not so fast! We'd like a few words first!
Officer—!
Never mind, Abigail—
Come come.

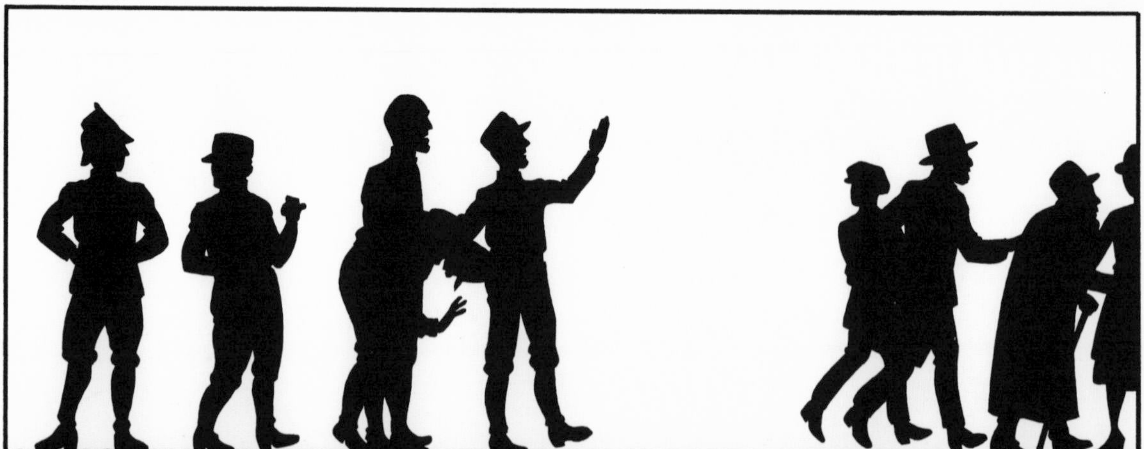

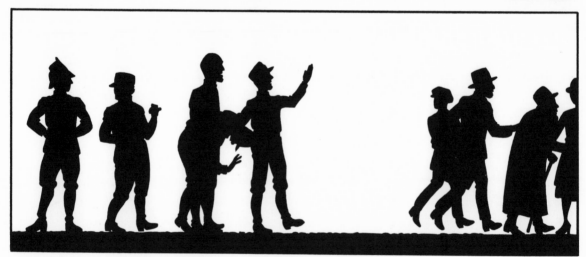

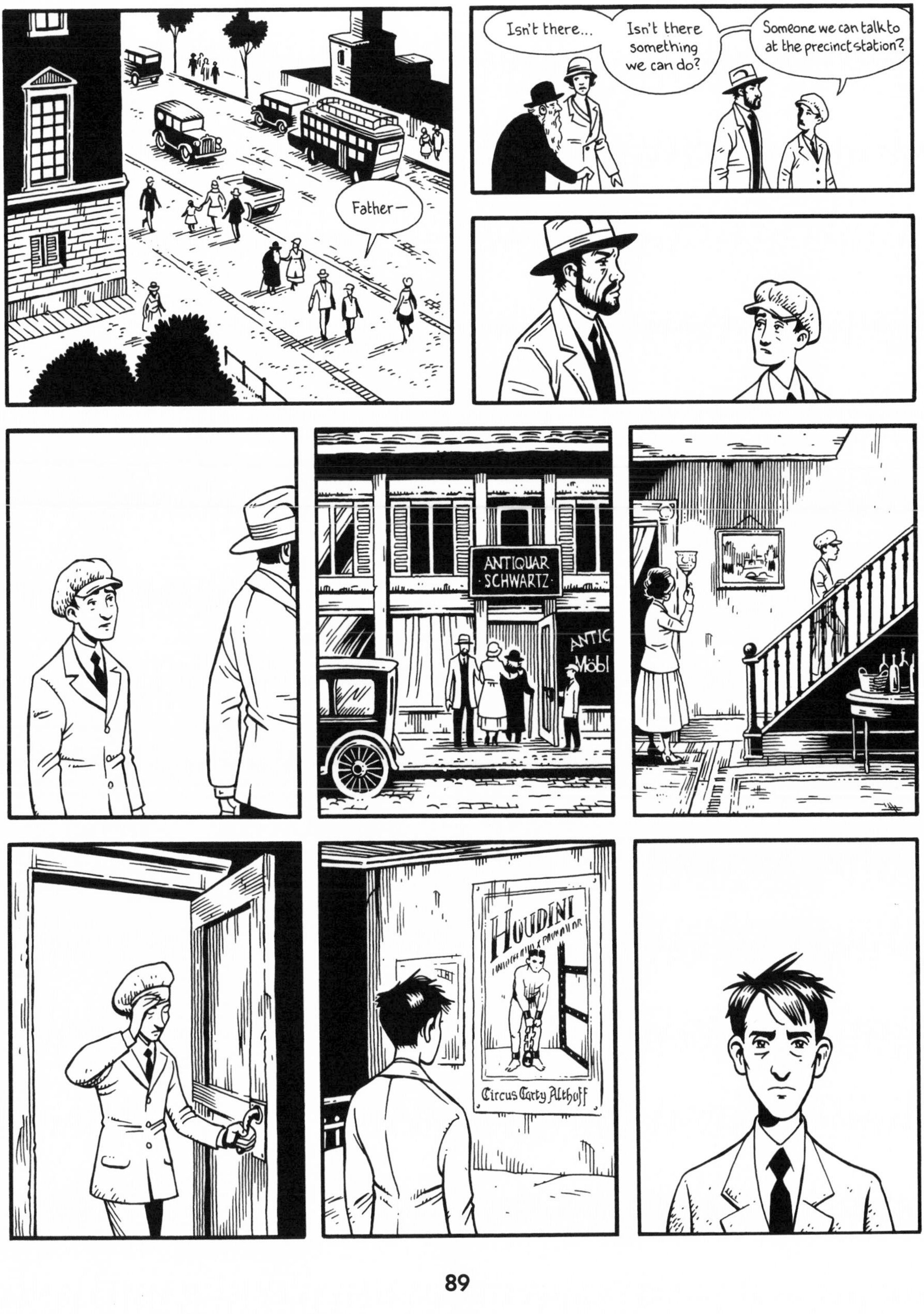
Father—
Isn't there...
Isn't there something we can do?
Someone we can talk to at the precinct station?
ANTIQUAR SCHWARTZ
ANTIC
Möbl
HOUDINI
Circus Carty Althoff

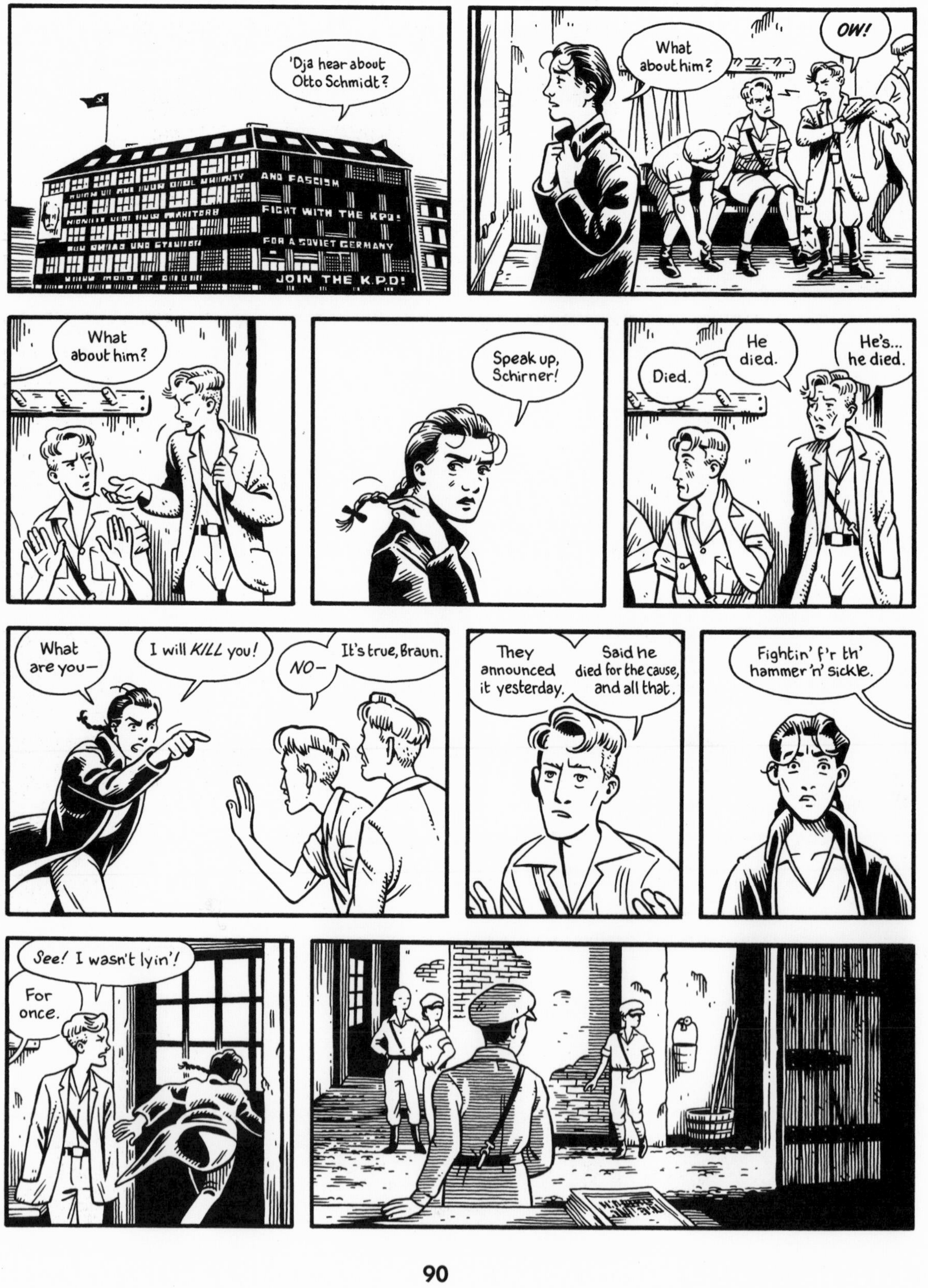
'Dja hear about Otto Schmidt?
AND FASCISM
FIGHT WITH THE KPD!
FOR A SOVIET GERMANY
JOIN THE K.P.D!
What about him?
OW!
What about him?
Speak up, Schirner!
Died.
He died.
He's... he died.
What are you—
I will *KILL* you!
NO—
It's true, Braun.
They announced it yesterday.
Said he died for the cause, and all that.
Fightin' f'r th' hammer 'n' sickle.
See! I wasn't lyin'!
For once.

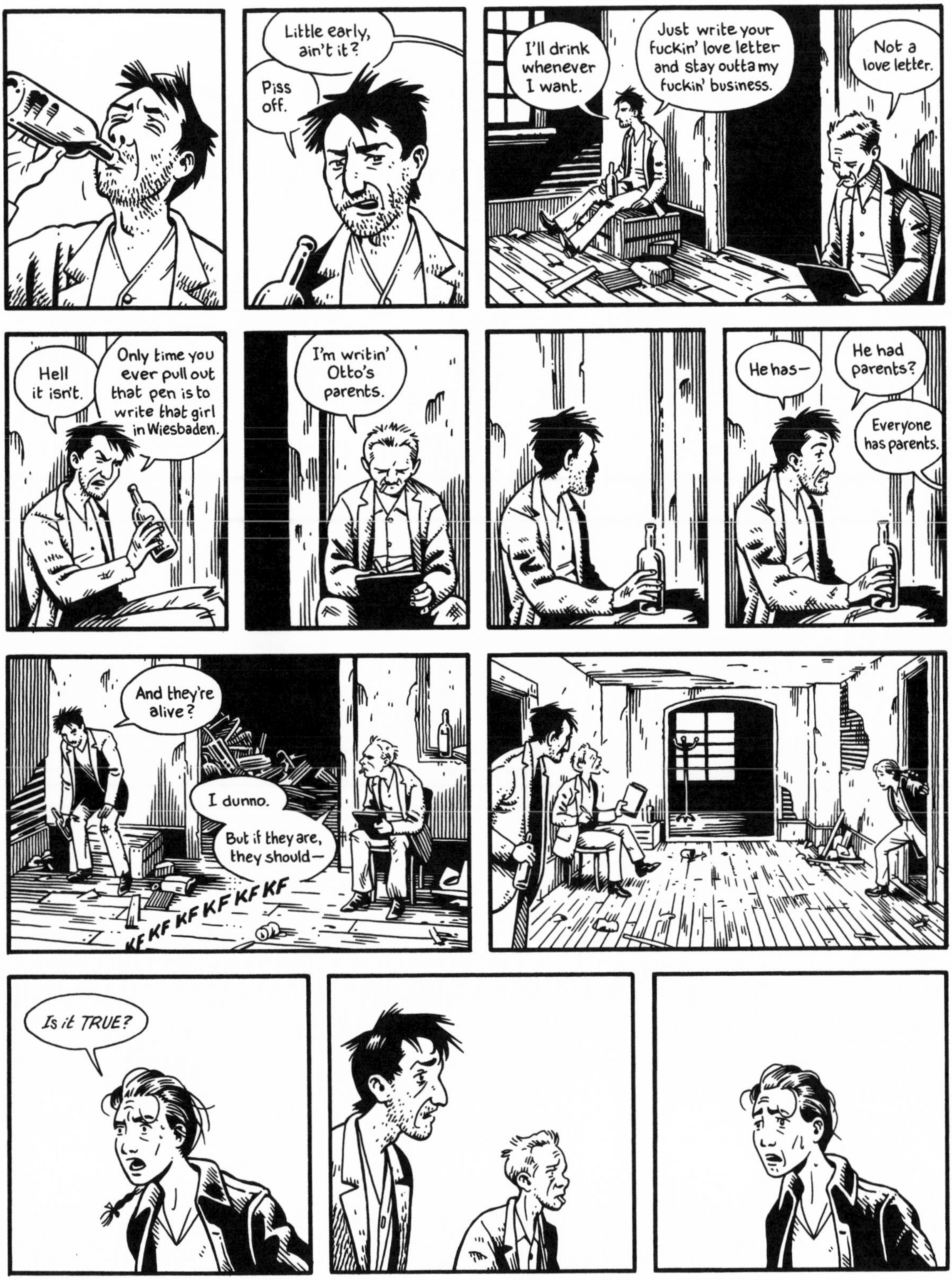
Little early, ain't it?
Piss off.
I'll drink whenever I want.
Just write your fuckin' love letter and stay outta my fuckin' business.
Not a love letter.
Hell it isn't.
Only time you ever pull out that pen is to write that girl in Wiesbaden.
I'm writin' Otto's parents.
He has—
He had parents?
Everyone has parents.
And they're alive?
I dunno.
But if they are, they should—
KF KF KF KF KF KF KF
Is it TRUE?

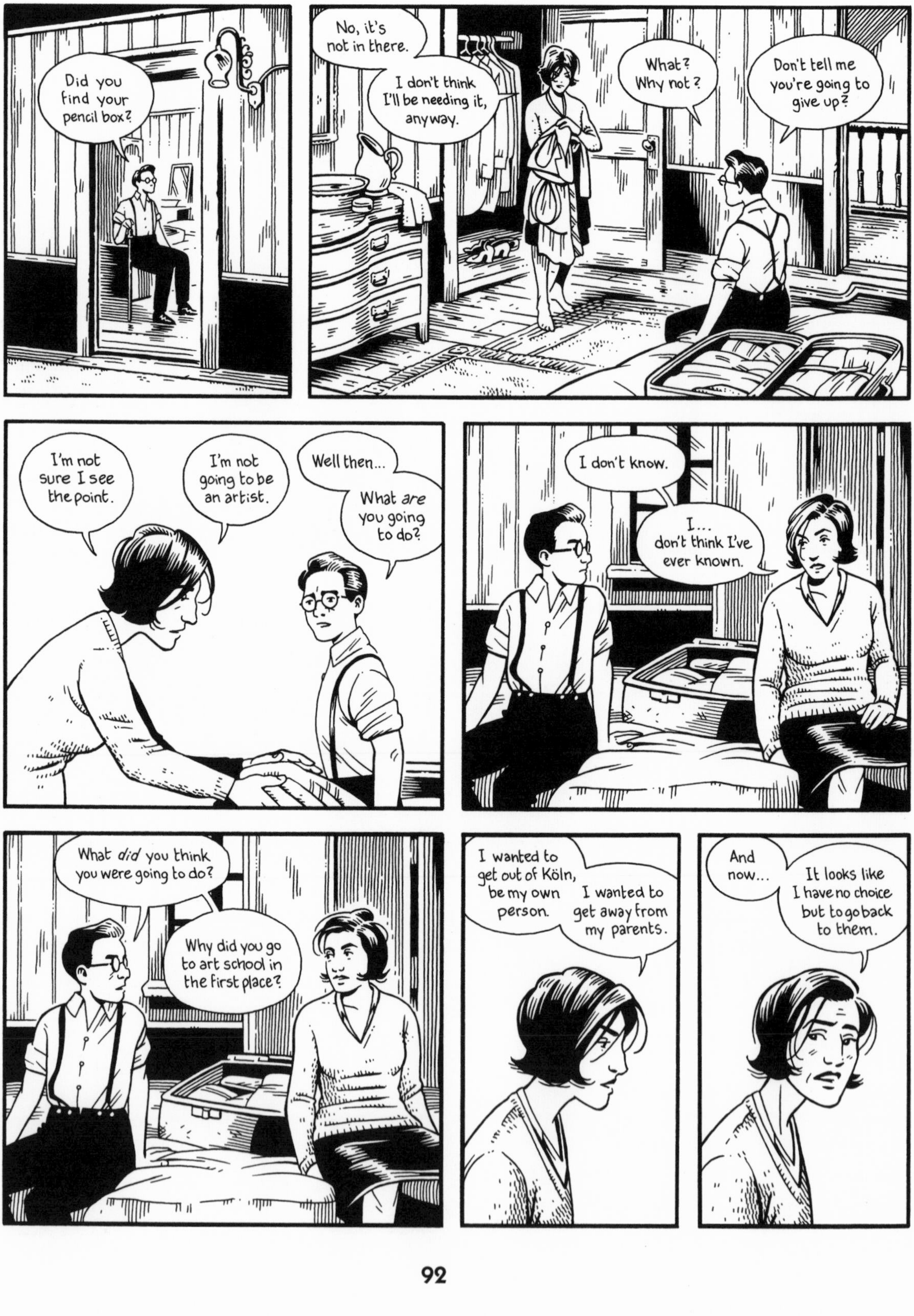
Did you find your pencil box?
No, it's not in there.
I don't think I'll be needing it, anyway.
What? Why not?
Don't tell me you're going to give up?
I'm not sure I see the point.
I'm not going to be an artist.
Well then...
What *are* you going to do?
I don't know.
I... don't think I've ever known.
What *did* you think you were going to do?
Why did you go to art school in the first place?
I wanted to get out of Köln, be my own person.
I wanted to get away from my parents.
And now...
It looks like I have no choice but to go back to them.

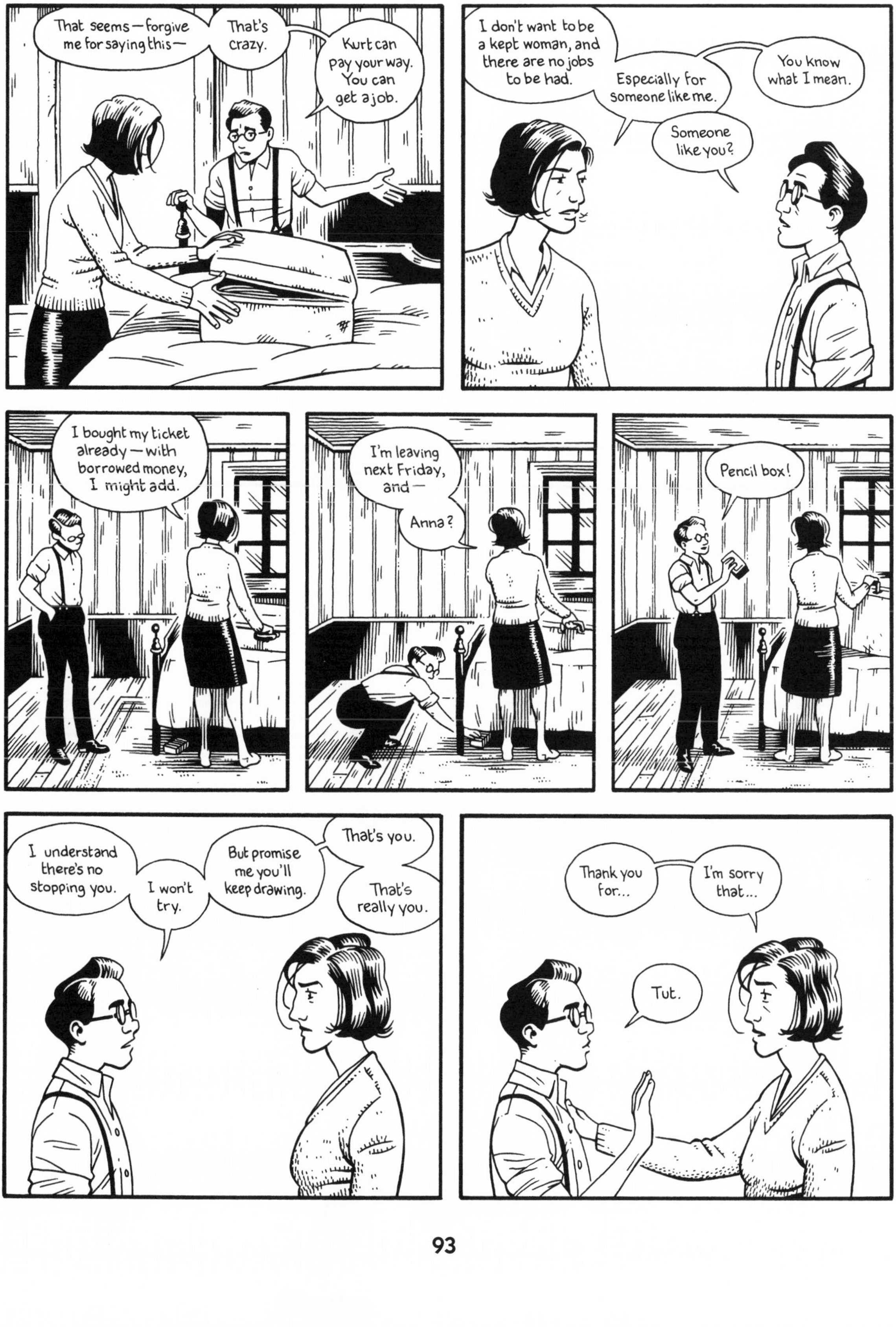

That seems—forgive me for saying this—
That's crazy.
Kurt can pay your way. You can get a job.
I don't want to be a kept woman, and there are no jobs to be had.
Especially for someone like me.
You know what I mean.
Someone like you?
I bought my ticket already—with borrowed money, I might add.
I'm leaving next Friday, and—
Anna?
Pencil box!
I understand there's no stopping you.
I won't try.
But promise me you'll keep drawing.
That's you.
That's really you.
Thank you for...
I'm sorry that...
Tut.

I'll walk you to the station on Friday.

All right.

I have a sick feeling in the pit of my stomach.

I used to wake up to a sense of possibility that flooded the streets like sunshine.

Now there's just sunshine.

And it's giving me a headache.

The shortcut through Tomaskirche cemetery may offer some relief.

What will I do?

Run back to Mother and Father.

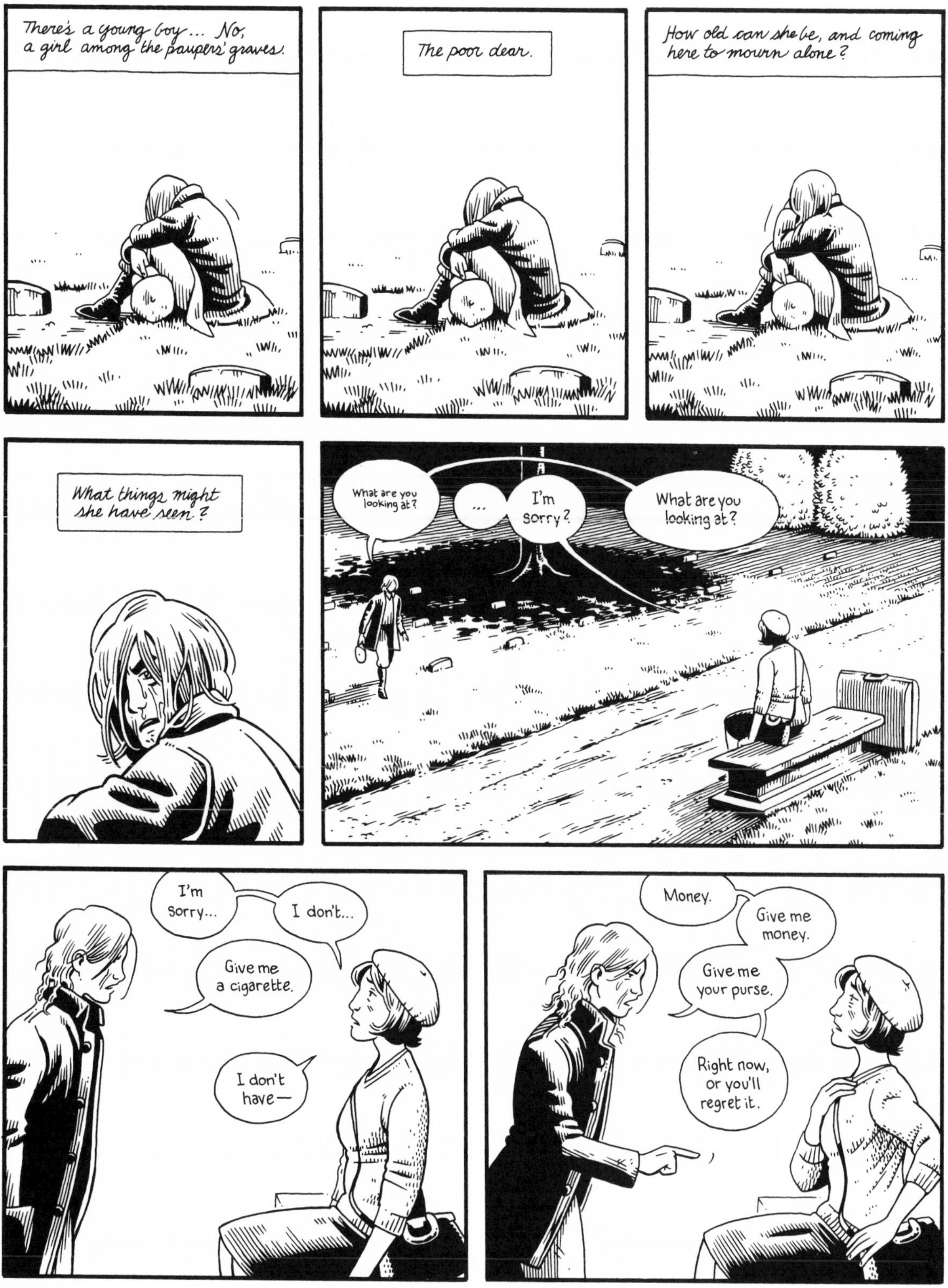
There's a young boy... No, a girl among the paupers' graves.
The poor dear.
How old can she be, and coming here to mourn alone?
What things might she have seen?
What are you looking at?
...
I'm sorry?
What are you looking at?
I'm sorry...
I don't...
Give me a cigarette.
I don't have—
Money.
Give me money.
Give me your purse.
Right now, or you'll regret it.

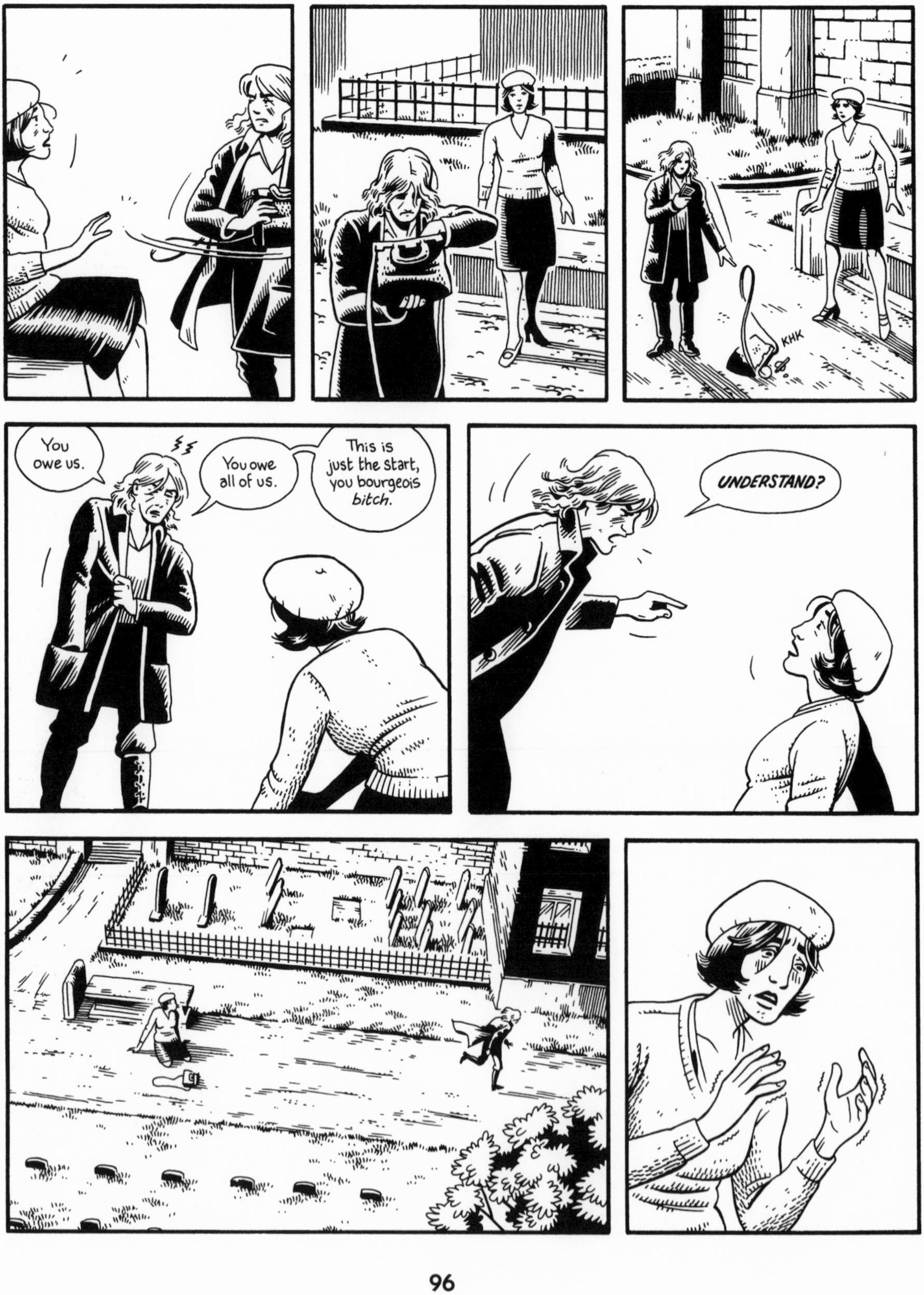
KHK
You owe us.
You owe all of us.
This is just the start, you bourgeois *bitch*.
UNDERSTAND?

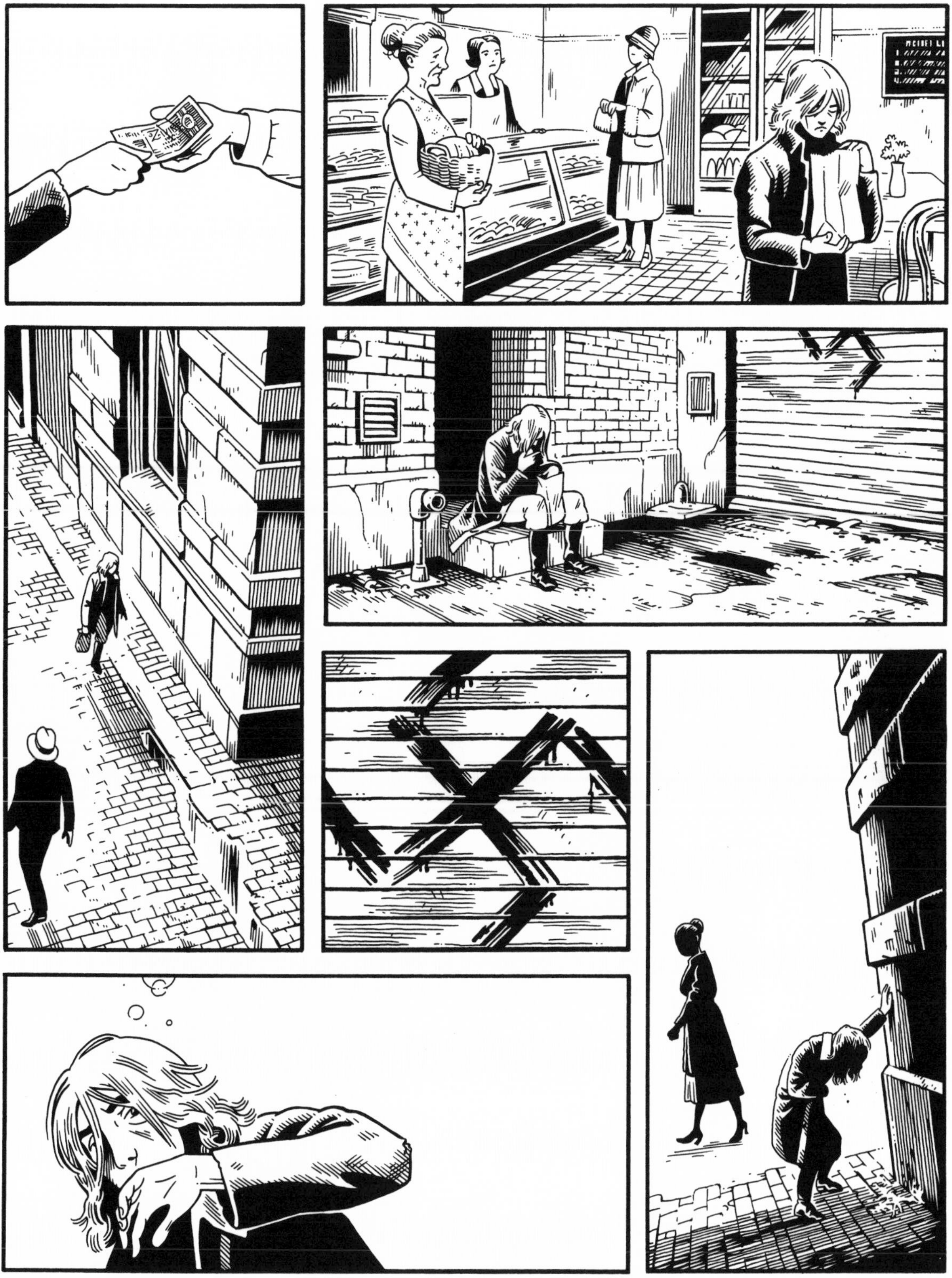

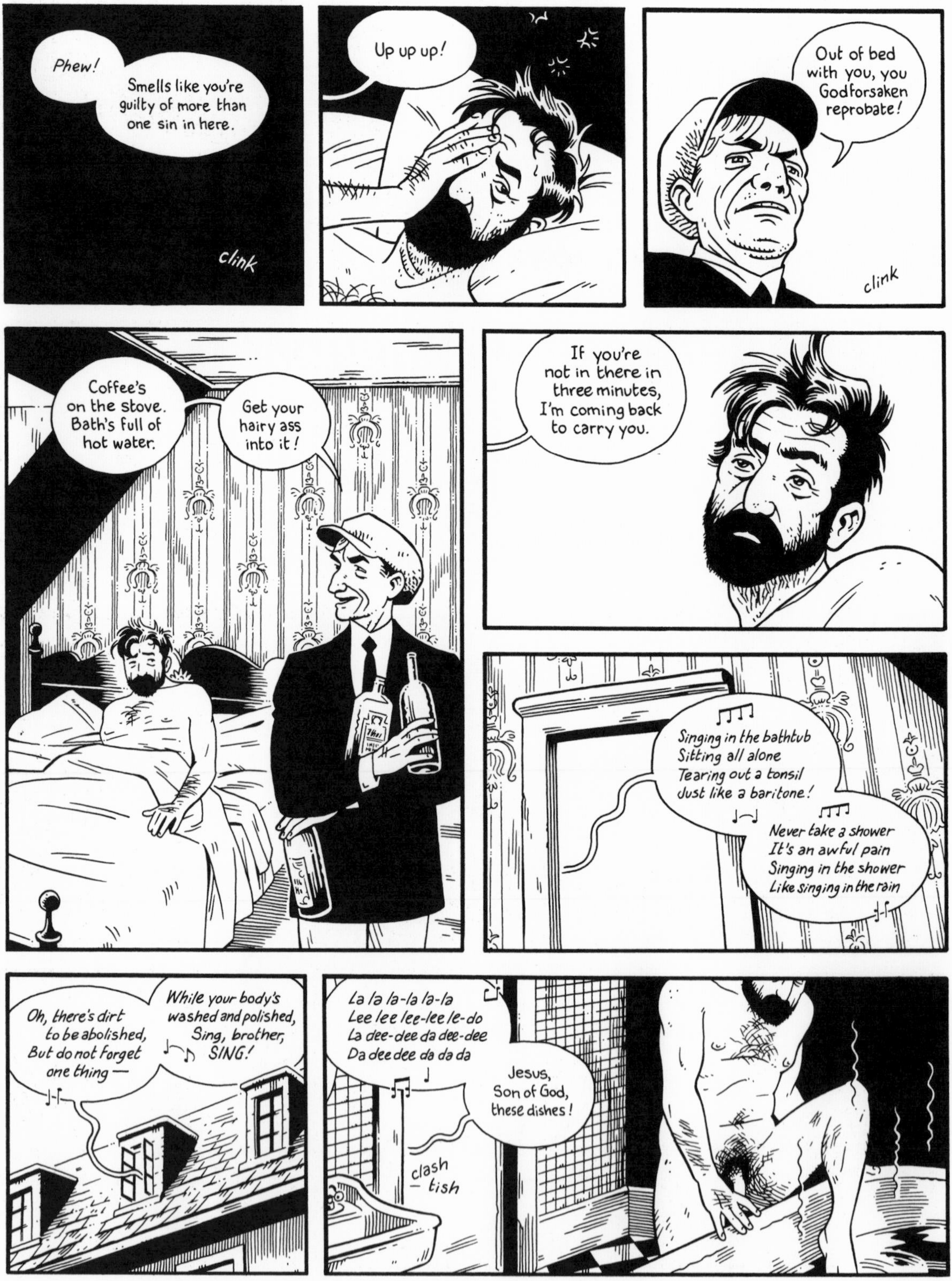

Phew!
Smells like you're guilty of more than one sin in here.
clink
Up up up!
Out of bed with you, you Godforsaken reprobate!
clink
Coffee's on the stove. Bath's full of hot water.
Get your hairy ass into it!
If you're not in there in three minutes, I'm coming back to carry you.
Singing in the bathtub
Sitting all alone
Tearing out a tonsil
Just like a baritone!
Never take a shower
It's an awful pain
Singing in the shower
Like singing in the rain
Oh, there's dirt to be abolished, But do not forget one thing—
While your body's washed and polished, Sing, brother, SING!
La la la-la la-la
Lee lee lee-lee le-do
La dee-dee da dee-dee
Da dee dee da da da
Jesus, Son of God, these dishes!
clash
— tish

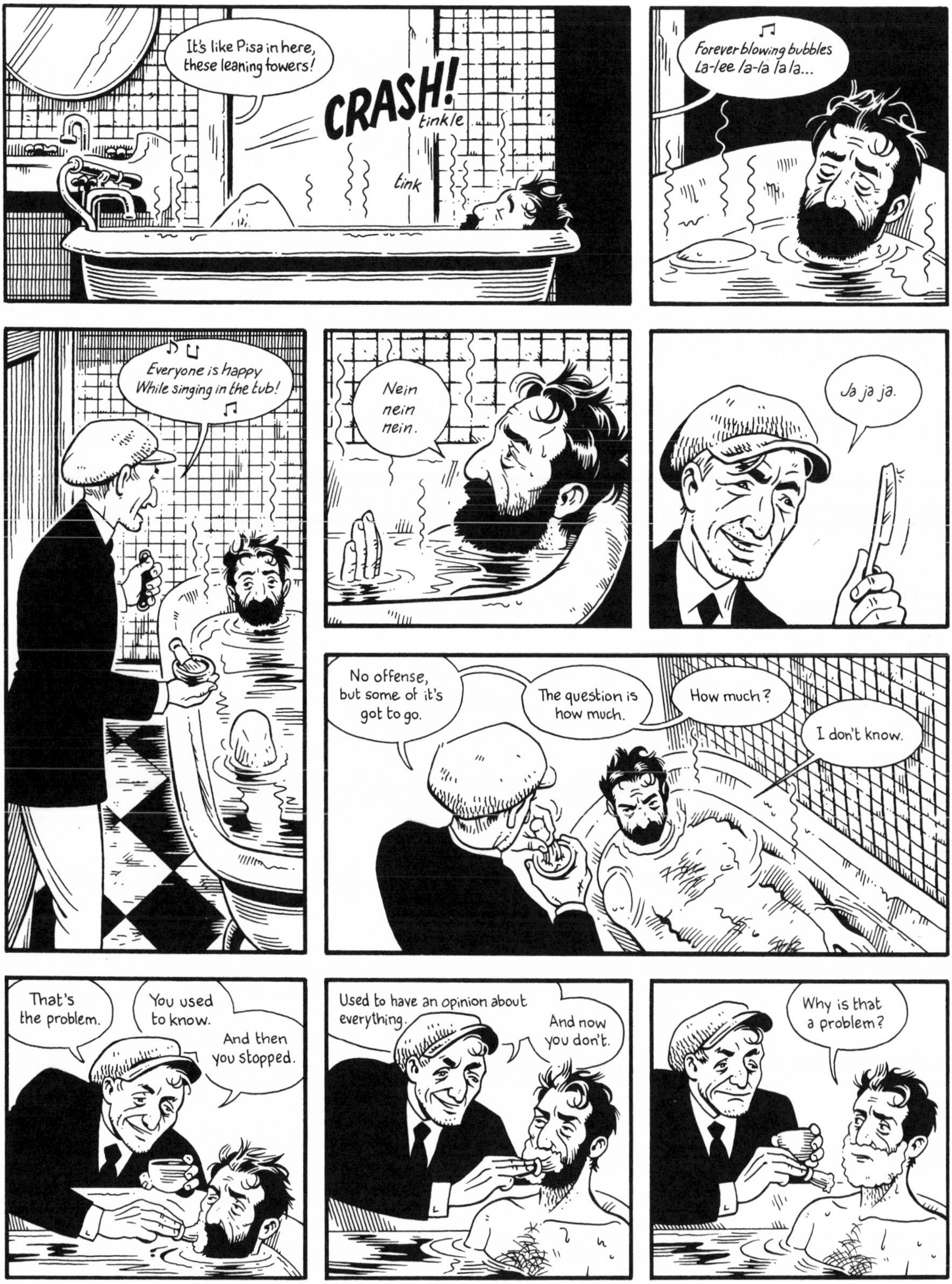

It's like Pisa in here, these leaning towers!
CRASH!
tinkle
tink
Forever blowing bubbles La-lee la-la la la...
Everyone is happy While singing in the tub!
Nein nein nein.
Ja ja ja.
No offense, but some of it's got to go.
The question is how much.
How much?
I don't know.
That's the problem.
You used to know.
And then you stopped.
Used to have an opinion about everything.
And now you don't.
Why is that a problem?

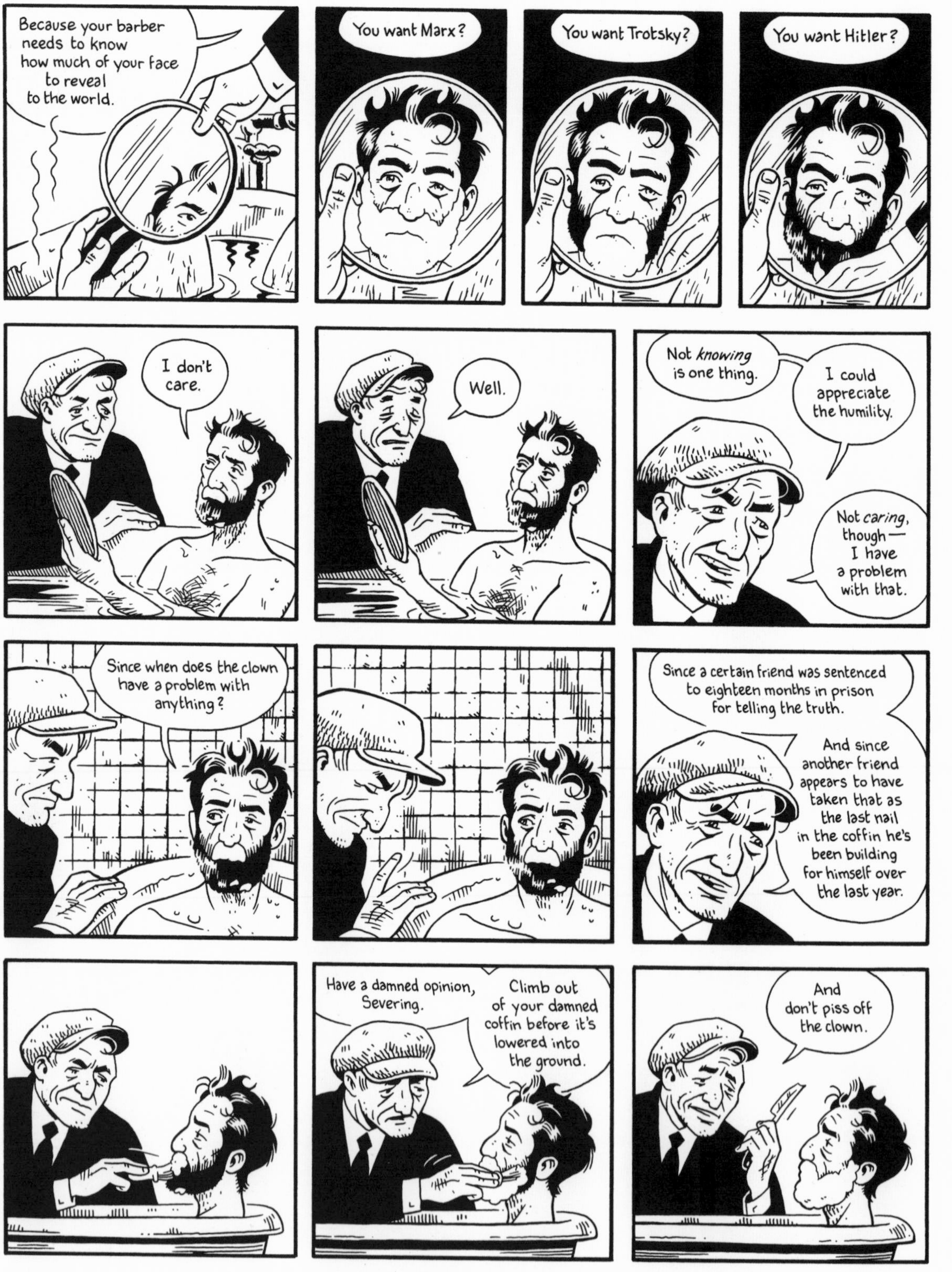
Because your barber needs to know how much of your face to reveal to the world.
You want Marx?
You want Trotsky?
You want Hitler?
I don't care.
Well.
Not *knowing* is one thing.
I could appreciate the humility.
Not *caring*, though— I have a problem with that.
Since when does the clown have a problem with anything?
Since a certain friend was sentenced to eighteen months in prison for telling the truth.
And since another friend appears to have taken that as the last nail in the coffin he's been building for himself over the last year.
Have a damned opinion, Severing.
Climb out of your damned coffin before it's lowered into the ground.
And don't piss off the clown.

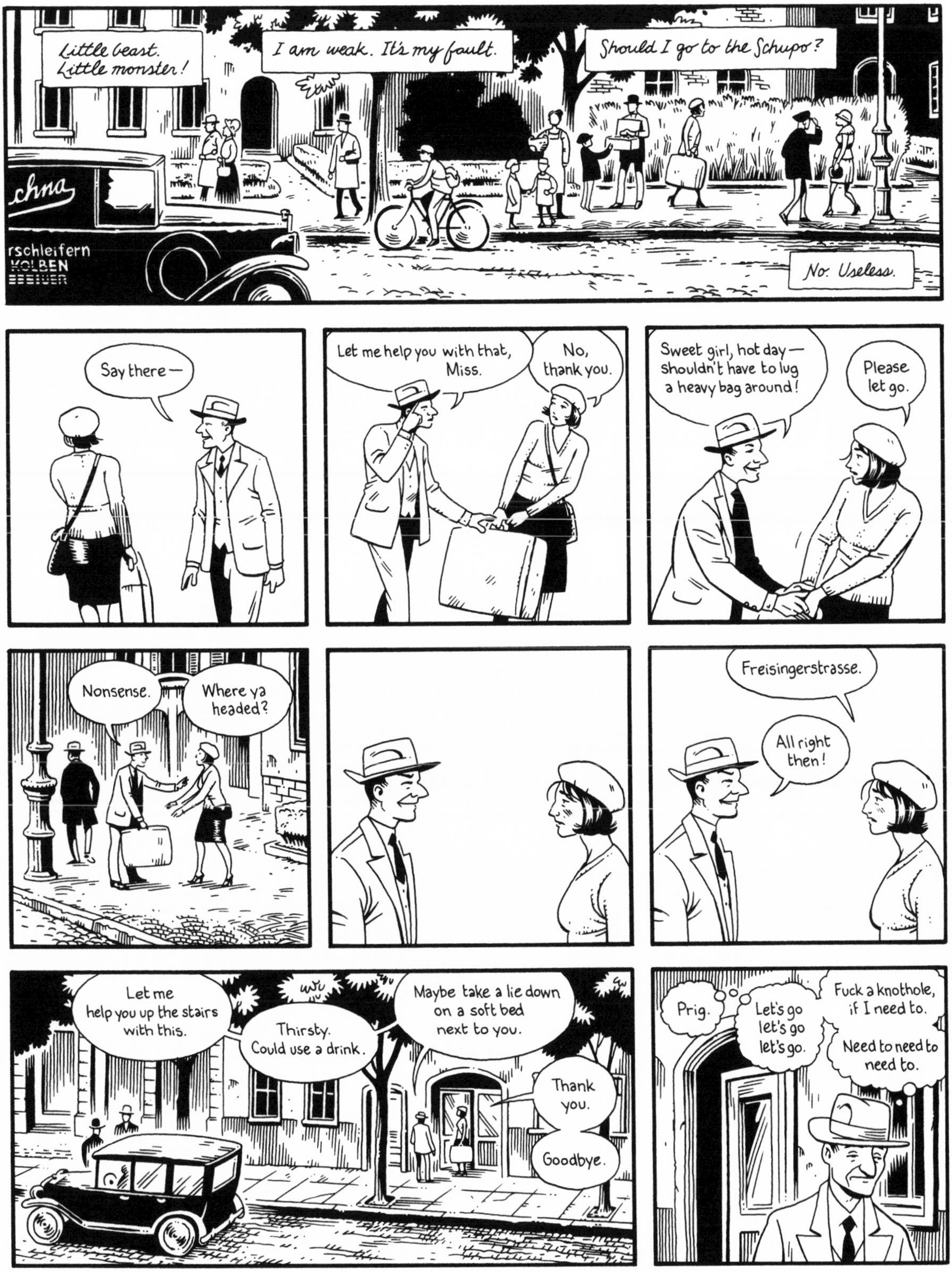
Little beast. Little monster!
I am weak. It's my fault.
Should I go to the Schupo?
chna
rschleifern
KOLBEN
No. Useless.
Say there—
Let me help you with that, Miss.
No, thank you.
Sweet girl, hot day—shouldn't have to lug a heavy bag around!
Please let go.
Nonsense.
Where ya headed?
Freisingerstrasse.
All right then!
Let me help you up the stairs with this.
Thirsty. Could use a drink.
Maybe take a lie down on a soft bed next to you.
Thank you.
Goodbye.
Prig.
Let's go let's go let's go.
Fuck a knothole, if I need to.
Need to need to need to.

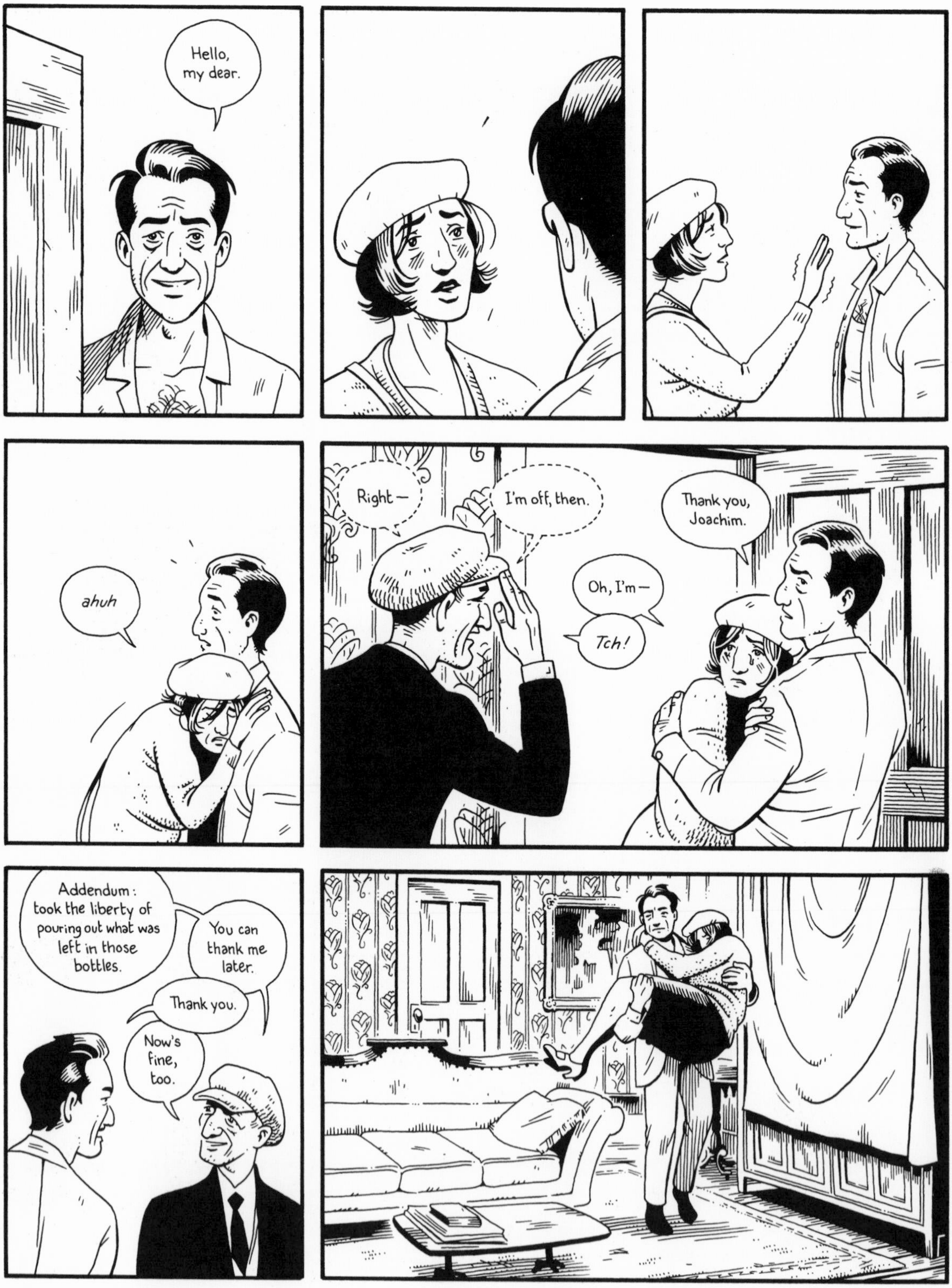

Hello, my dear.
ahuh
Right—
I'm off, then.
Thank you, Joachim.
Oh, I'm—
Tch!
Addendum: took the liberty of pouring out what was left in those bottles.
You can thank me later.
Thank you.
Now's fine, too.

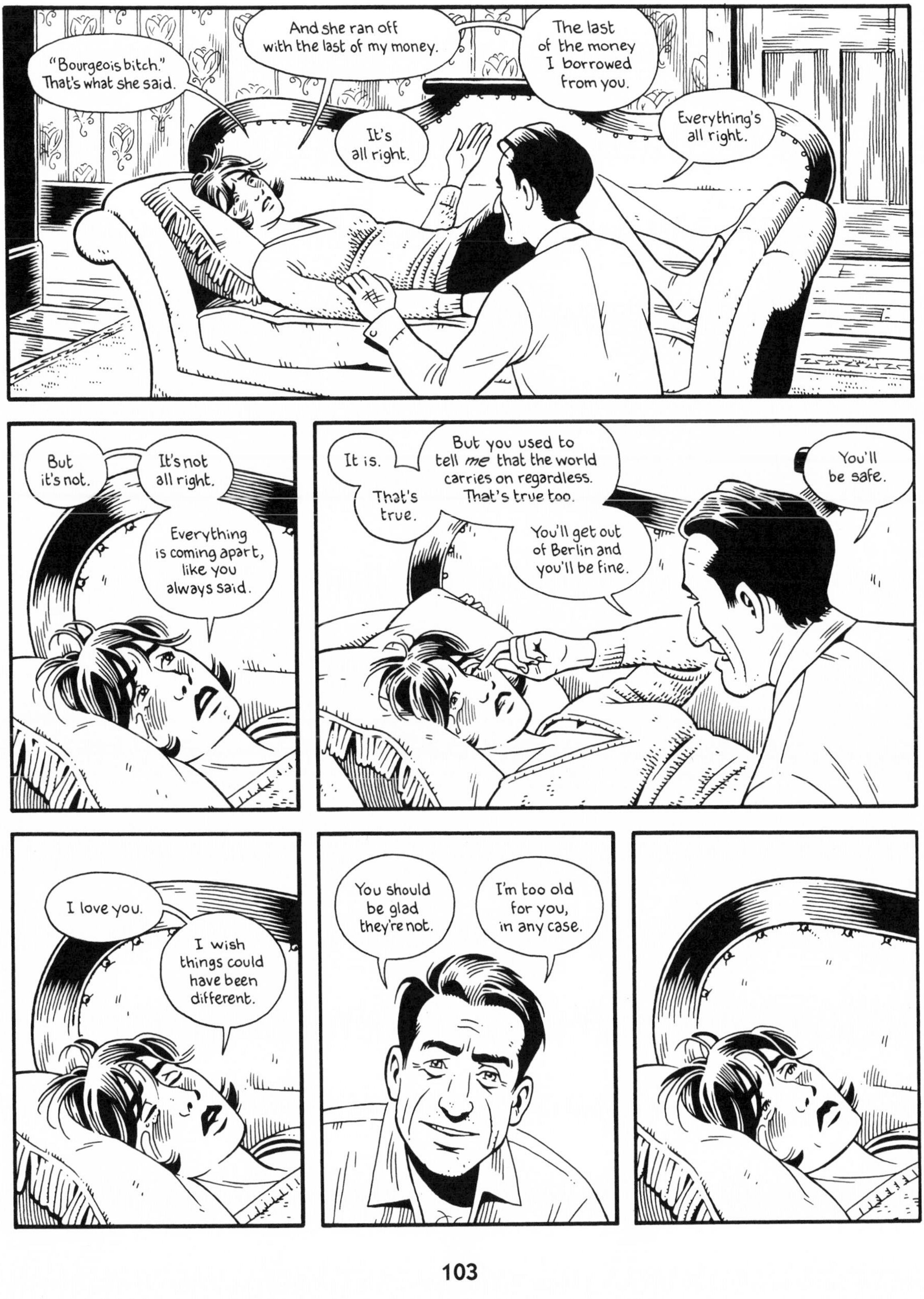
"Bourgeois bitch." That's what she said.
And she ran off with the last of my money.
The last of the money I borrowed from you.
It's all right.
Everything's all right.
But it's not.
It's not all right.
Everything is coming apart, like you always said.
It is.
That's true.
But you used to tell *me* that the world carries on regardless. That's true too.
You'll get out of Berlin and you'll be fine.
You'll be safe.
I love you.
I wish things could have been different.
You should be glad they're not.
I'm too old for you, in any case.

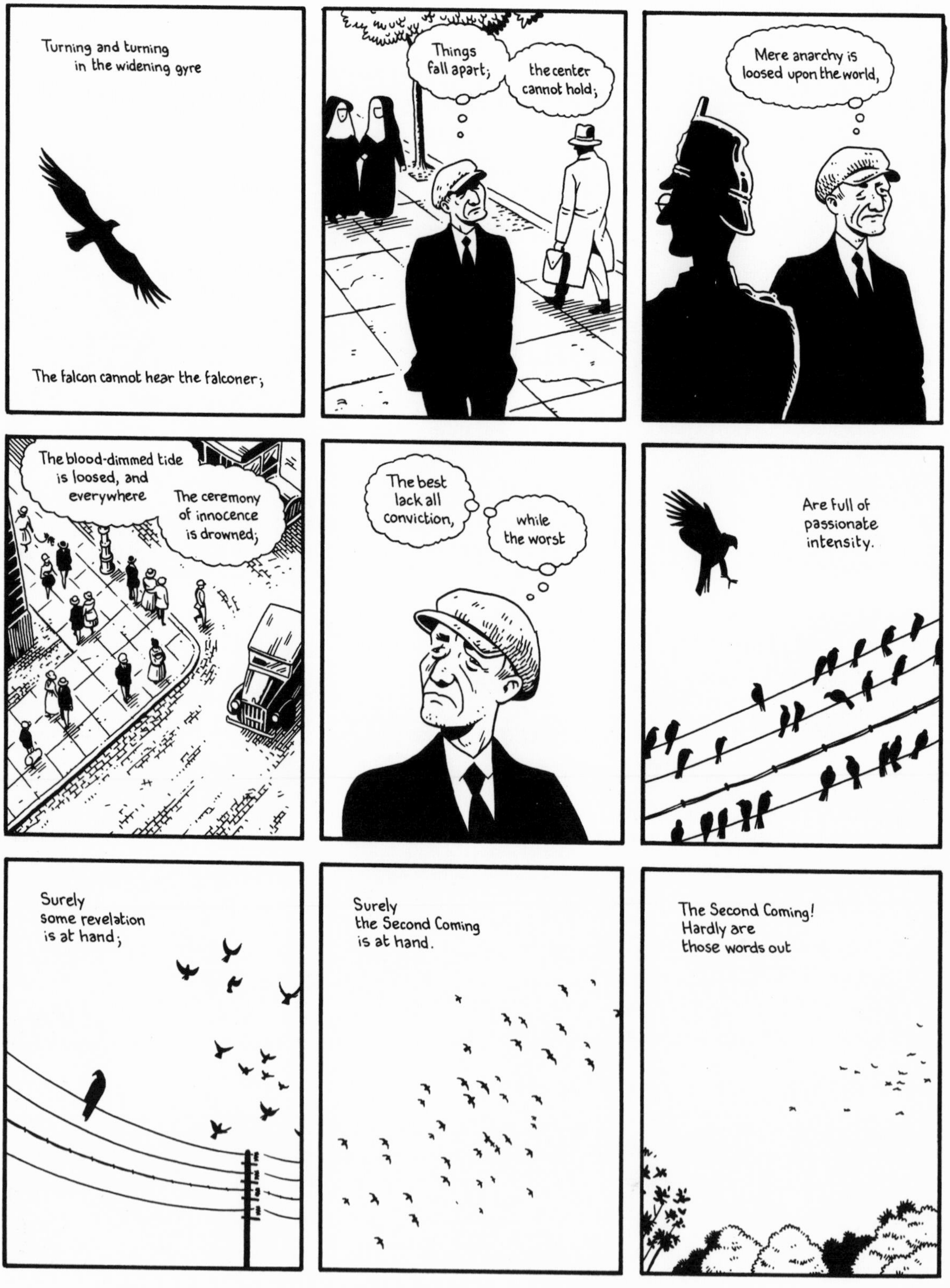

Turning and turning
in the widening gyre
The falcon cannot hear the falconer;
Things fall apart;
the center cannot hold;
Mere anarchy is loosed upon the world,
The blood-dimmed tide is loosed, and everywhere
The ceremony of innocence is drowned;
The best lack all conviction,
while the worst
Are full of passionate intensity.
Surely some revelation is at hand;
Surely the Second Coming is at hand.
The Second Coming! Hardly are those words out

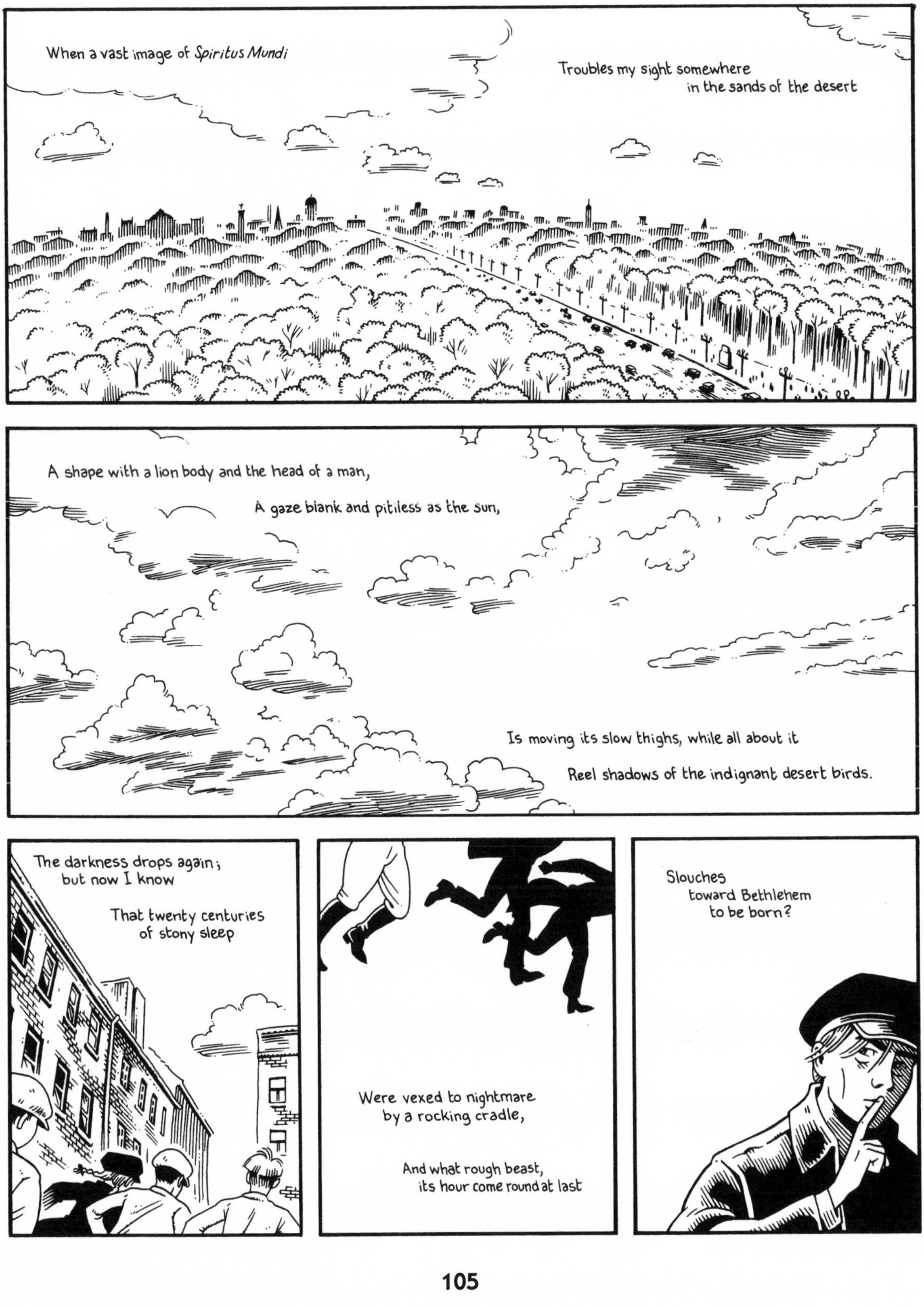
When a vast image of *Spiritus Mundi*
Troubles my sight somewhere in the sands of the desert
A shape with a lion body and the head of a man,
A gaze blank and pitiless as the sun,
Is moving its slow thighs, while all about it
Reel shadows of the indignant desert birds.
The darkness drops again; but now I know
That twenty centuries of stony sleep
Were vexed to nightmare by a rocking cradle,
And what rough beast, its hour come round at last
Slouches toward Bethlehem to be born?

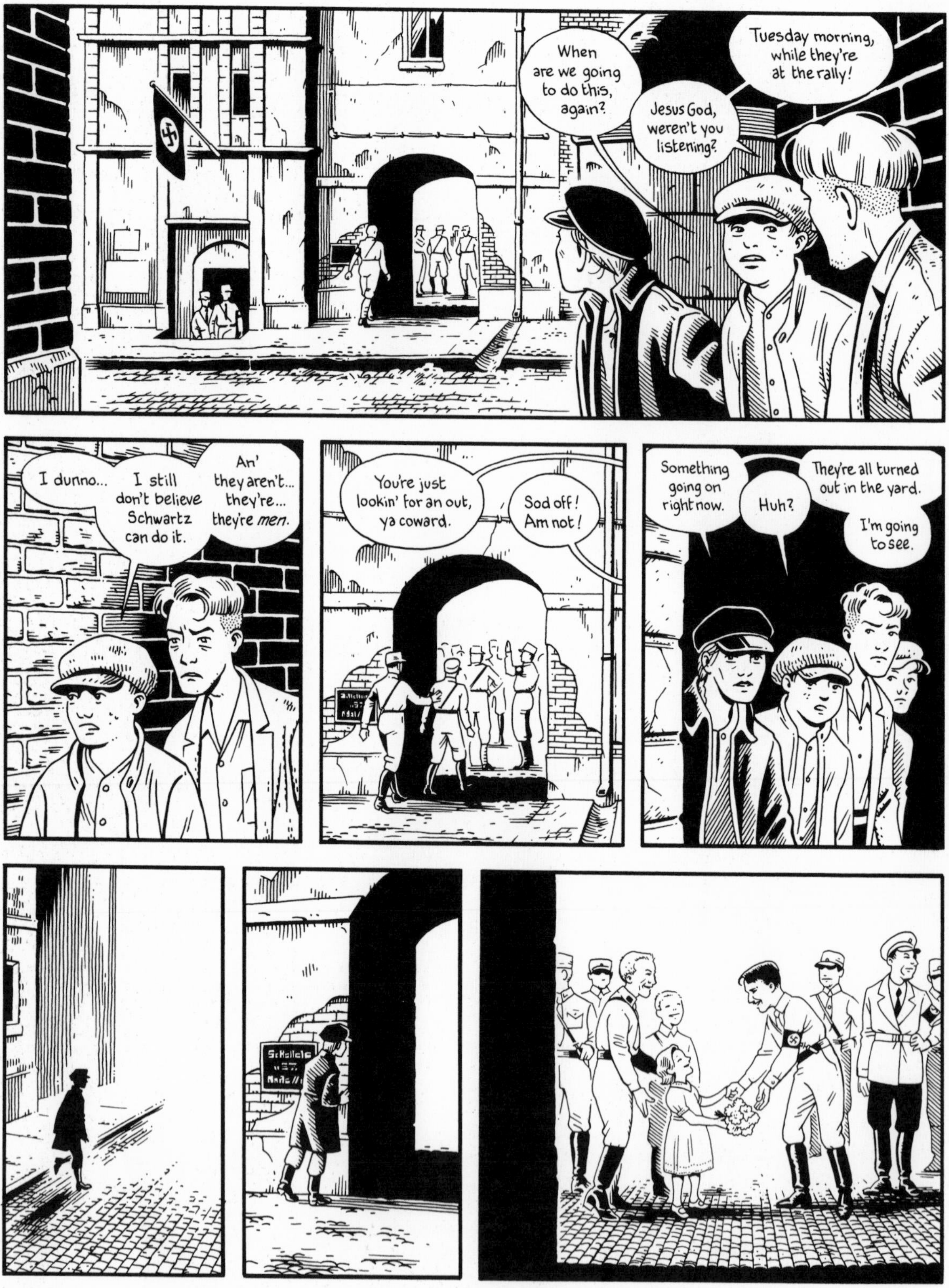
When are we going to do this, again?
Jesus God, weren't you listening?
Tuesday morning, while they're at the rally!
I dunno...
I still don't believe Schwartz can do it.
An' they aren't... they're... they're *men*.
You're just lookin' for an out, ya coward.
Sod off! Am not!
Something going on right now.
Huh?
They're all turned out in the yard.
I'm going to see.

5

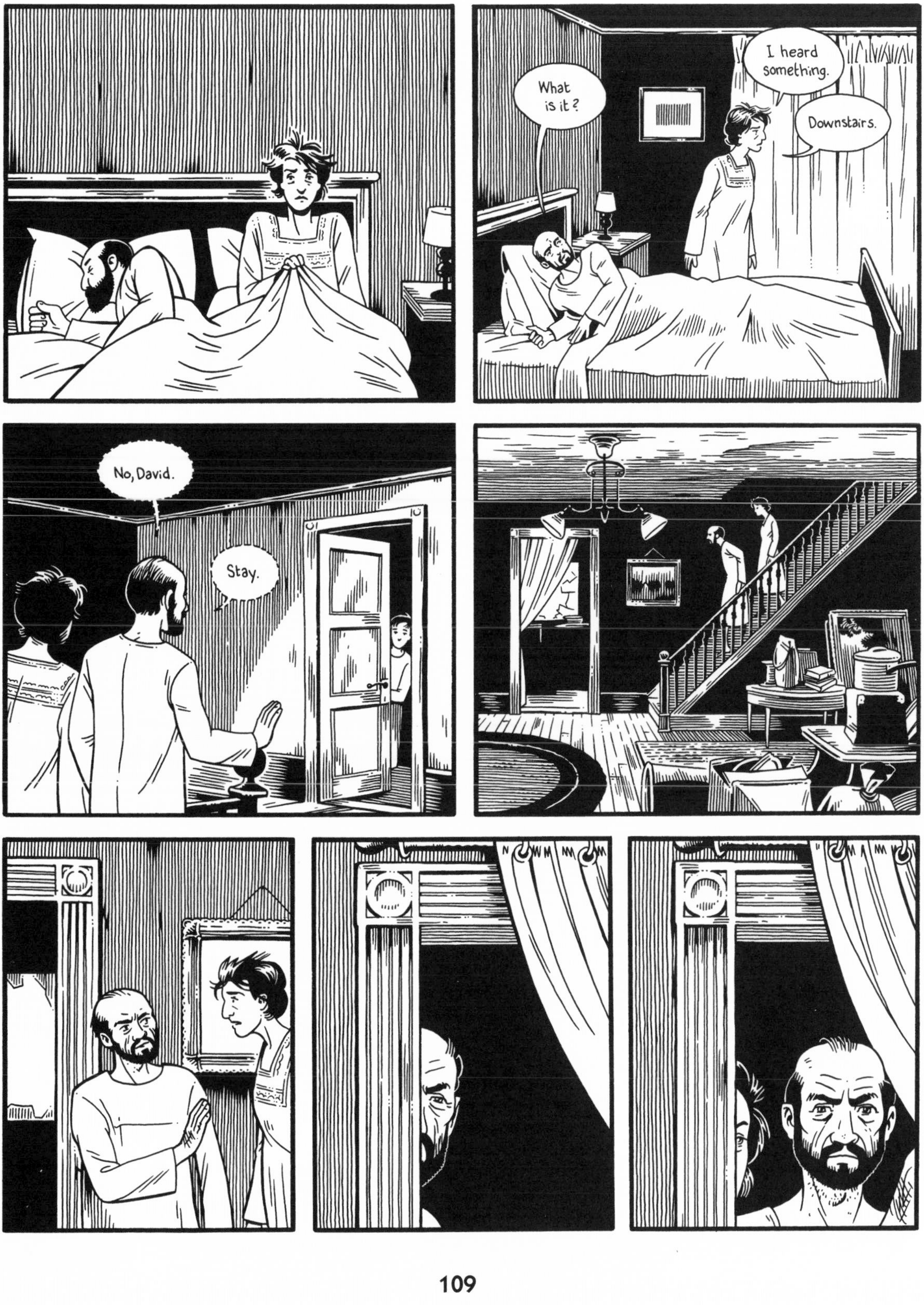
I heard something.
What is it?
Downstairs.
No, David.
Stay.

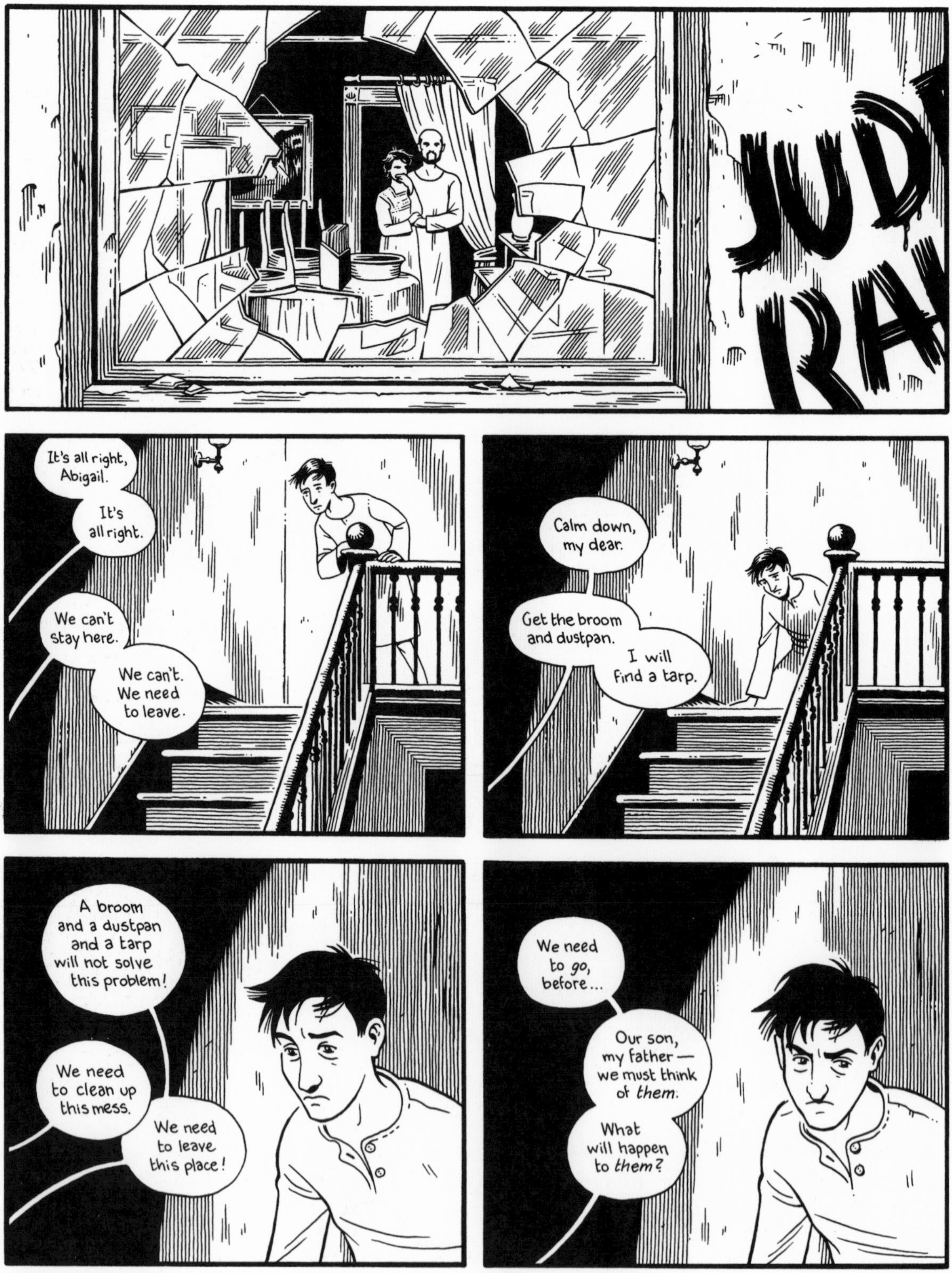
It's all right, Abigail.
It's all right.
We can't stay here.
We can't. We need to leave.
Calm down, my dear.
Get the broom and dustpan.
I will find a tarp.
A broom and a dustpan and a tarp will not solve this problem!
We need to clean up this mess.
We need to leave this place!
We need to *go*, before...
Our son, my father — we must think of *them*.
What will happen to *them*?

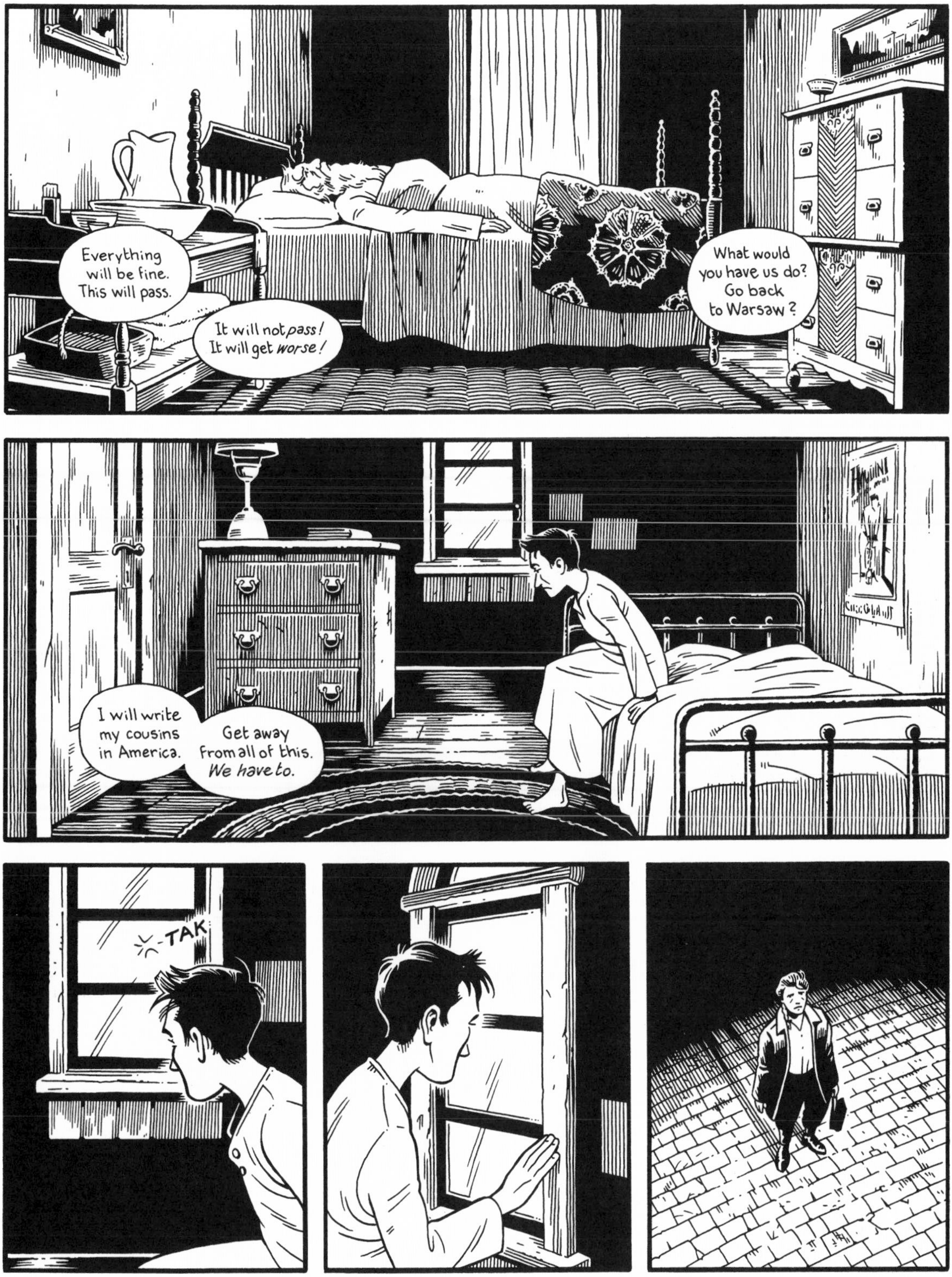
Everything will be fine. This will pass.
It will not *pass*! It will get *worse*!
What would you have us do? Go back to Warsaw?
I will write my cousins in America.
Get away from all of this. *We have to.*
TAK

Blockleiter Braun, reporting!

Don't get ahead of yourself, kid.

What d'you think, Elga?

Your brother pass inspection?

His shirt is too wrinkled.

Poppa—!

Heinz! Maintain!

If you can't maintain in the face of a six-year-old, you're not Trooper material!

She's right — looks like you slept in it.

But we don't have time t'iron.

Told you!

I'm using the iron.

And step it up, Fischer!

We've got...

Seventeen minutes to get to the rally.

Seventeen minutes.

I heard you.

I don't want any laggards.

Why you lookin' at me?

Someone is *Blockleiter* here, and it's not your son.

The *Führer* demands punctuality.

Anyone showing up late reflects badly on *me*.

We will not be late, sir.

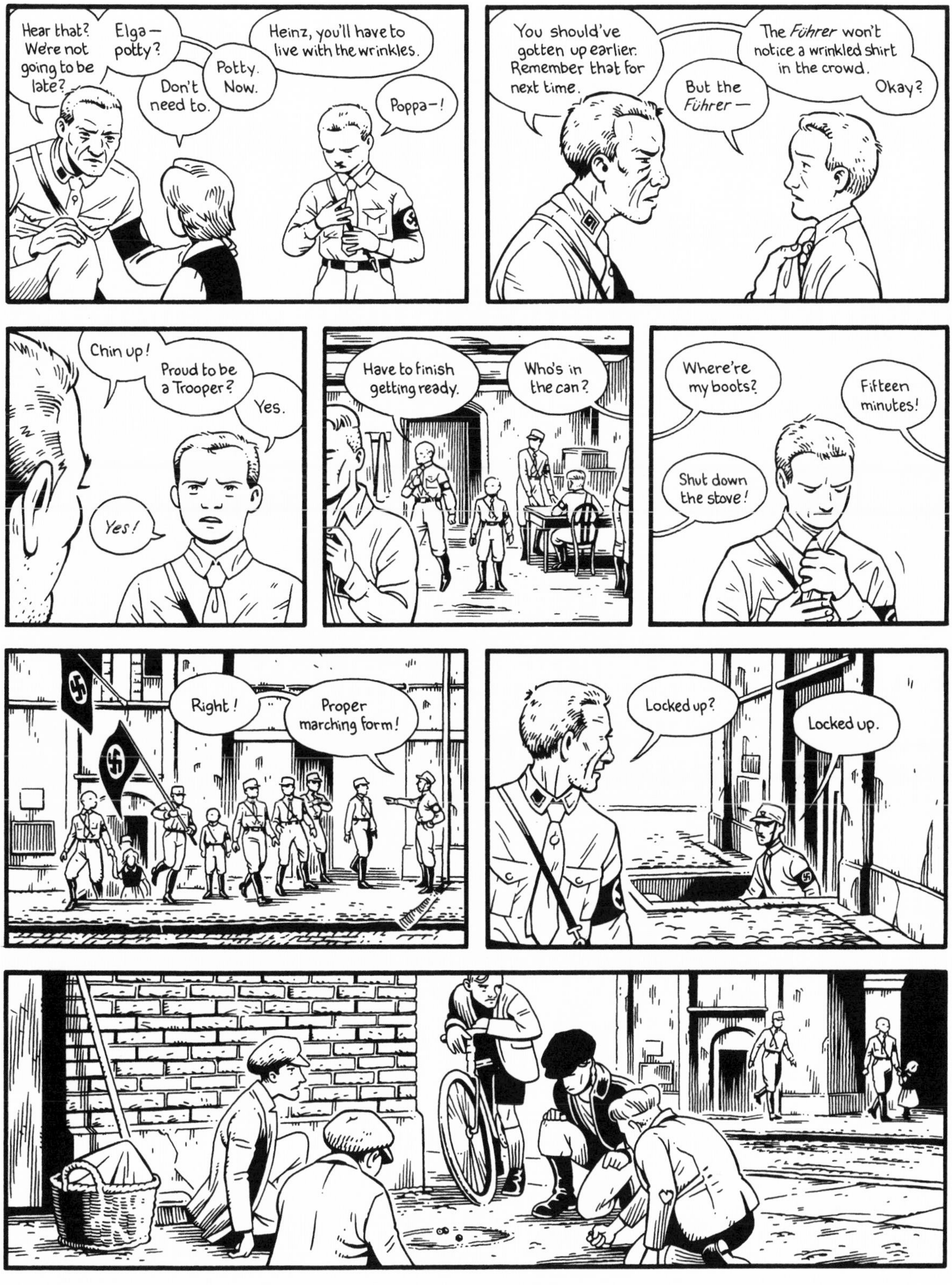
Hear that? We're not going to be late?
Elga— potty?
Heinz, you'll have to live with the wrinkles.
Potty. Now.
Don't need to.
Poppa—!
You should've gotten up earlier. Remember that for next time.
But the *Führer*—
The *Führer* won't notice a wrinkled shirt in the crowd.
Okay?
Chin up!
Proud to be a Trooper?
Yes.
Yes!
Have to finish getting ready.
Who's in the can?
Where're my boots?
Fifteen minutes!
Shut down the stove!
Right!
Proper marching form!
Locked up?
Locked up.

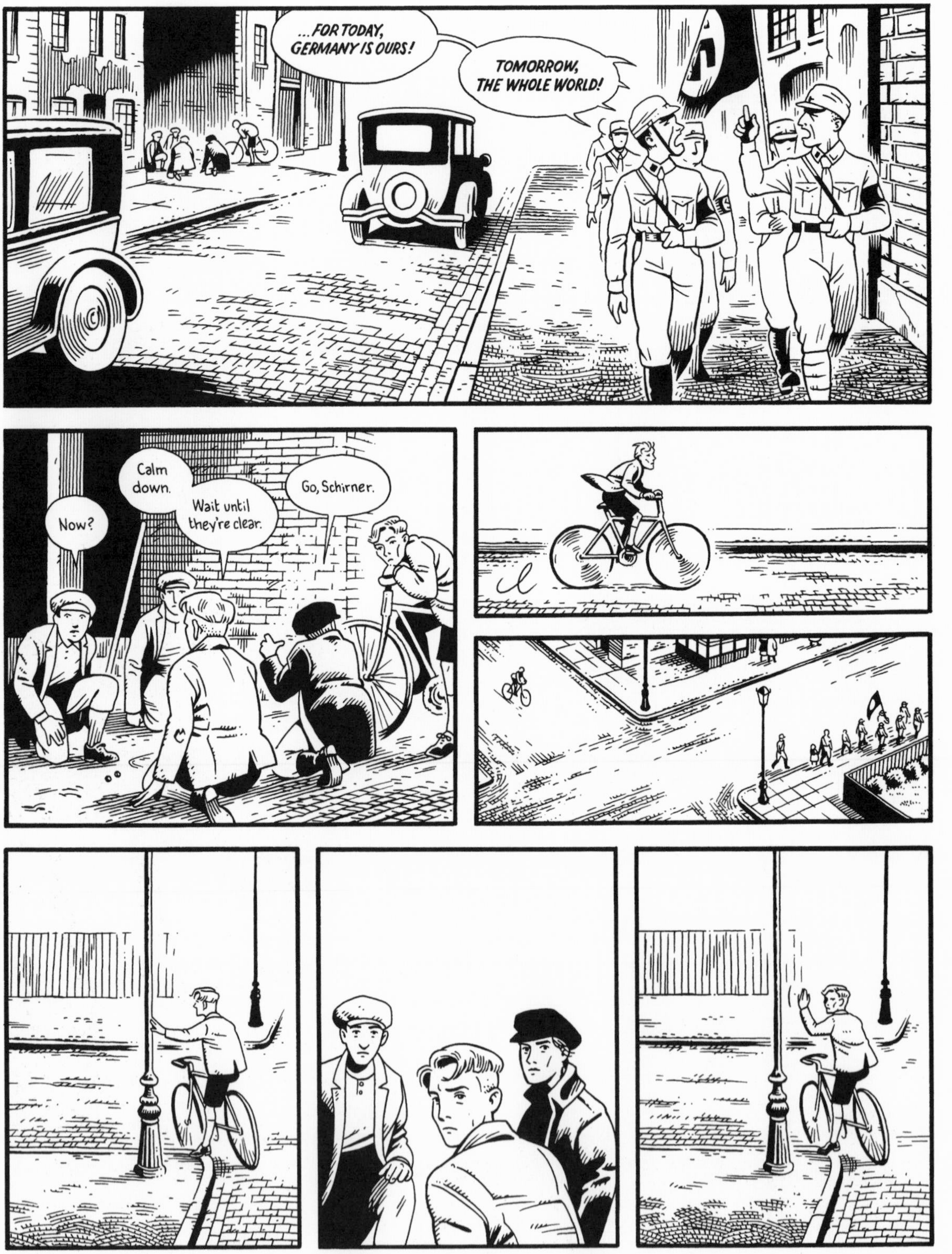
...FOR TODAY, GERMANY IS OURS!
TOMORROW, THE WHOLE WORLD!
Now?
Calm down.
Wait until they're clear.
Go, Schirner.

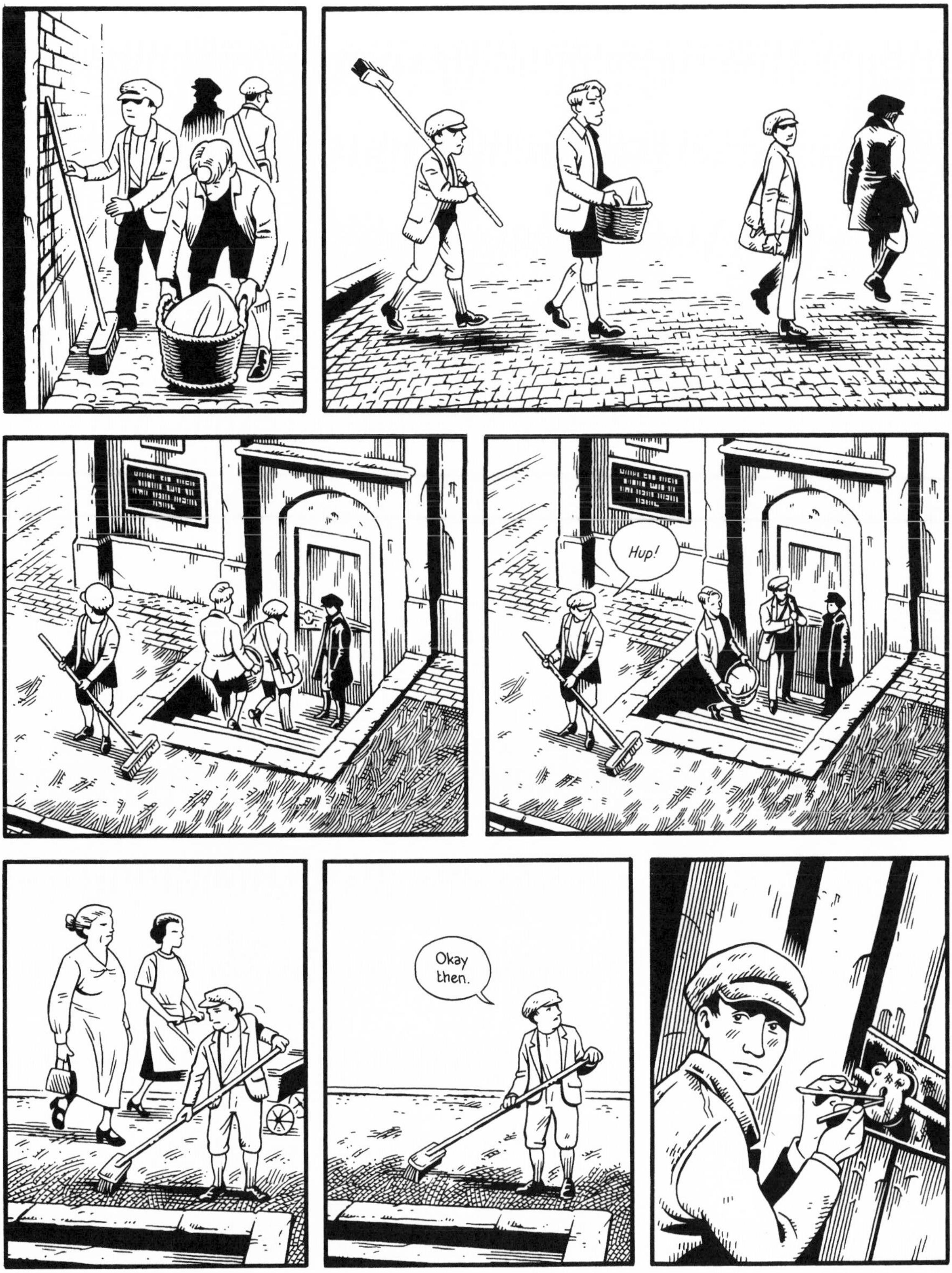
Hup!
Okay then.

Come on, come on!
I'm not...
I...
Don't go soft on us, Schiff.
Jesus Christ.
Out of the way, then.
UMSONST WAREN DIE OPFER
Don't just stand there—
Get the food!

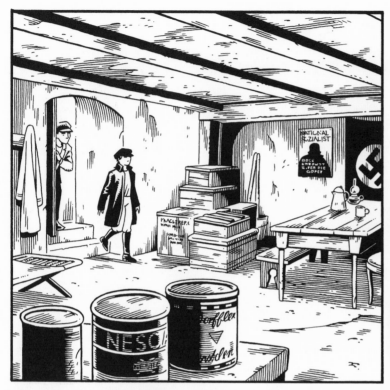

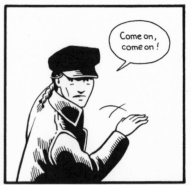

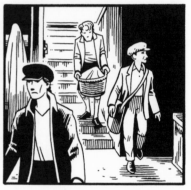

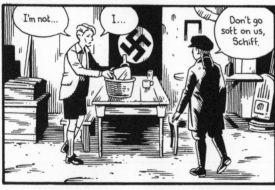

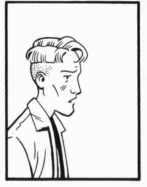

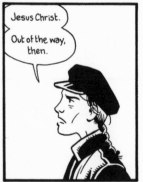

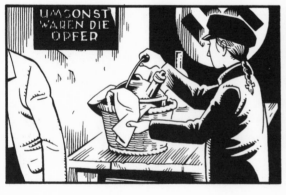

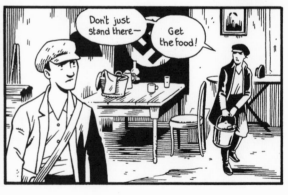

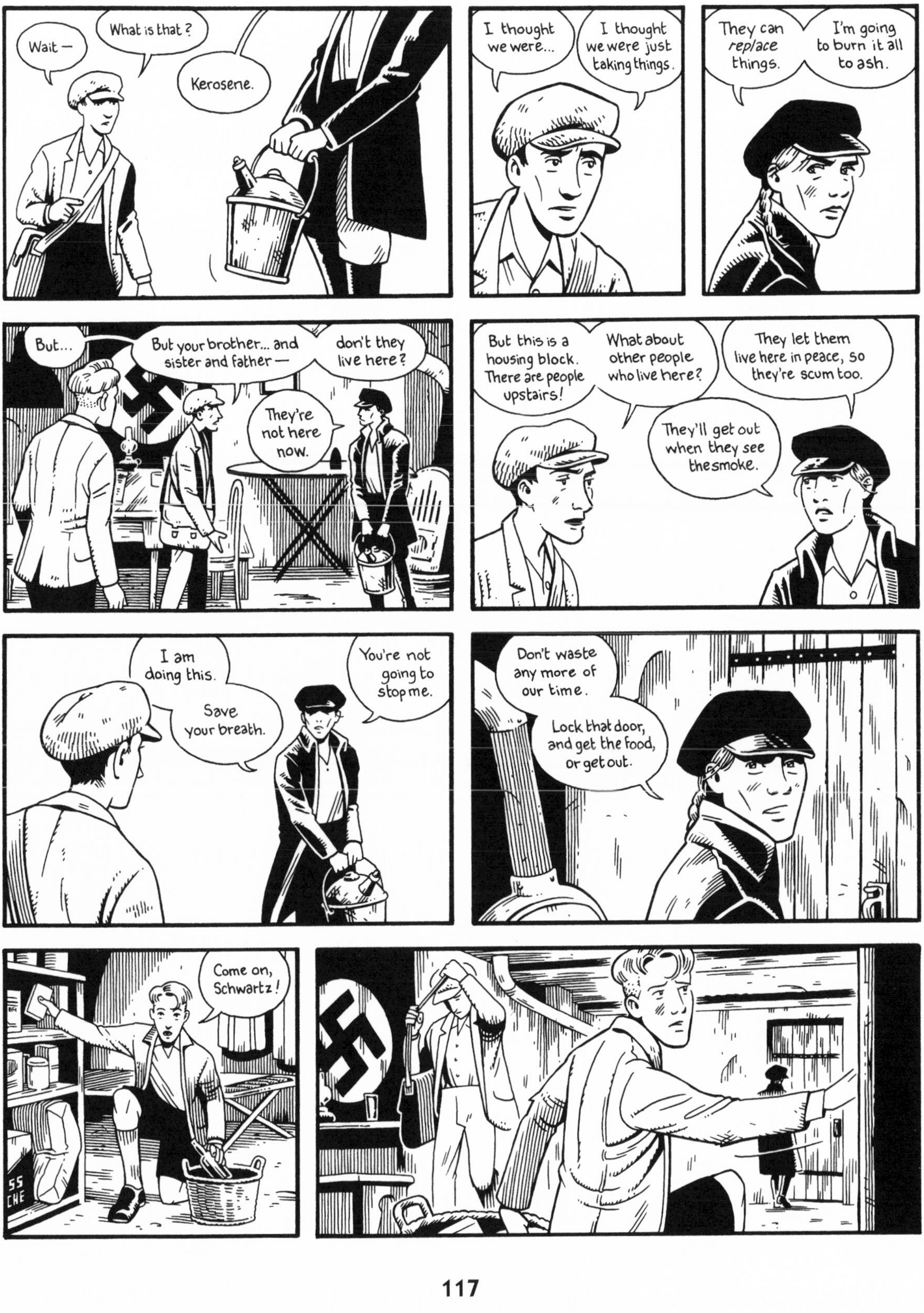
Wait —
What is that?
Kerosene.
I thought we were...
I thought we were just taking things.
They can *replace* things.
I'm going to burn it all to ash.
But...
But your brother... and sister and father —
don't they live here?
They're not here now.
But this is a housing block. There are people upstairs!
What about other people who live here?
They let them live here in peace, so they're scum too.
They'll get out when they see the smoke.
I am doing this.
Save your breath.
You're not going to stop me.
Don't waste any more of our time.
Lock that door, and get the food, or get out.
Come on, Schwartz!

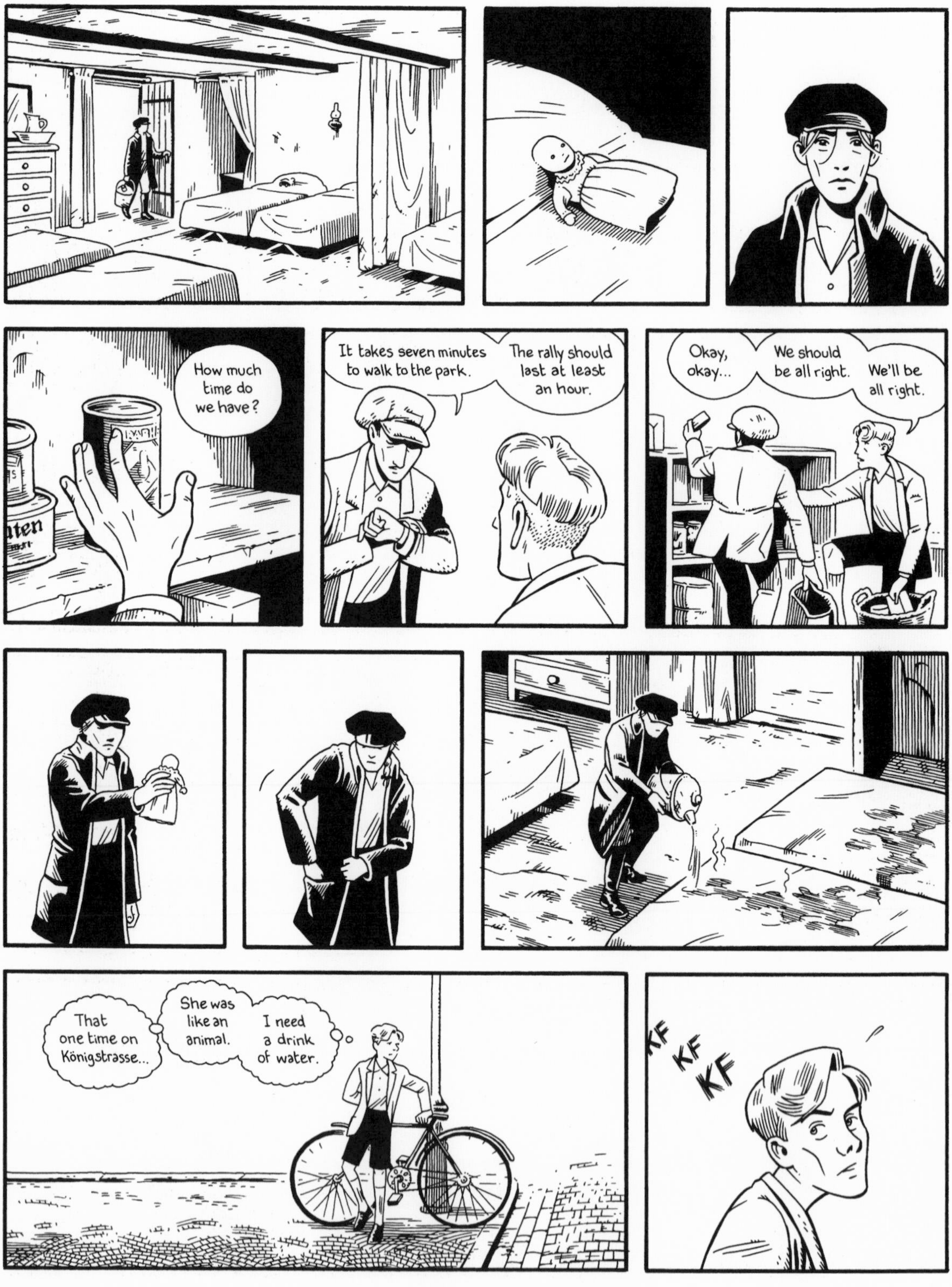
How much time do we have?
It takes seven minutes to walk to the park.
The rally should last at least an hour.
Okay, okay...
We should be all right.
We'll be all right.
That one time on Königstrasse...
She was like an animal.
I need a drink of water.
KF KF KF

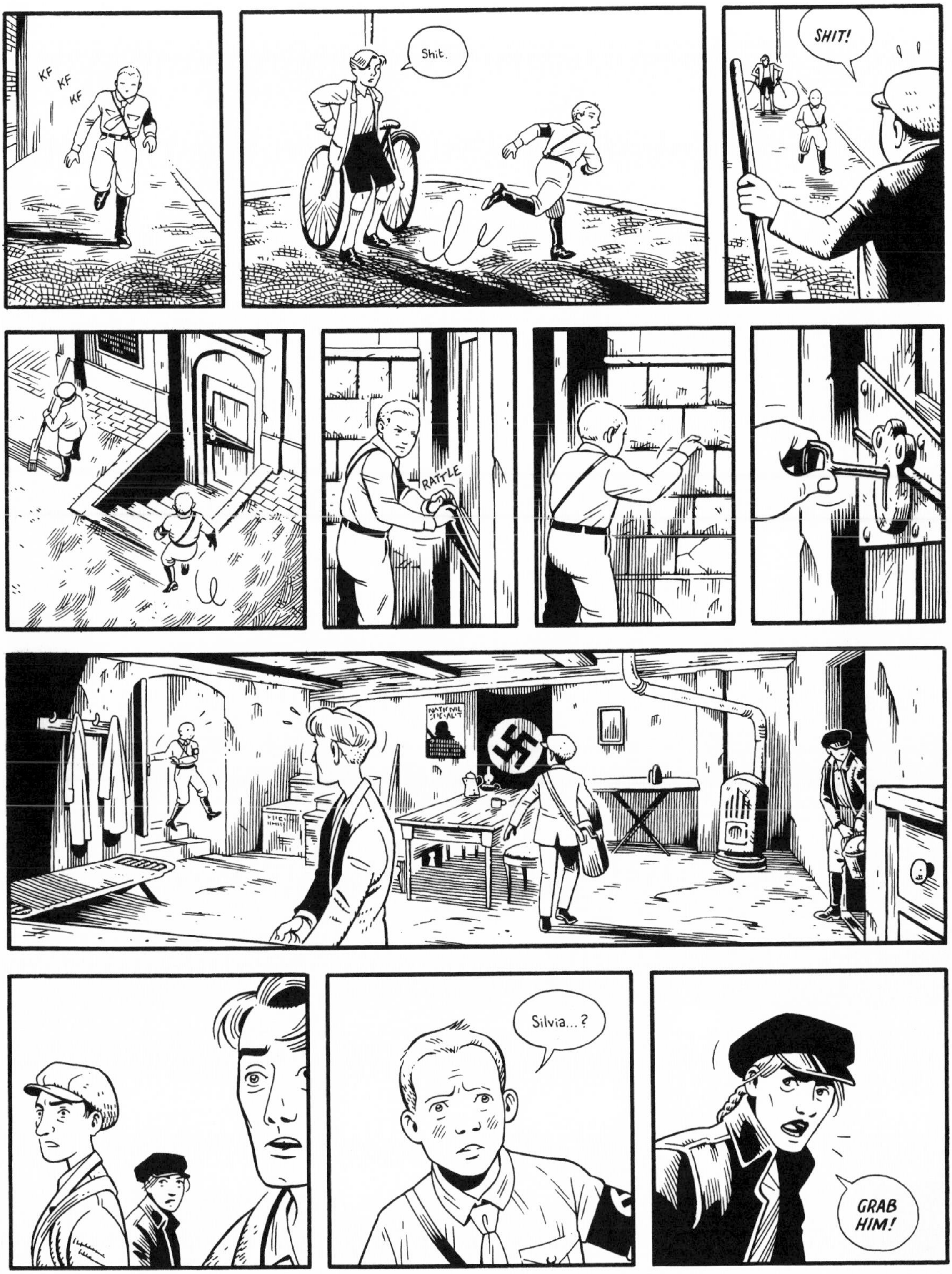
KF
KF
KF
Shit.
SHIT!
RATTLE
NATIONAL SOCIALIST
Silvia...?
GRAB HIM!

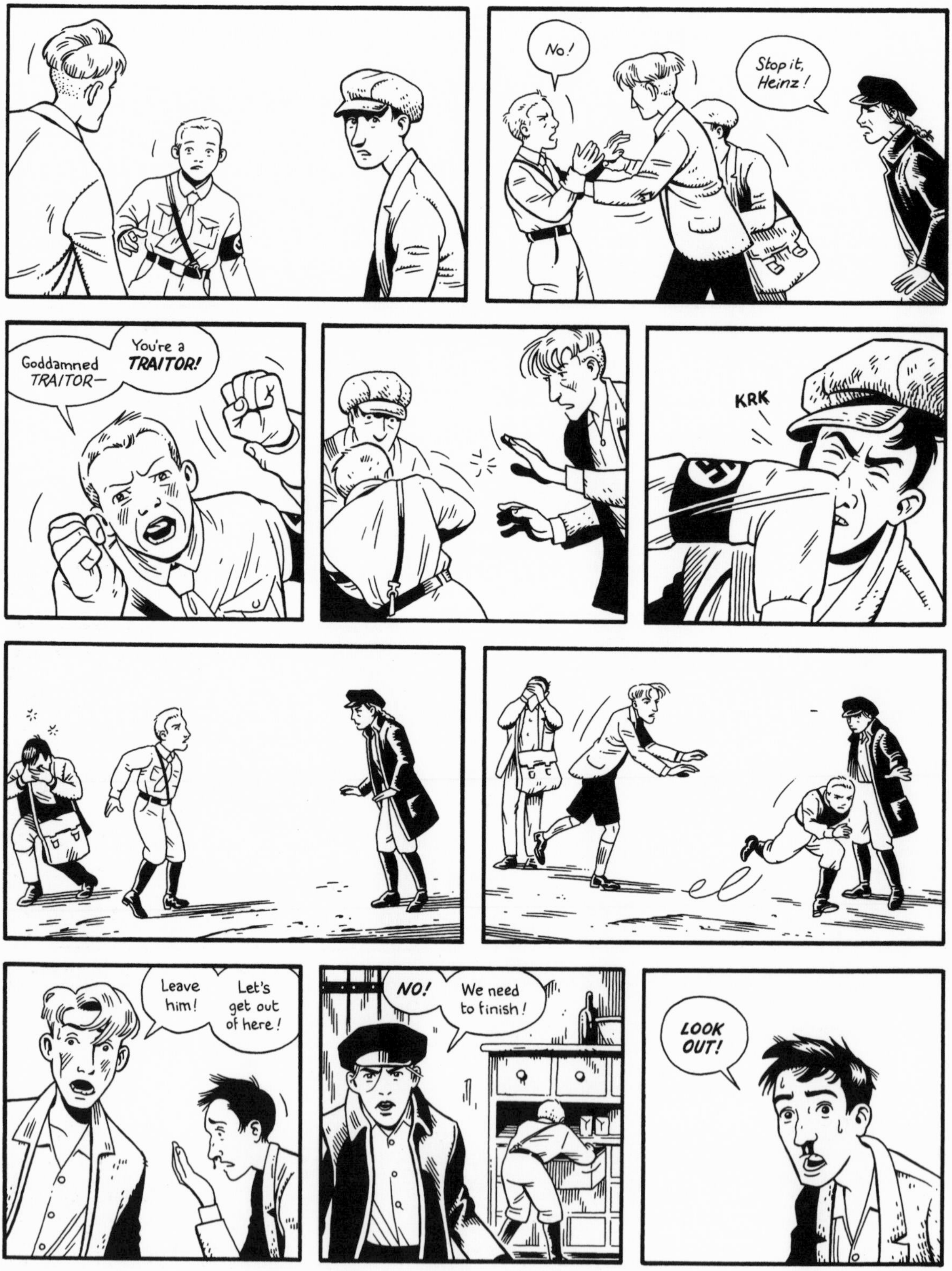

No!
Stop it, Heinz!
Goddamned TRAITOR—
You're a TRAITOR!
KRK
Leave him!
Let's get out of here!
NO!
We need to finish!
LOOK OUT!

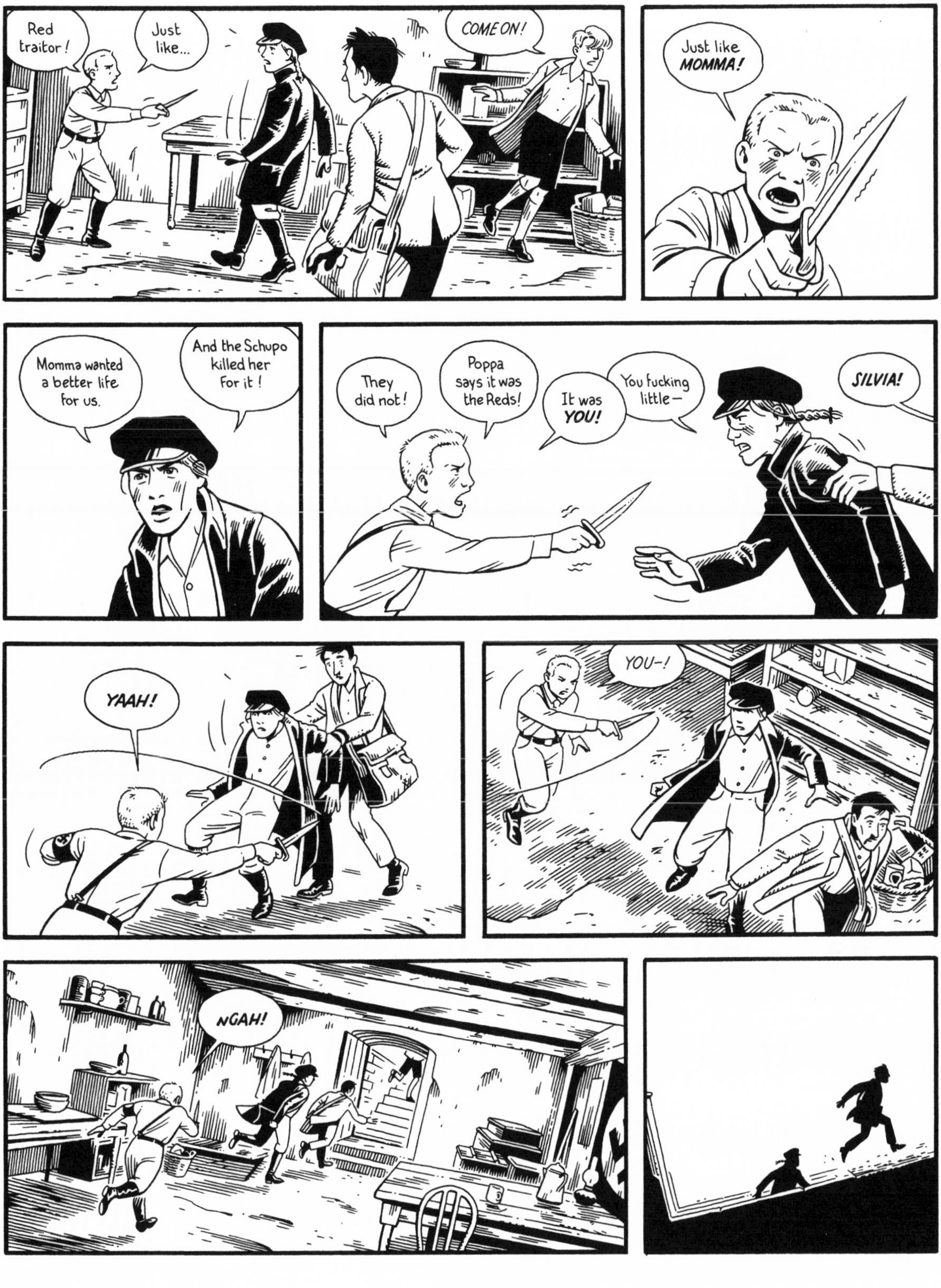
Red traitor!
Just like...
COME ON!
Just like MOMMA!
Momma wanted a better life for us.
And the Schupo killed her for it!
They did not!
Poppa says it was the Reds!
It was YOU!
You fucking little—
SILVIA!
YAAH!
YOU–!
NGAH!

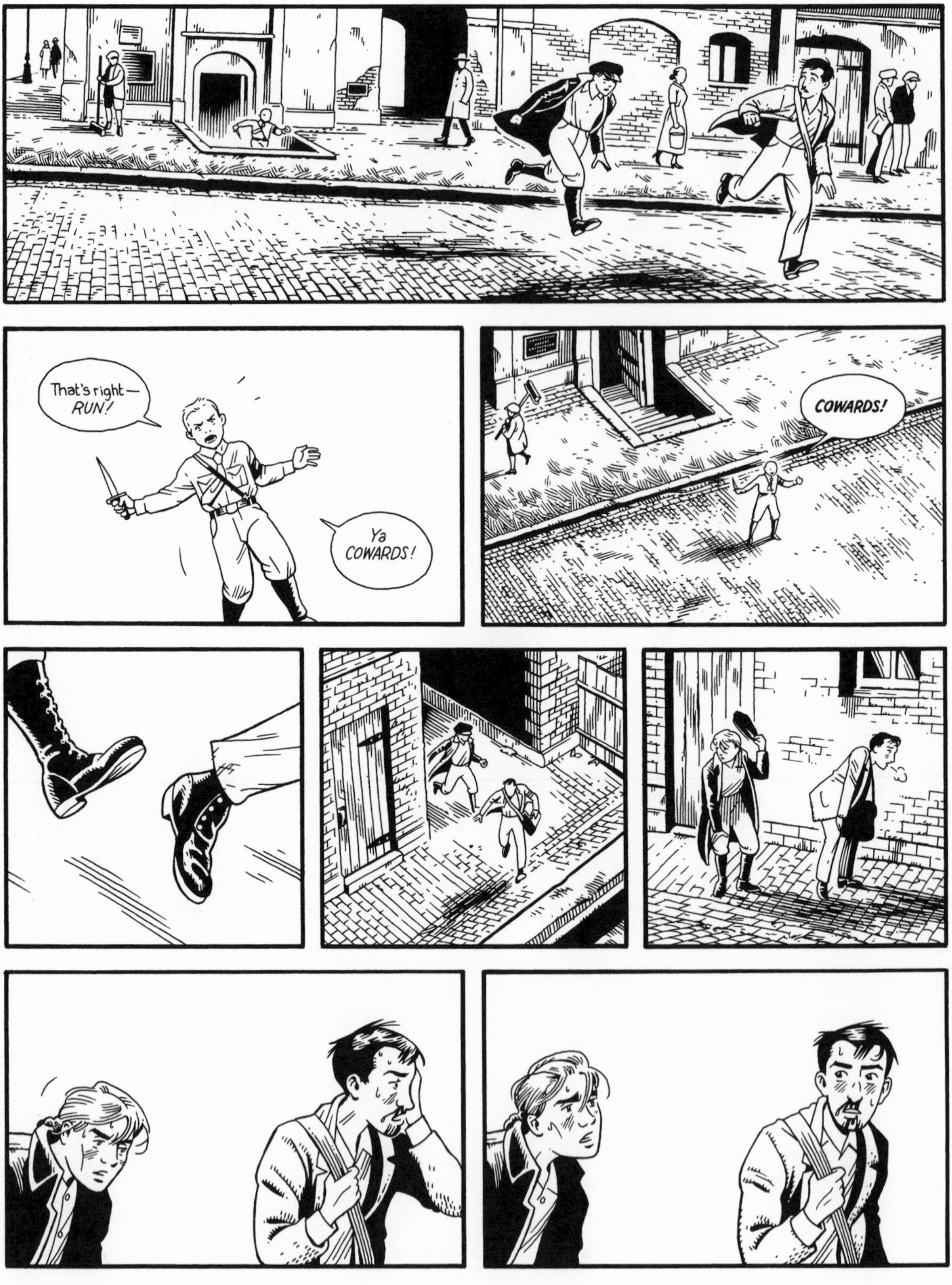
That's right—
RUN!
Ya COWARDS!
COWARDS!

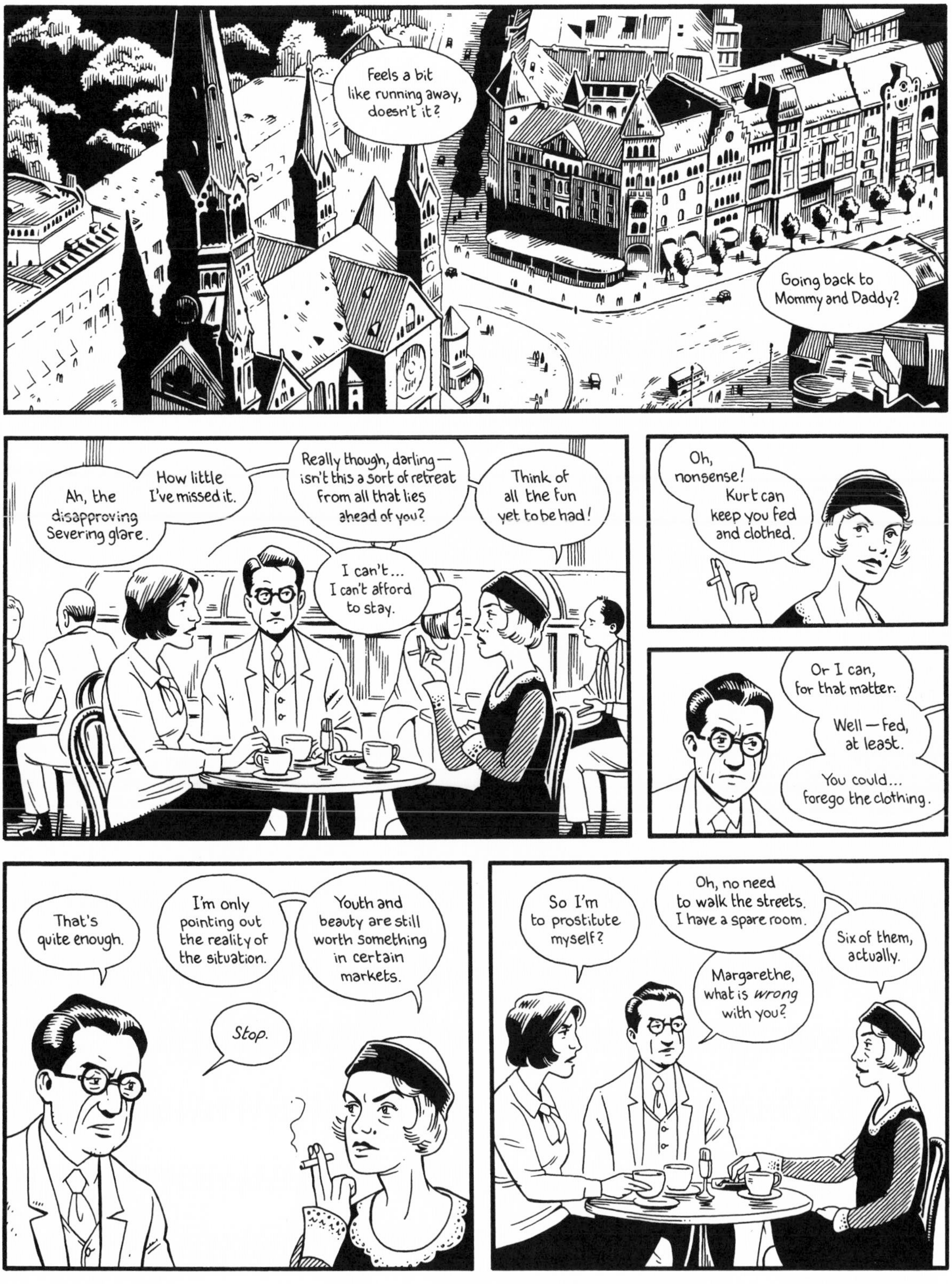

Feels a bit like running away, doesn't it?
Going back to Mommy and Daddy?
Ah, the disapproving Severing glare.
How little I've missed it.
Really though, darling — isn't this a sort of retreat from all that lies ahead of you?
Think of all the fun yet to be had!
I can't... I can't afford to stay.
Oh, nonsense! Kurt can keep you fed and clothed.
Or I can, for that matter.
Well — fed, at least.
You could... forego the clothing.
That's quite enough.
I'm only pointing out the reality of the situation.
Youth and beauty are still worth something in certain markets.
Stop.
So I'm to prostitute myself?
Oh, no need to walk the streets. I have a spare room.
Six of them, actually.
Margarethe, what is *wrong* with you?

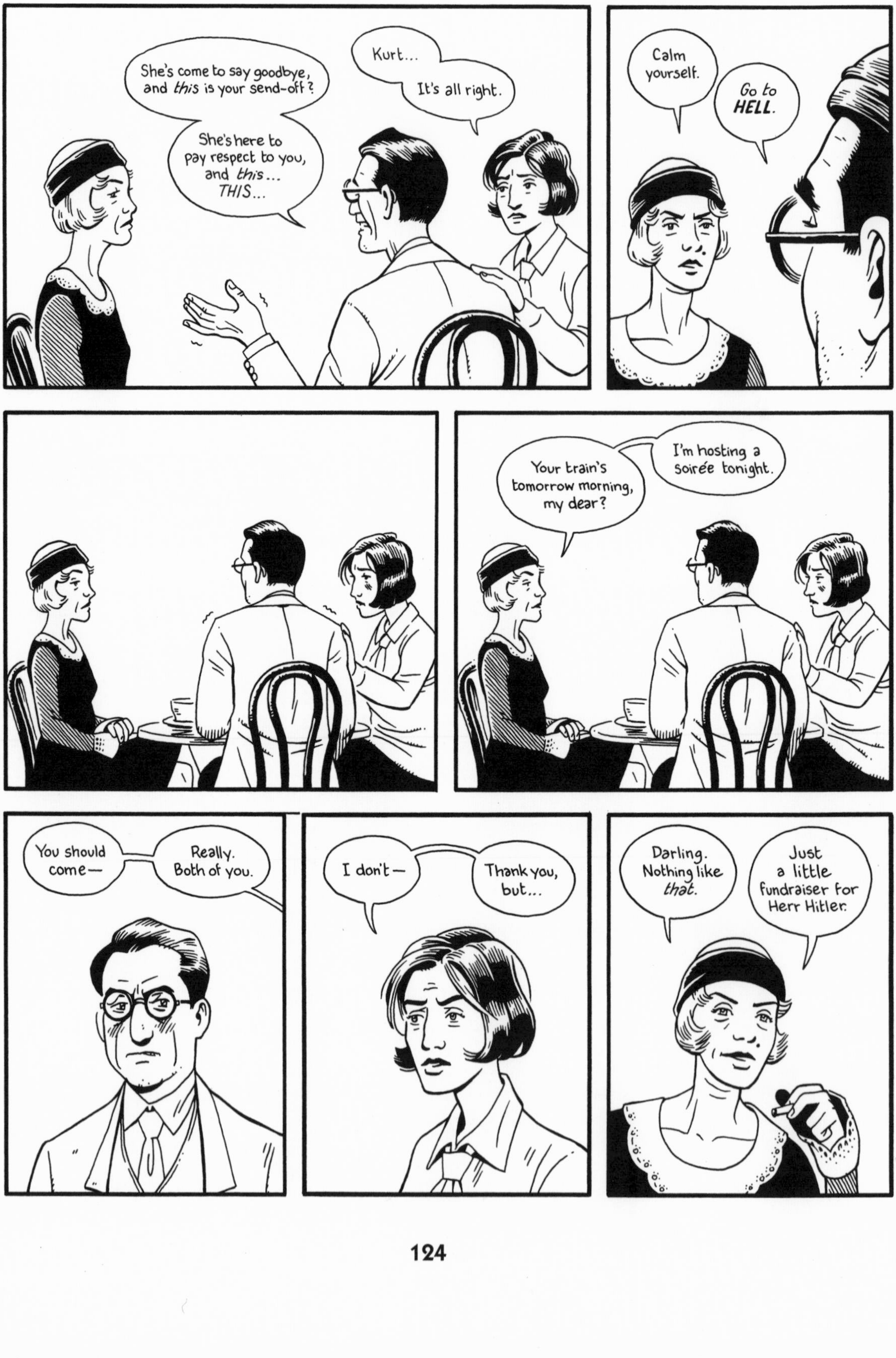

She's come to say goodbye, and *this* is your send-off?
She's here to pay respect to you, and *this*... *THIS*...
Kurt...
It's all right.
Calm yourself.
Go to ***HELL***.
Your train's tomorrow morning, my dear?
I'm hosting a soirée tonight.
You should come—
Really. Both of you.
I don't—
Thank you, but...
Darling. Nothing like *that*.
Just a little fundraiser for Herr Hitler.

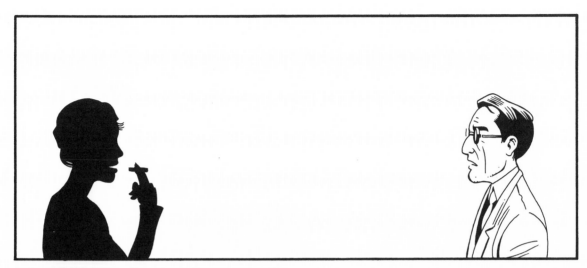

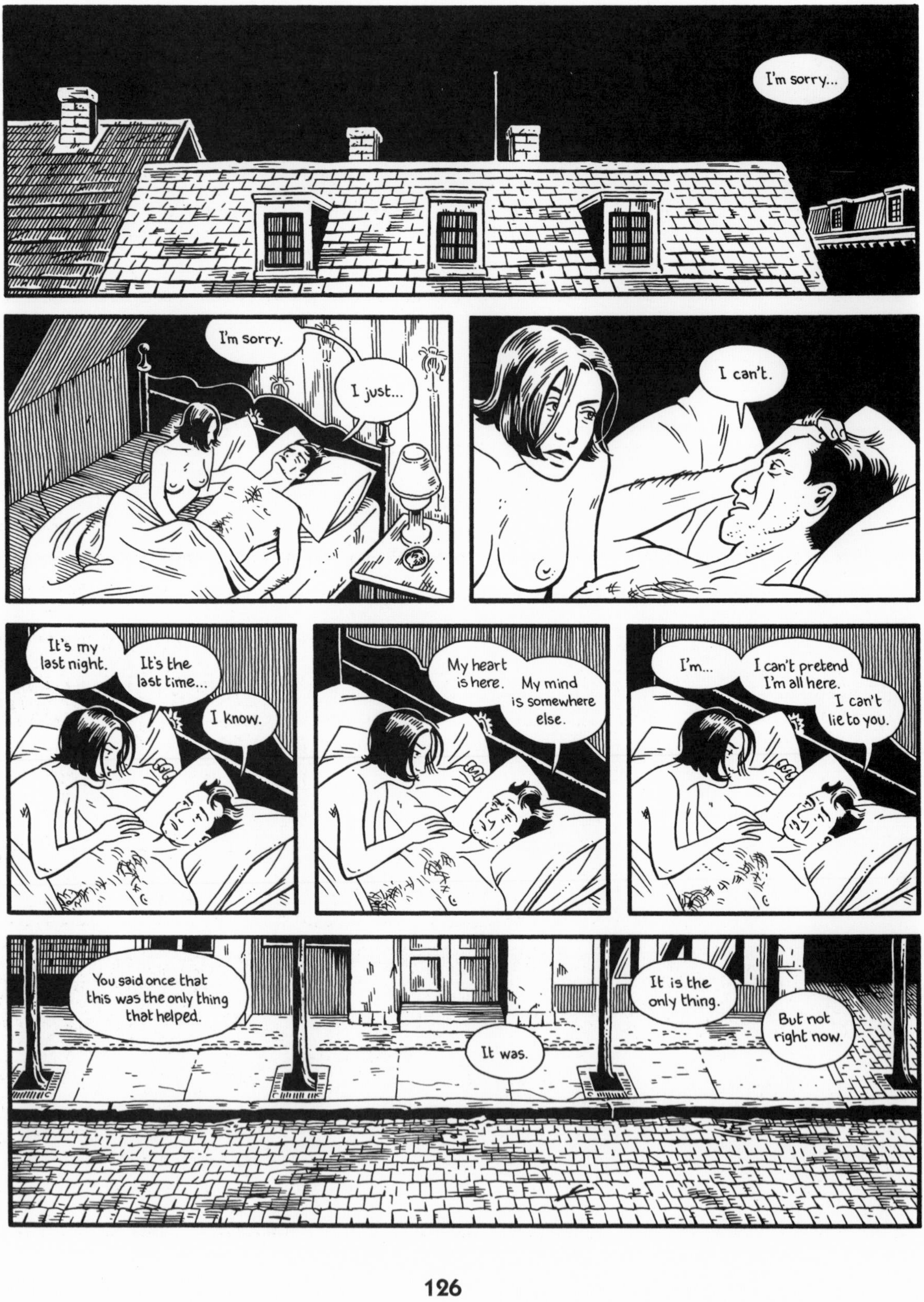
I'm sorry...
I'm sorry.
I just...
I can't.
It's my last night.
It's the last time...
I know.
My heart is here.
My mind is somewhere else.
I'm...
I can't pretend I'm all here.
I can't lie to you.
You said once that this was the only thing that helped.
It was.
It is the only thing.
But not right now.

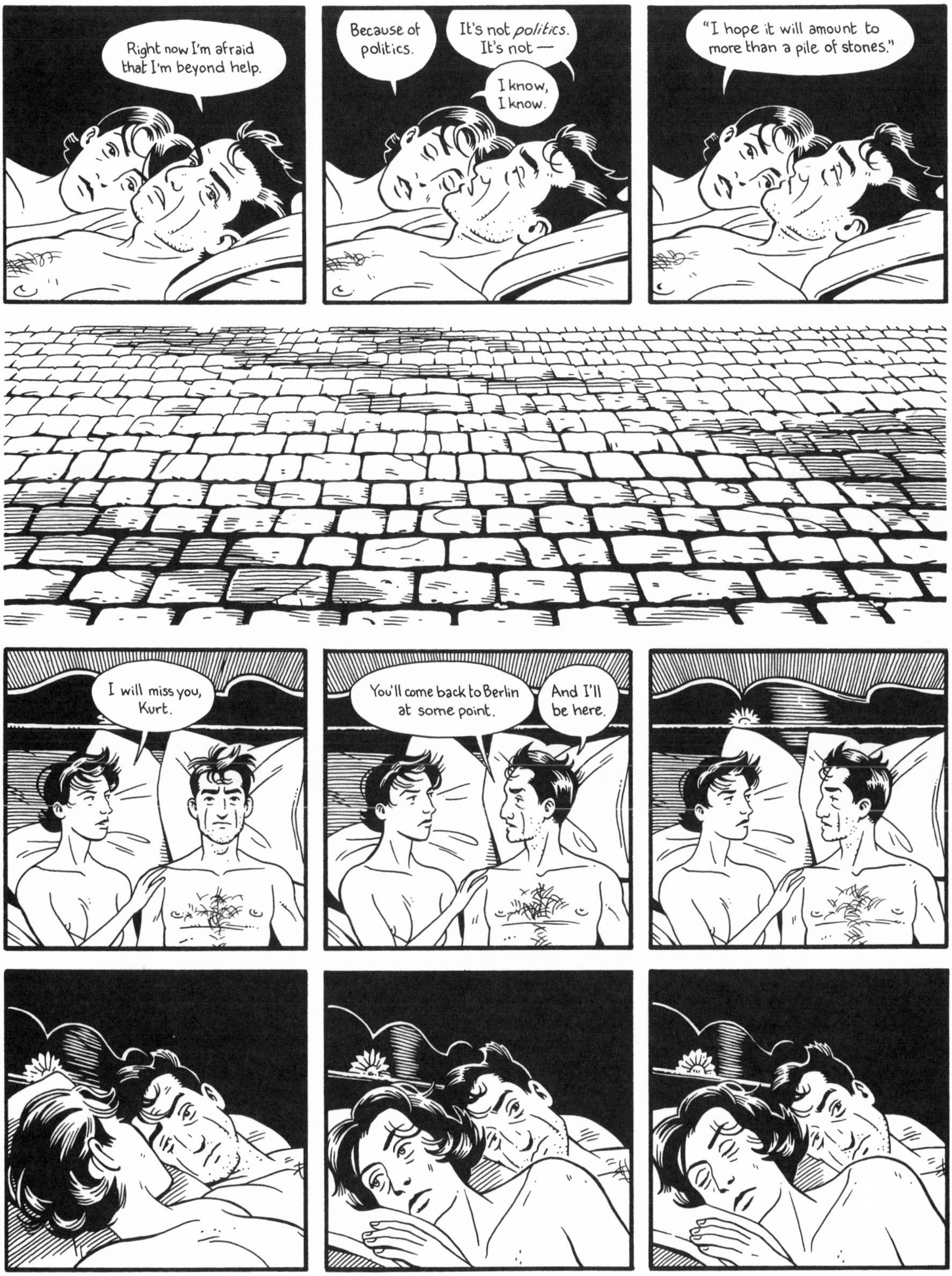
Right now I'm afraid that I'm beyond help.
Because of politics.
It's not *politics*. It's not —
I know, I know.
"I hope it will amount to more than a pile of stones."
I will miss you, Kurt.
You'll come back to Berlin at some point.
And I'll be here.

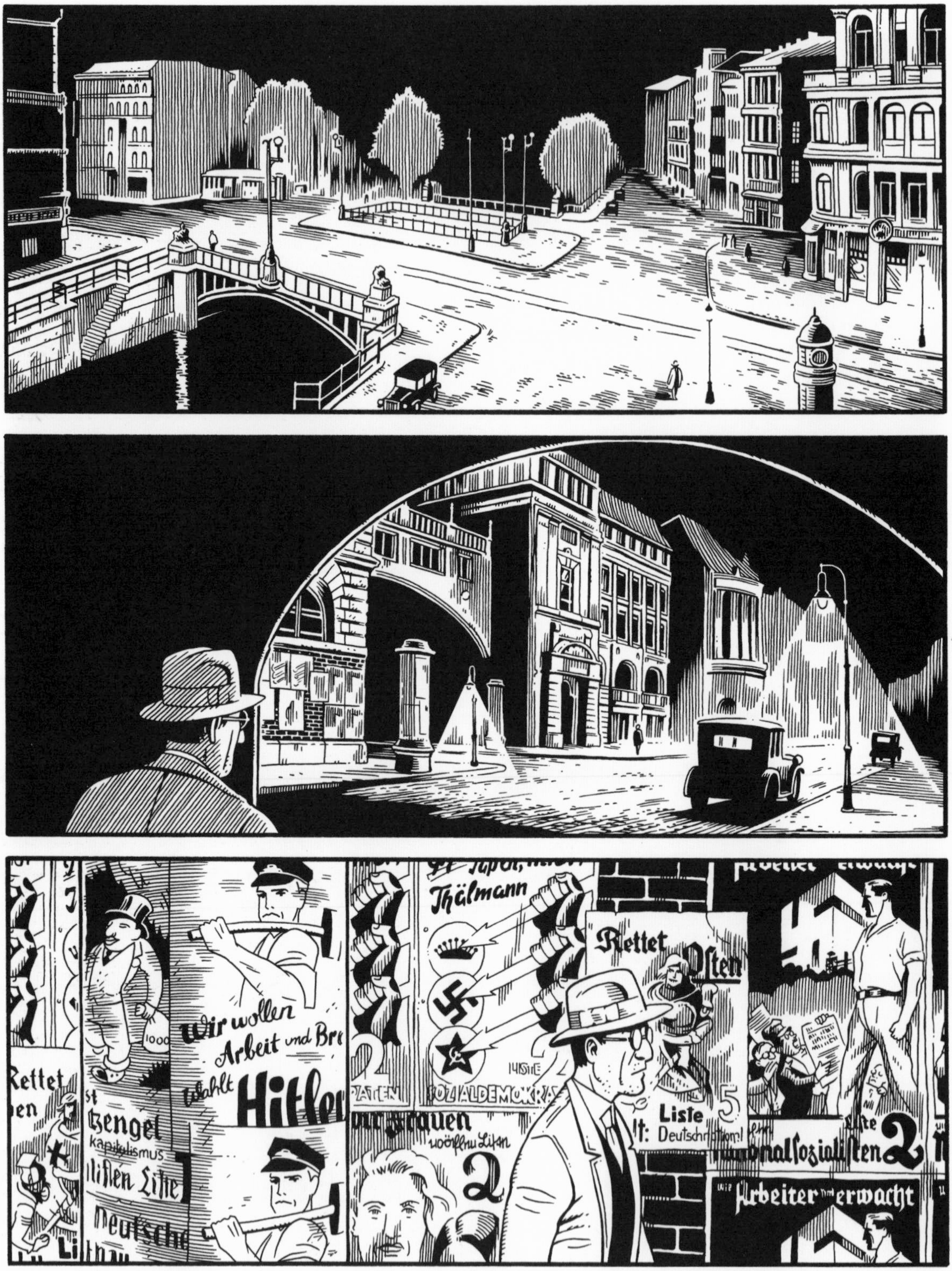
Thälmann
Rettet
Osten
Wir wollen
Arbeit
Wählt Hitler
kapitalismus
Liste
5
Rettet
Sozialdemokra
2
Arbeiter
erwacht

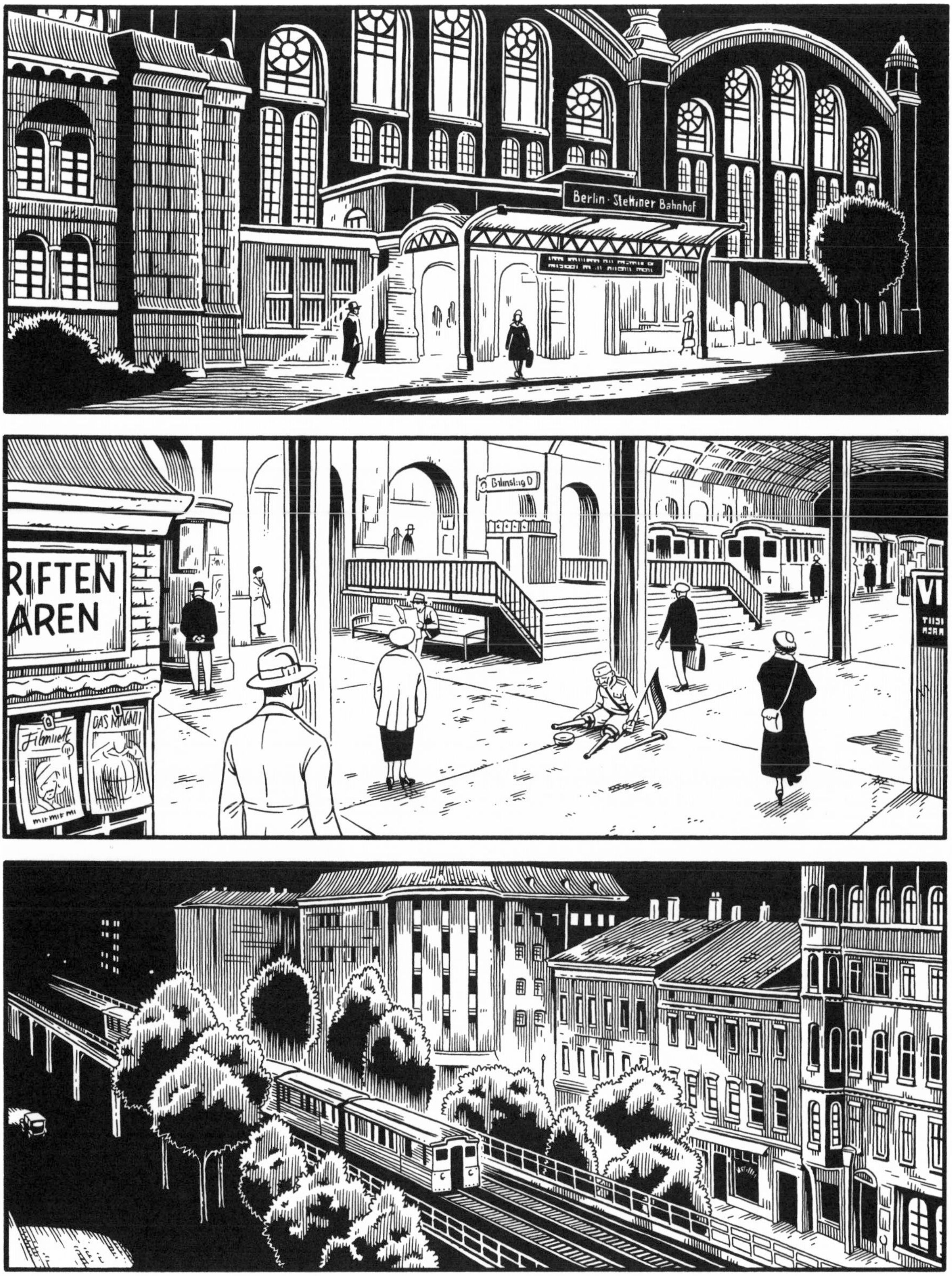
Berlin · Stettiner Bahnhof
RIFTEN
AREN

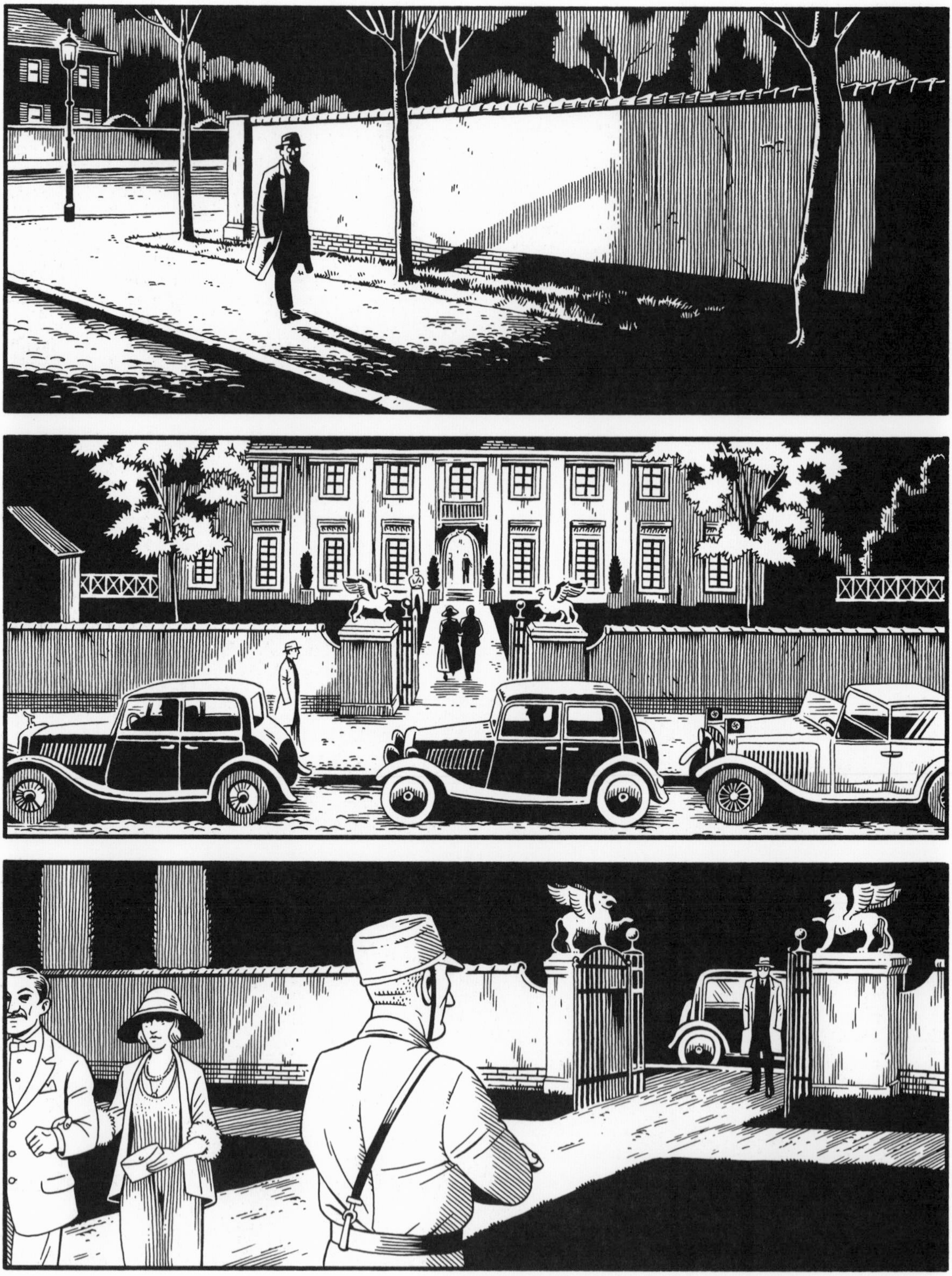

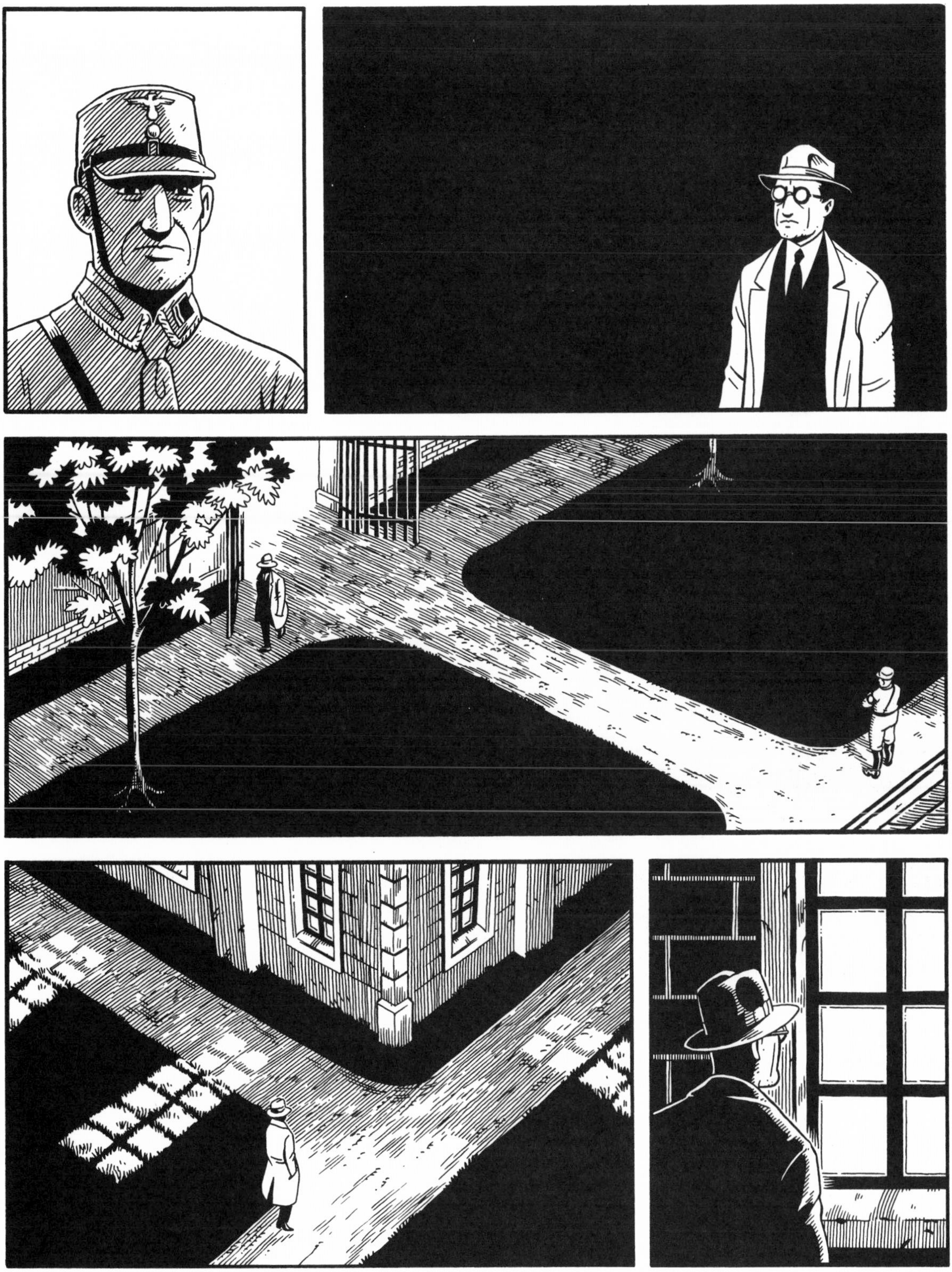

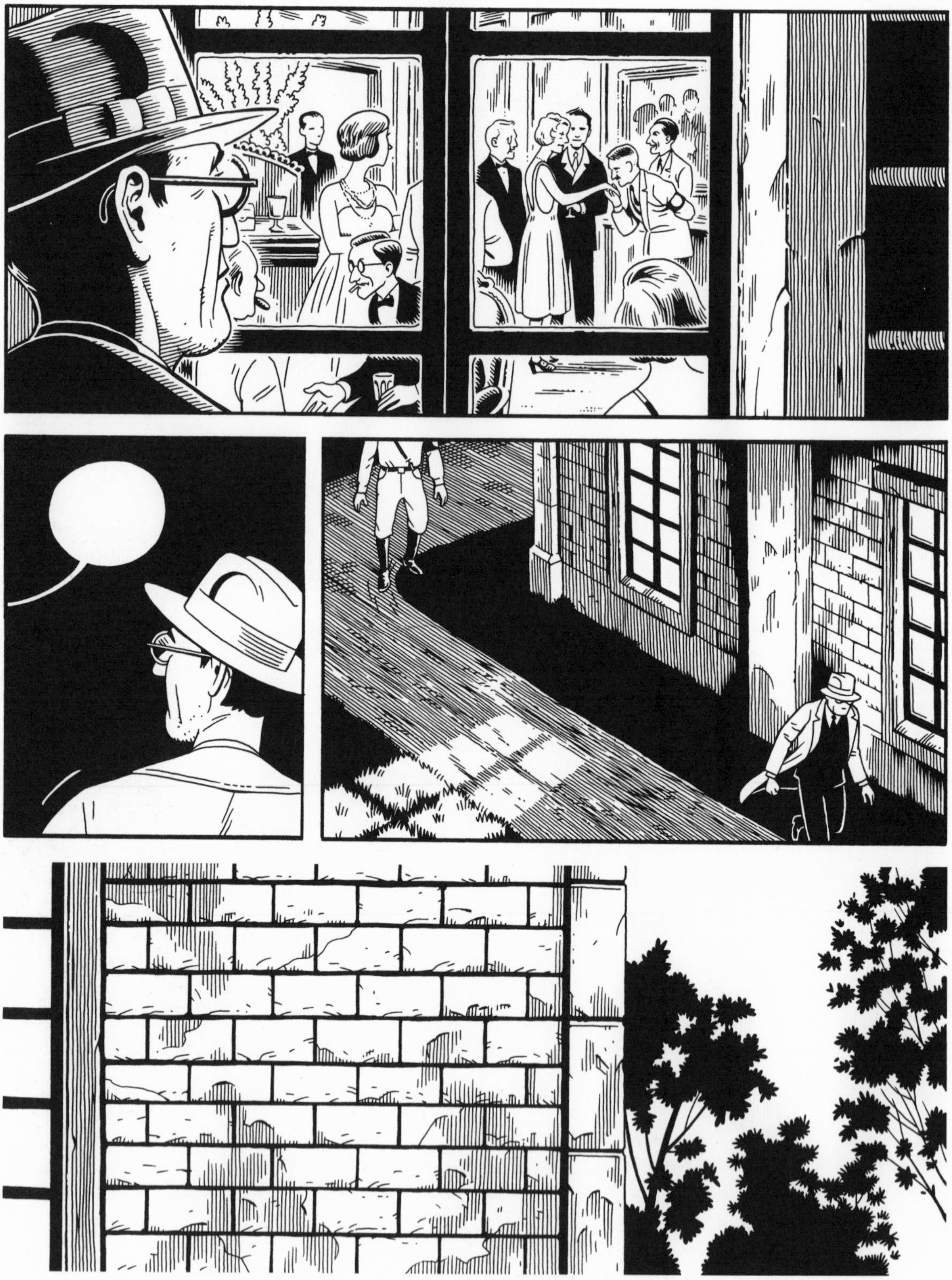

6

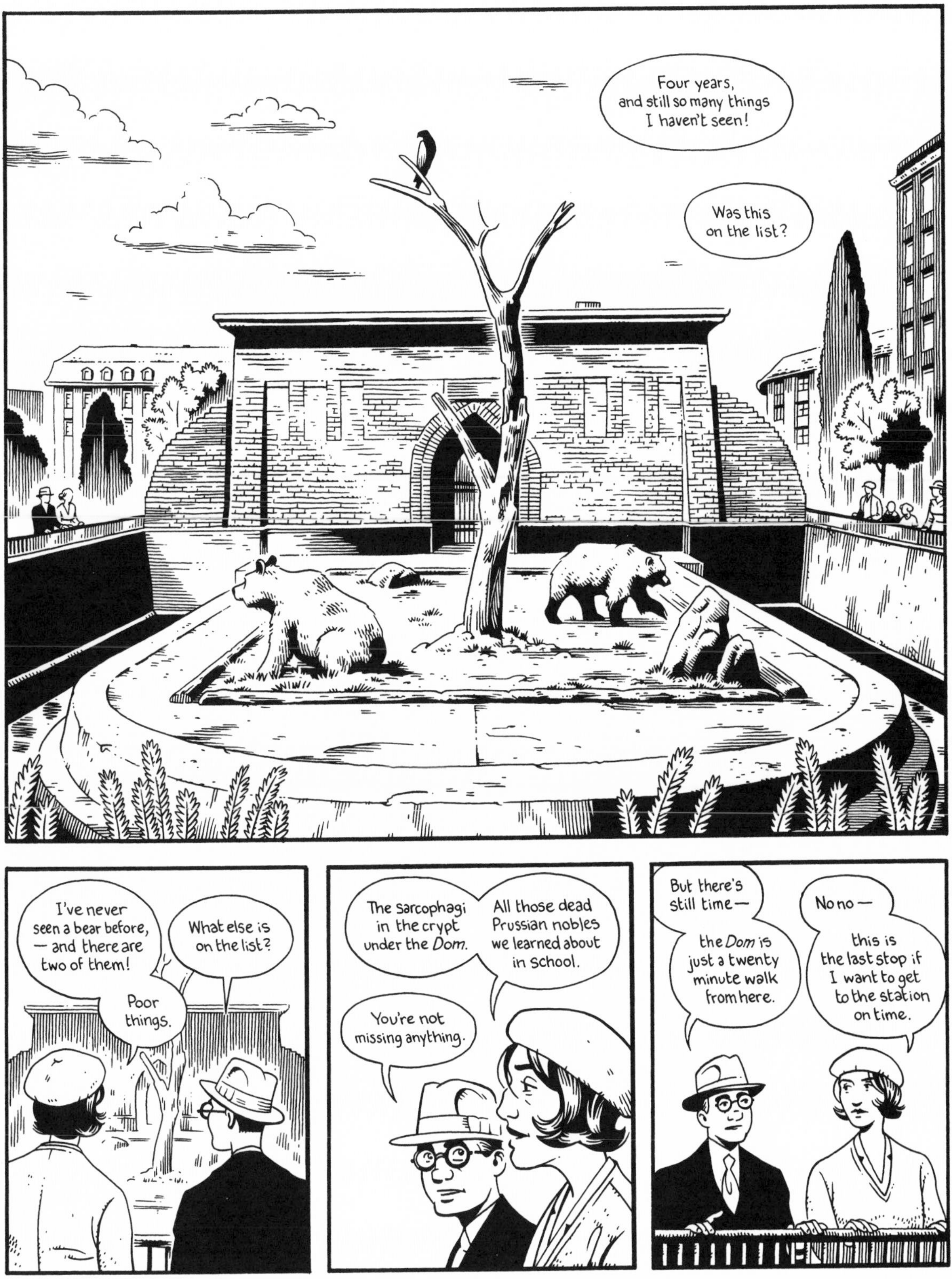
Four years, and still so many things I haven't seen!
Was this on the list?
I've never seen a bear before, — and there are two of them!
Poor things.
What else is on the list?
The sarcophagi in the crypt under the *Dom*.
All those dead Prussian nobles we learned about in school.
You're not missing anything.
But there's still time —
the *Dom* is just a twenty minute walk from here.
No no —
this is the last stop if I want to get to the station on time.

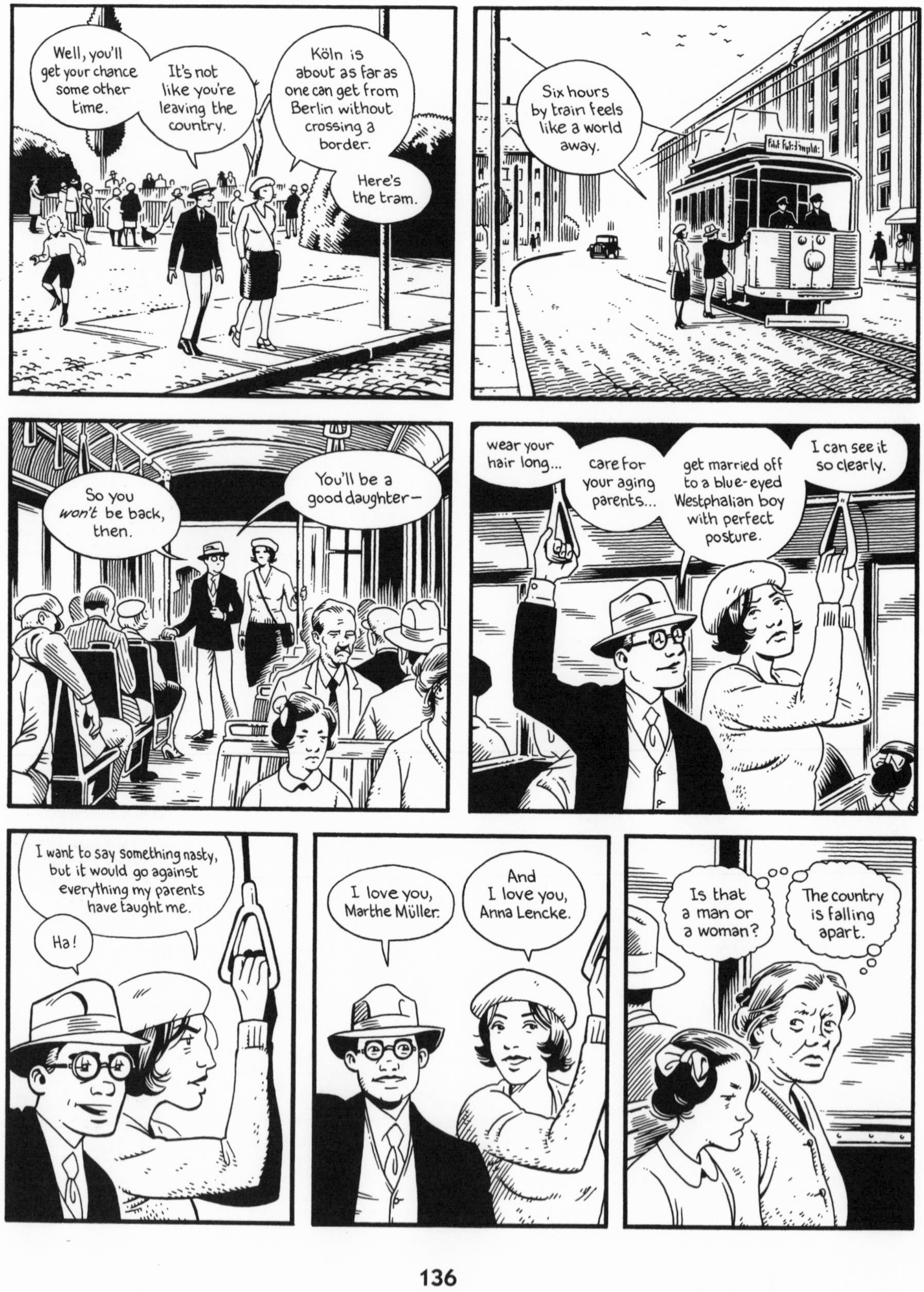
Well, you'll get your chance some other time.
It's not like you're leaving the country.
Köln is about as far as one can get from Berlin without crossing a border.
Here's the tram.
Six hours by train feels like a world away.
So you *won't* be back, then.
You'll be a good daughter—
wear your hair long...
care for your aging parents...
get married off to a blue-eyed Westphalian boy with perfect posture.
I can see it so clearly.
I want to say something nasty, but it would go against everything my parents have taught me.
Ha!
I love you, Marthe Müller.
And I love you, Anna Lencke.
Is that a man or a woman?
The country is falling apart.

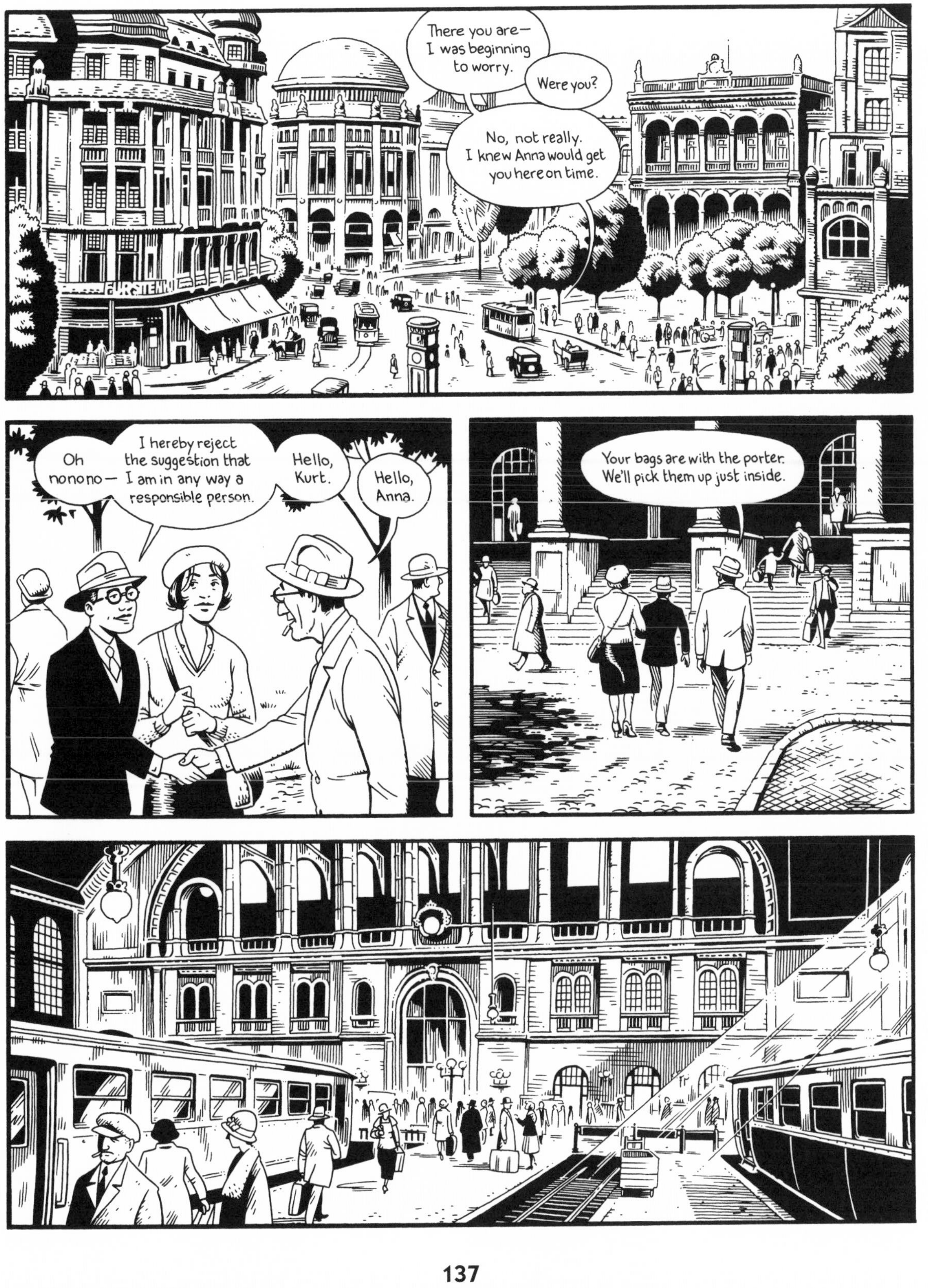

There you are— I was beginning to worry.
Were you?
No, not really. I knew Anna would get you here on time.
Oh nonono—
I hereby reject the suggestion that I am in any way a responsible person.
Hello, Kurt.
Hello, Anna.
Your bags are with the porter. We'll pick them up just inside.

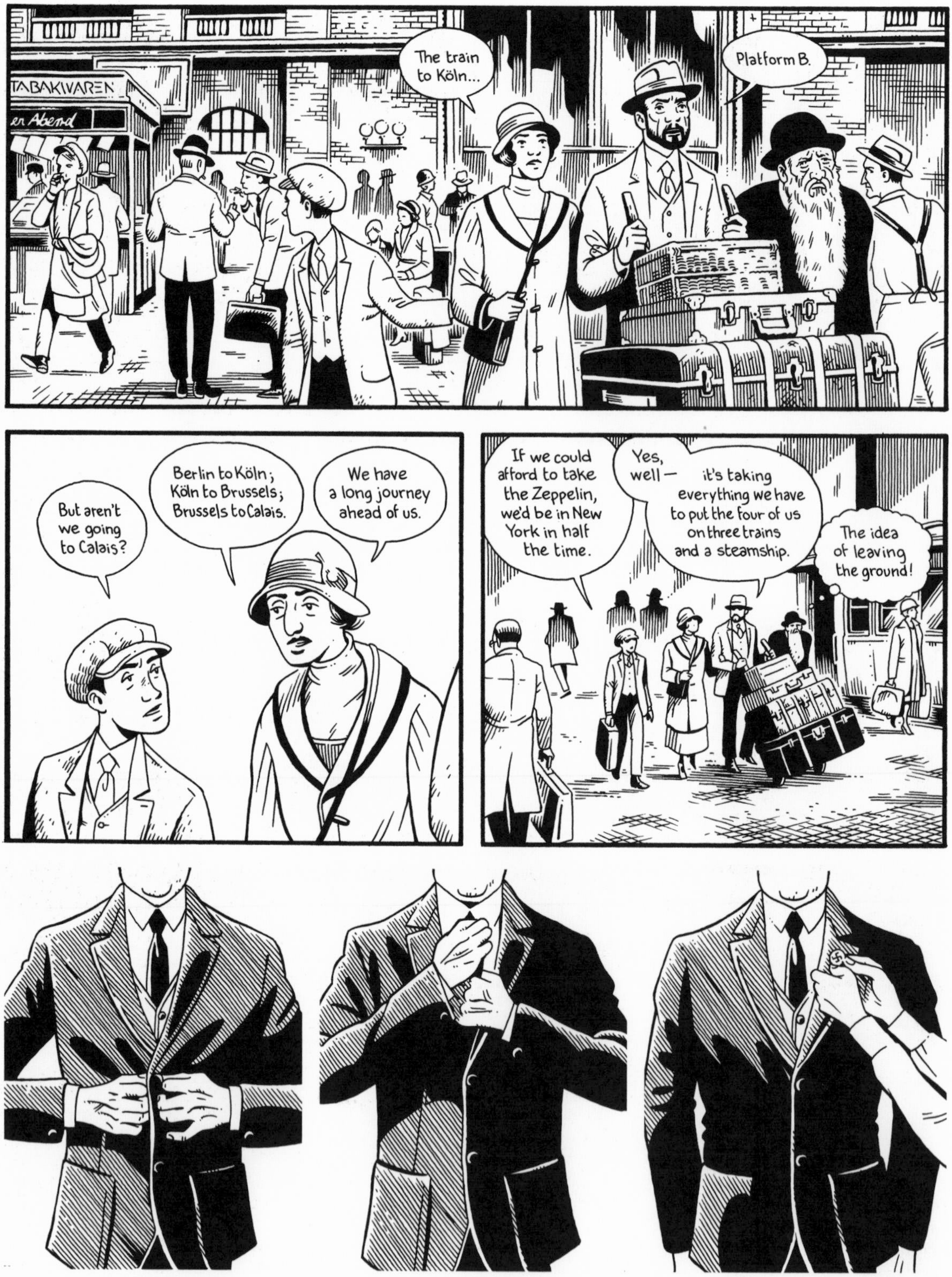
TABAKWAREN
The train to Köln...
Platform B.
But aren't we going to Calais?
Berlin to Köln; Köln to Brussels; Brussels to Calais.
We have a long journey ahead of us.
If we could afford to take the Zeppelin, we'd be in New York in half the time.
Yes, well—
it's taking everything we have to put the four of us on three trains and a steamship.
The idea of leaving the ground!

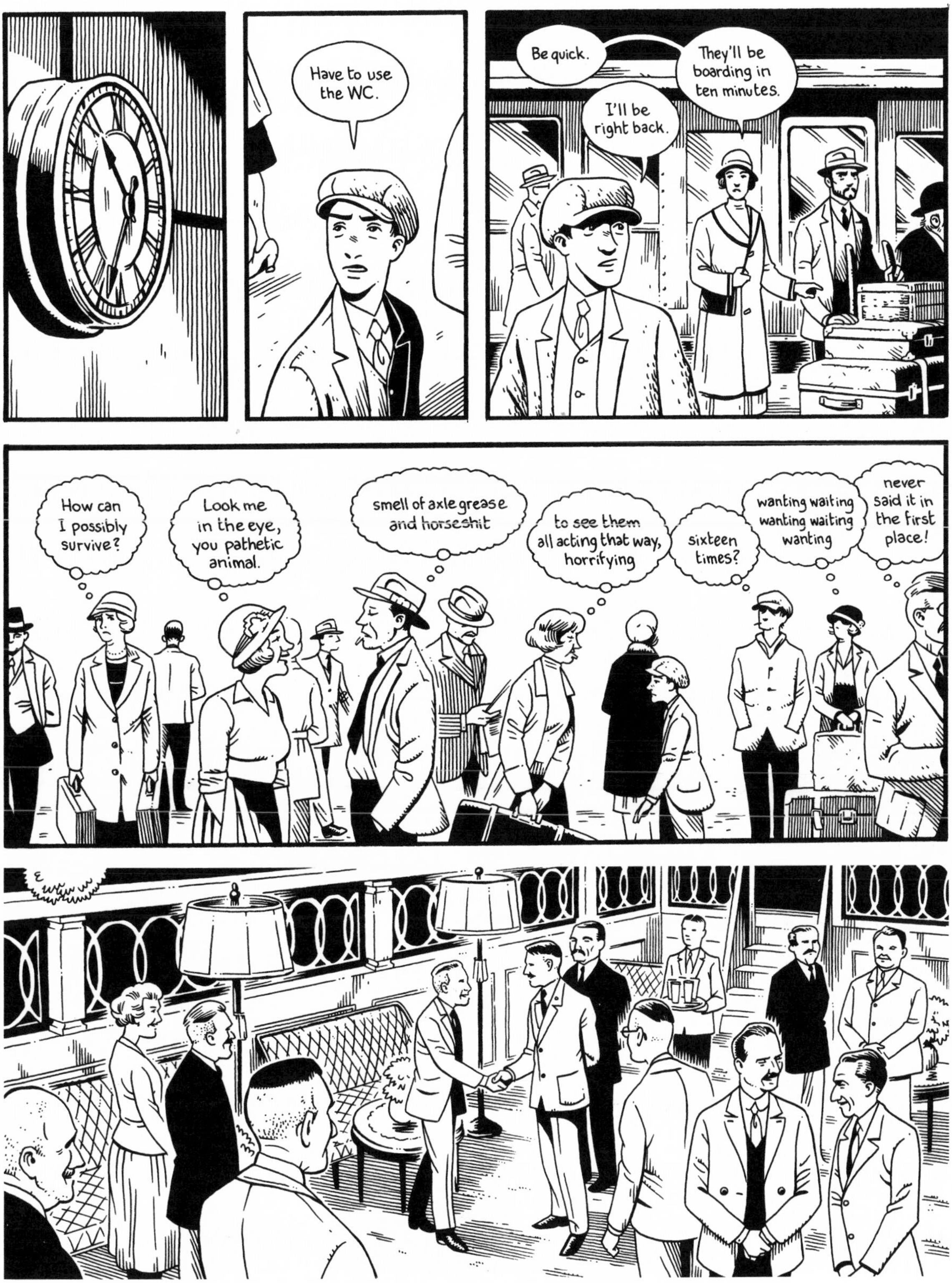

Have to use the WC.
Be quick.
They'll be boarding in ten minutes.
I'll be right back.
How can I possibly survive?
Look me in the eye, you pathetic animal.
smell of axle grease ~~and horseshit~~
~~to see them~~ all acting that way, horrifying
sixteen times?
wanting waiting wanting waiting wanting
never said it in the first place!

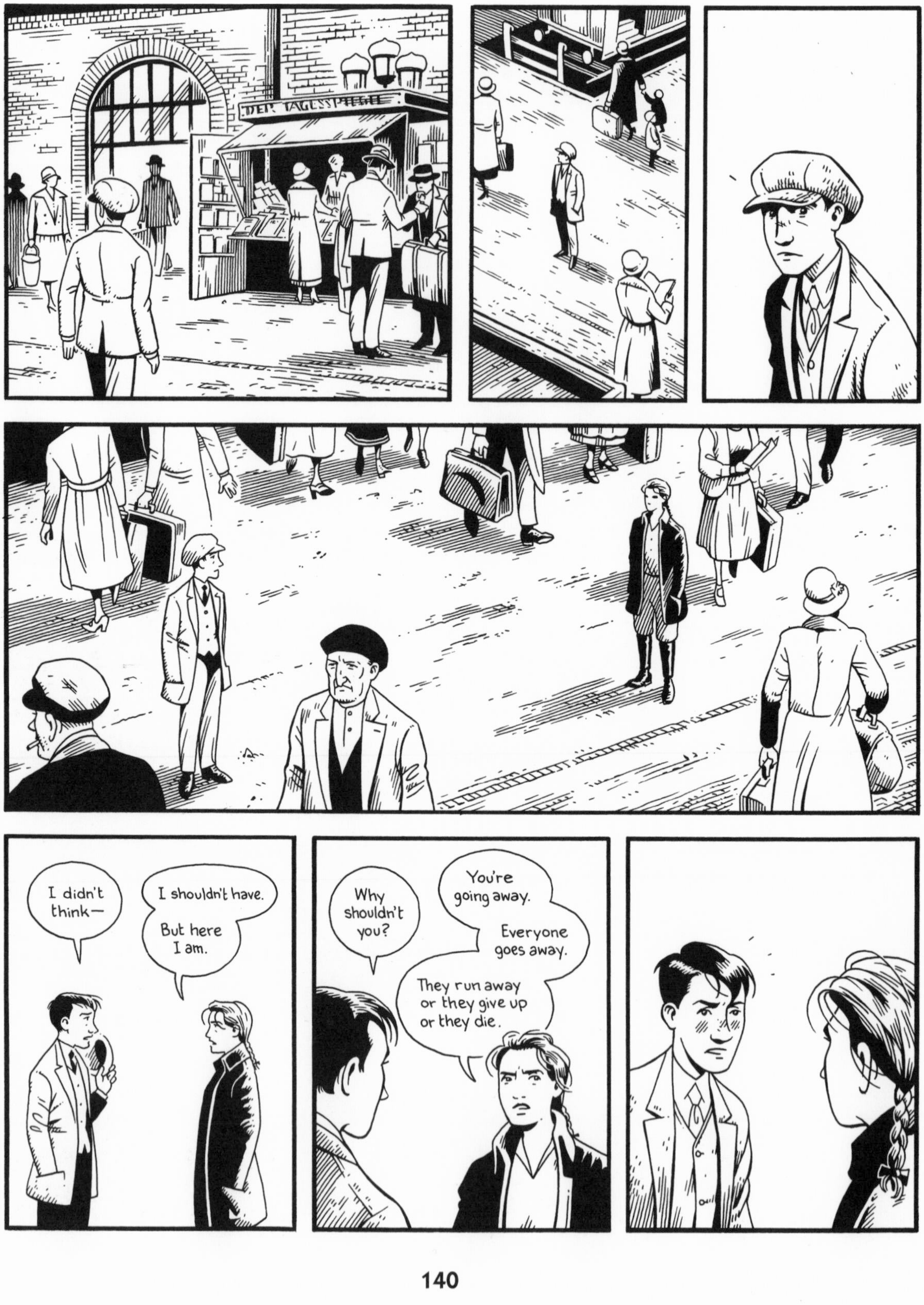
DER TAGESSPIEGEL
I didn't think—
I shouldn't have.
But here I am.
Why shouldn't you?
You're going away.
Everyone goes away.
They run away or they give up or they die.

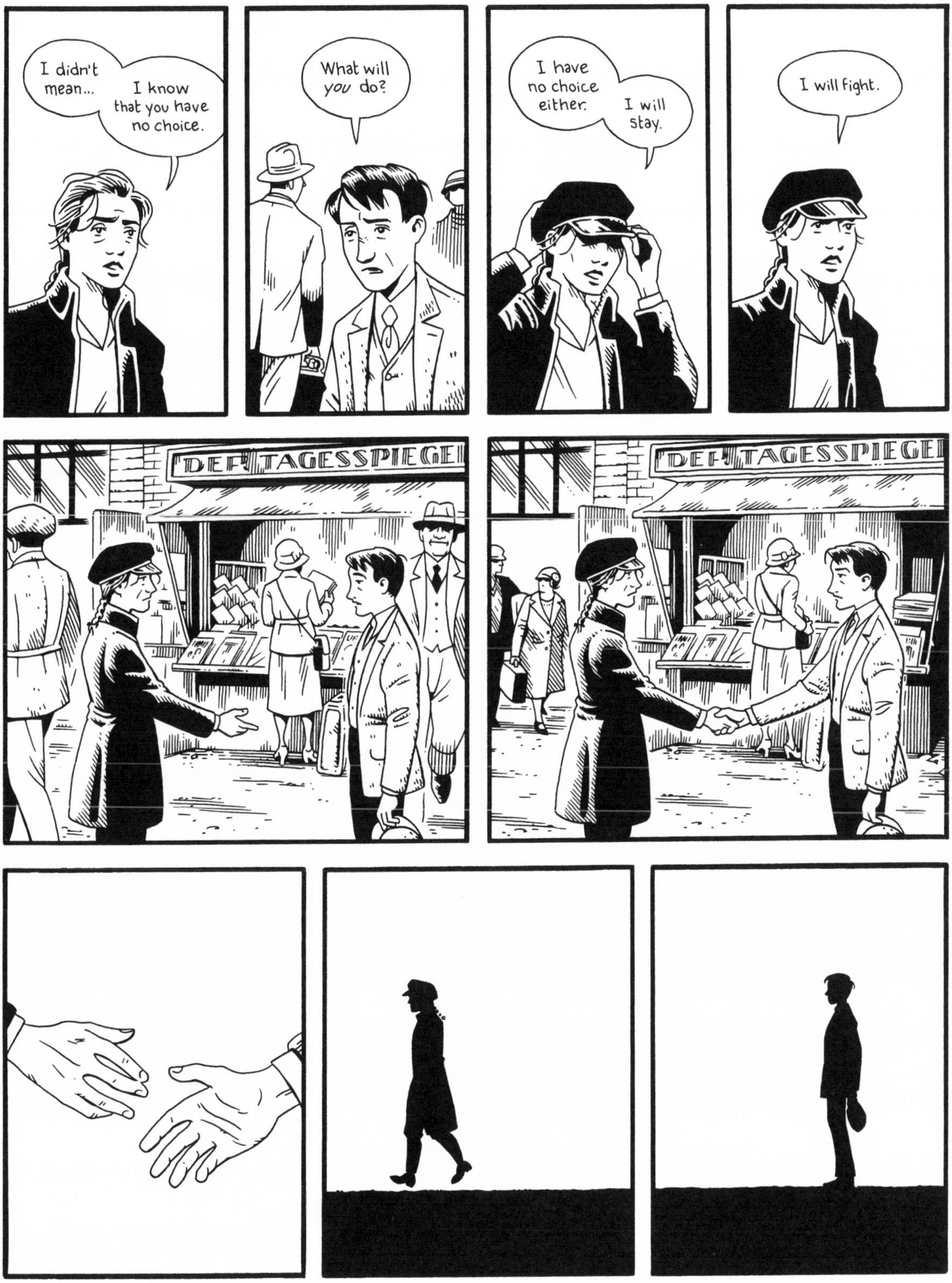
I didn't mean...
I know that you have no choice.
What will you do?
I have no choice either.
I will stay.
I will fight.
DER TAGESSPIEGE
DER TAGESSPIEGE

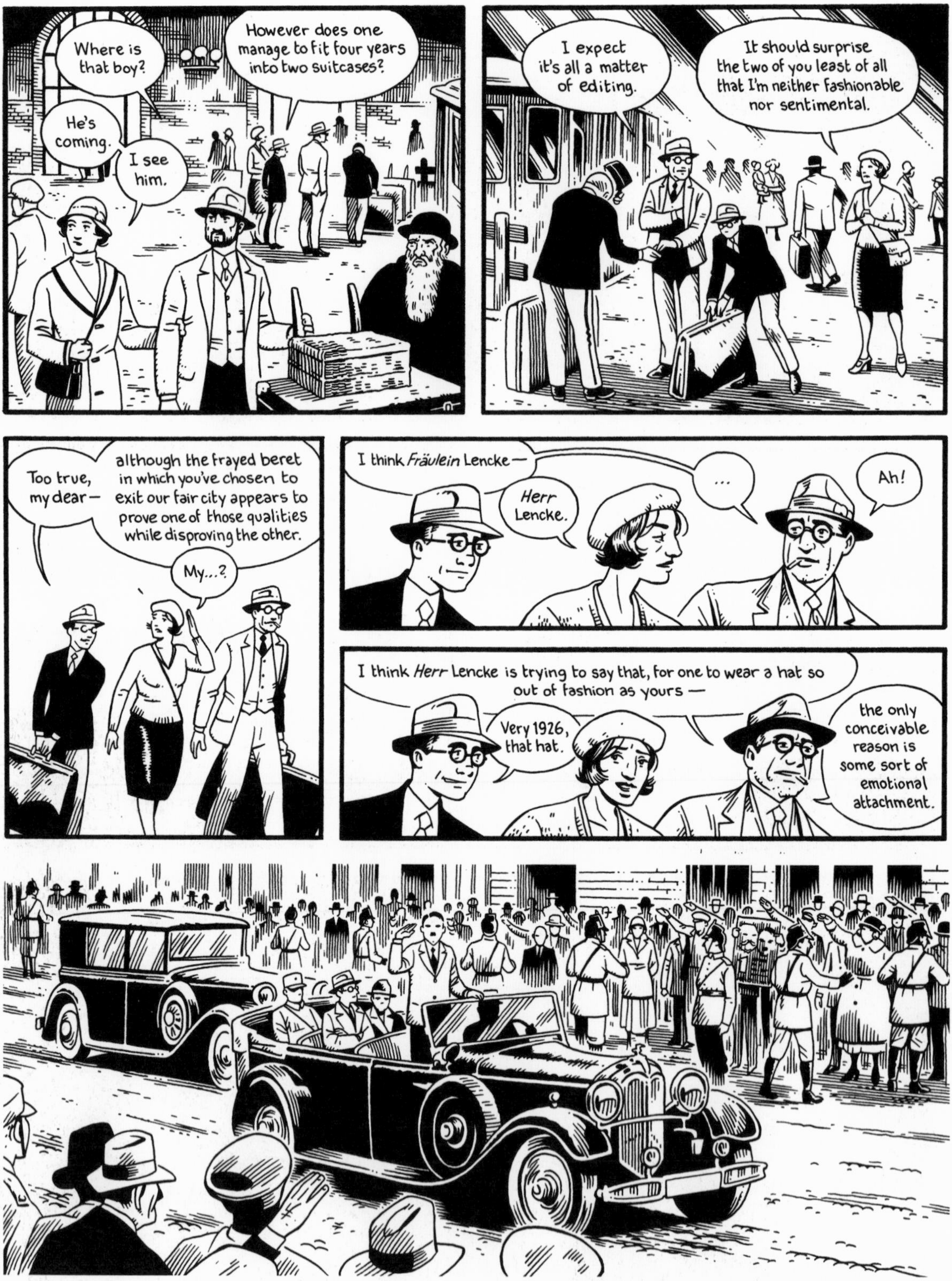
Where is that boy?
However does one manage to fit four years into two suitcases?
He's coming.
I see him.
I expect it's all a matter of editing.
It should surprise the two of you least of all that I'm neither fashionable nor sentimental.
Too true, my dear—
although the frayed beret in which you've chosen to exit our fair city appears to prove one of those qualities while disproving the other.
My...?
I think *Fräulein* Lencke—
Herr Lencke.
...
Ah!
I think *Herr* Lencke is trying to say that, for one to wear a hat so out of fashion as yours —
Very 1926, that hat.
the only conceivable reason is some sort of emotional attachment.

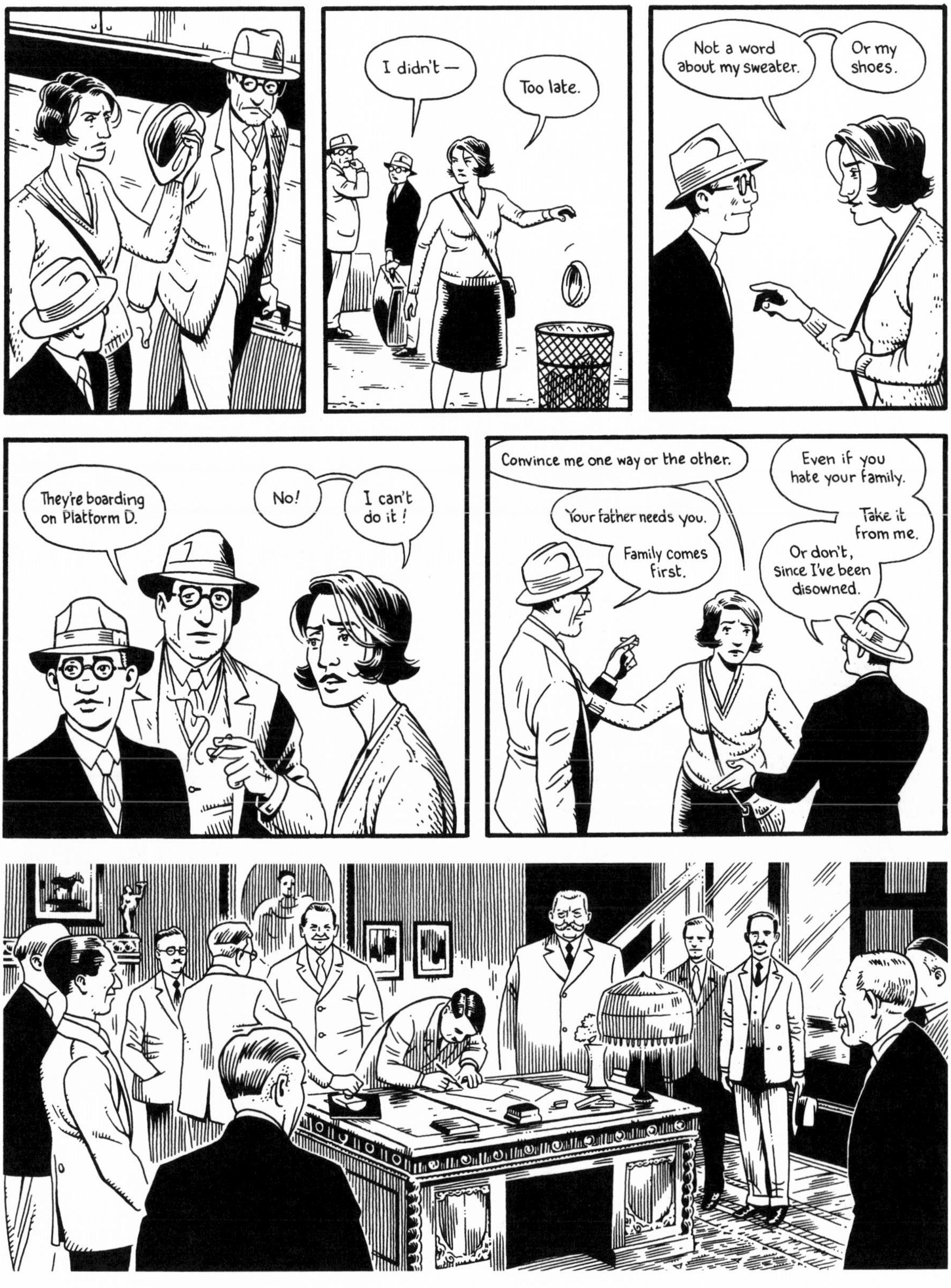
I didn't —
Too late.
Not a word about my sweater.
Or my shoes.
They're boarding on Platform D.
No!
I can't do it!
Convince me one way or the other.
Your father needs you.
Family comes first.
Even if you hate your family.
Take it from me.
Or don't, since I've been disowned.

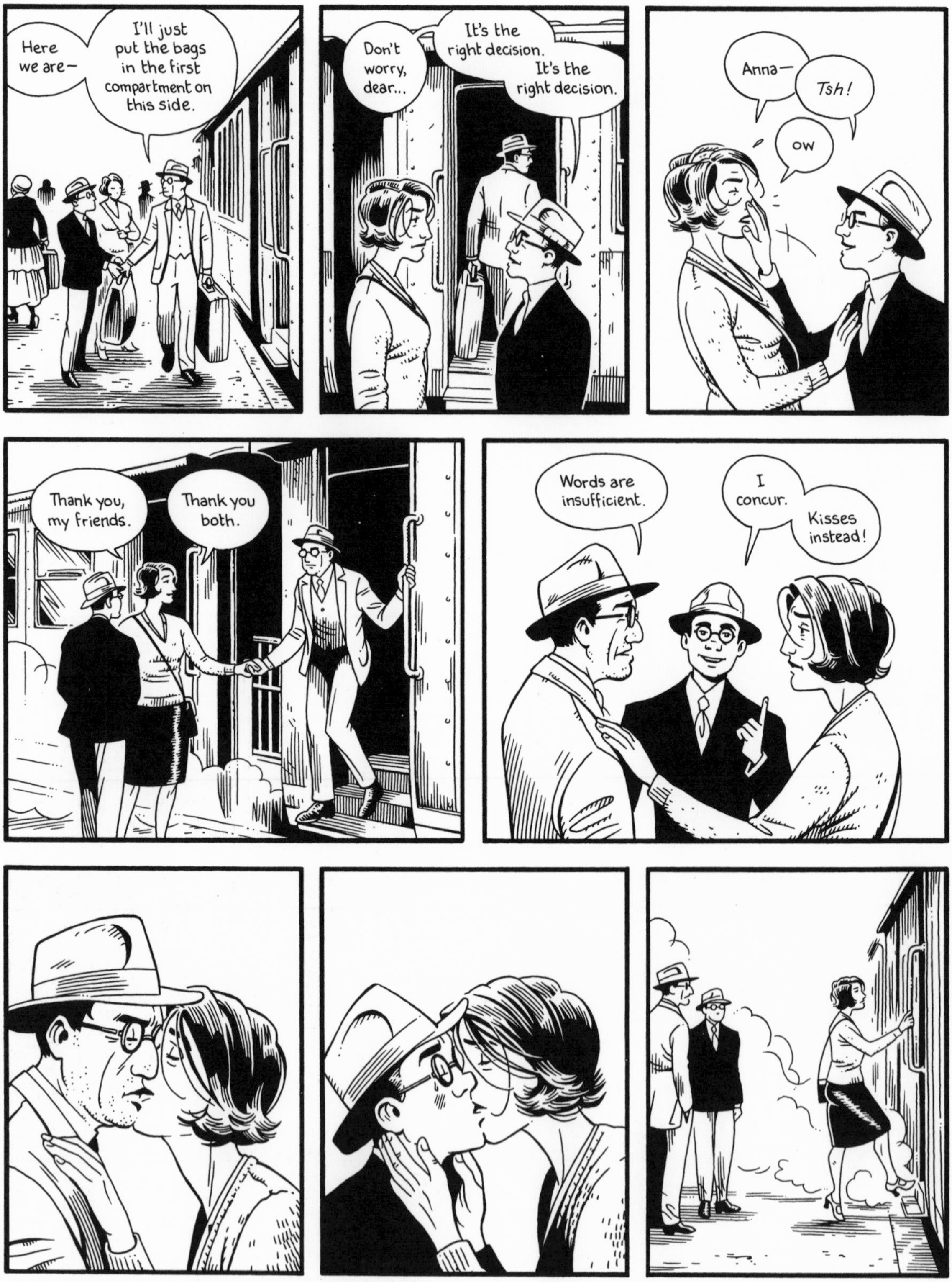
Here we are—
I'll just put the bags in the first compartment on this side.
Don't worry, dear...
It's the right decision.
It's the right decision.
Anna—
Tsh!
ow
Thank you, my friends.
Thank you both.
Words are insufficient.
I concur.
Kisses instead!

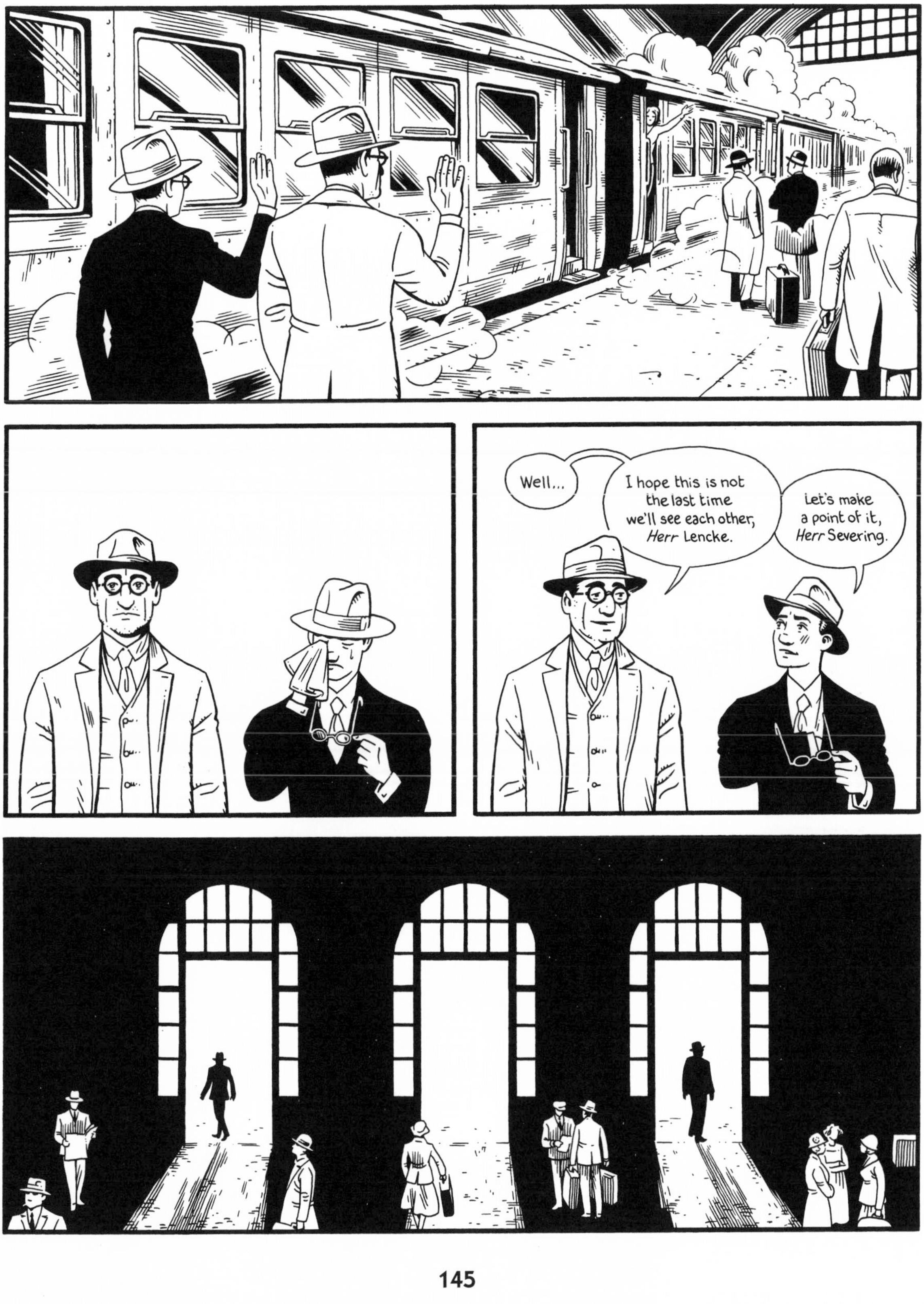

Well...
I hope this is not the last time we'll see each other, *Herr* Lencke.
Let's make a point of it, *Herr* Severing.

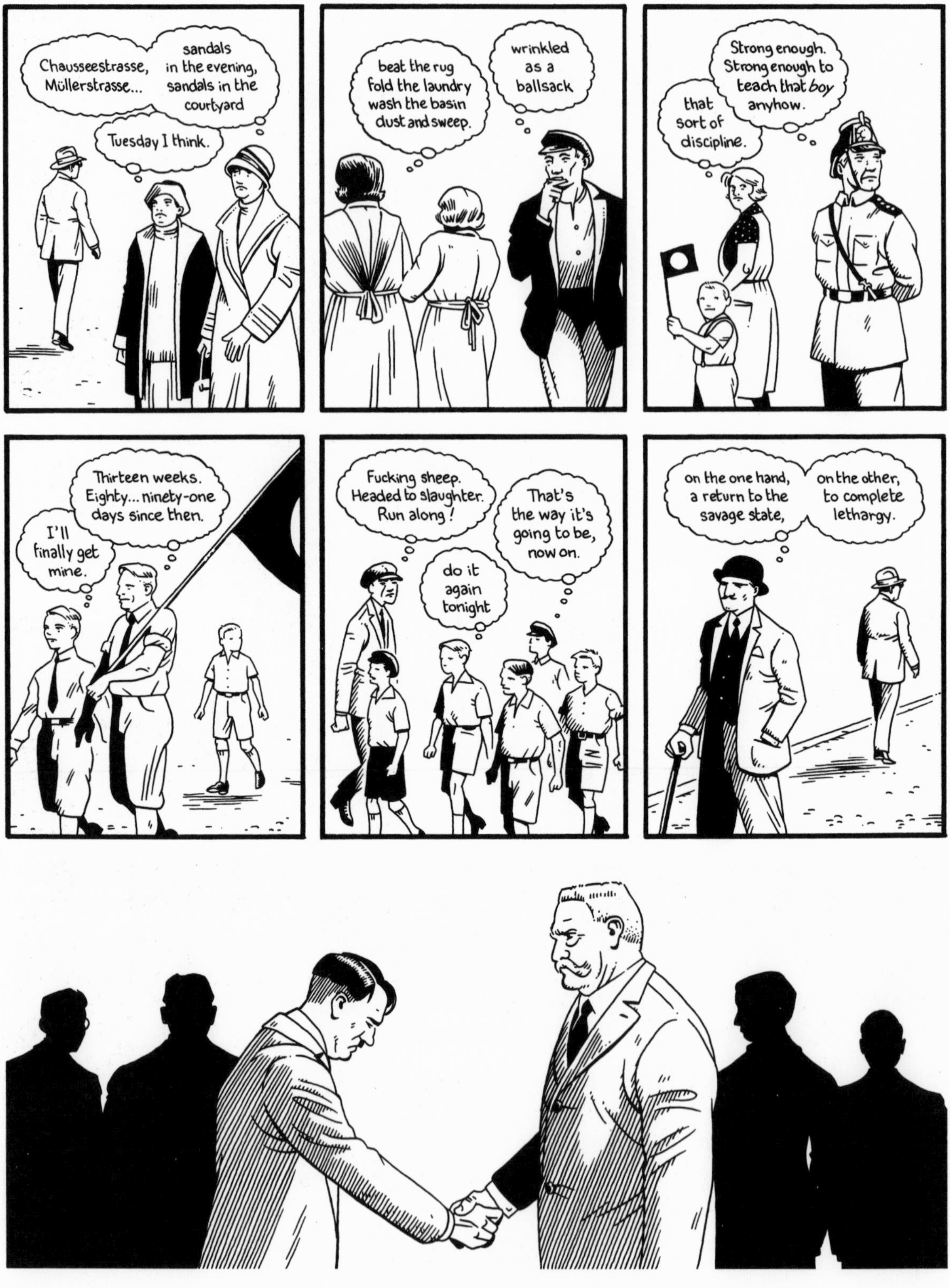

Chausseestrasse, Müllerstrasse...
sandals in the evening, sandals in the courtyard
Tuesday I think.
beat the rug fold the laundry wash the basin dust and sweep.
wrinkled as a ballsack
that sort of discipline.
Strong enough. Strong enough to teach that *boy* anyhow.
I'll finally get mine.
Thirteen weeks. Eighty... ninety-one days since then.
Fucking sheep. Headed to slaughter. Run along!
do it again tonight
That's the way it's going to be, now on.
on the one hand, a return to the savage state,
on the other, to complete lethargy.

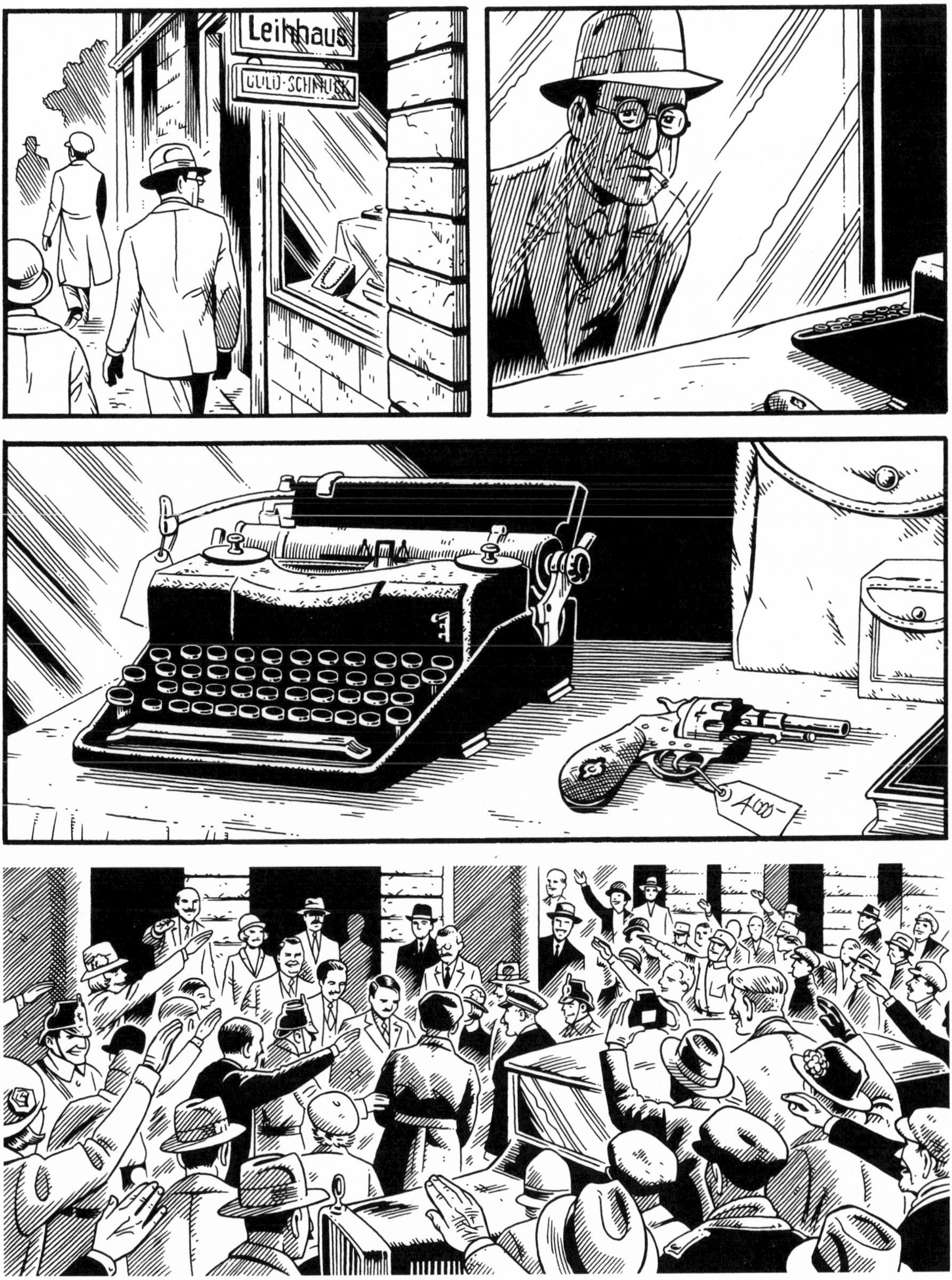
Leihhaus
GOLD·SCHMUCK

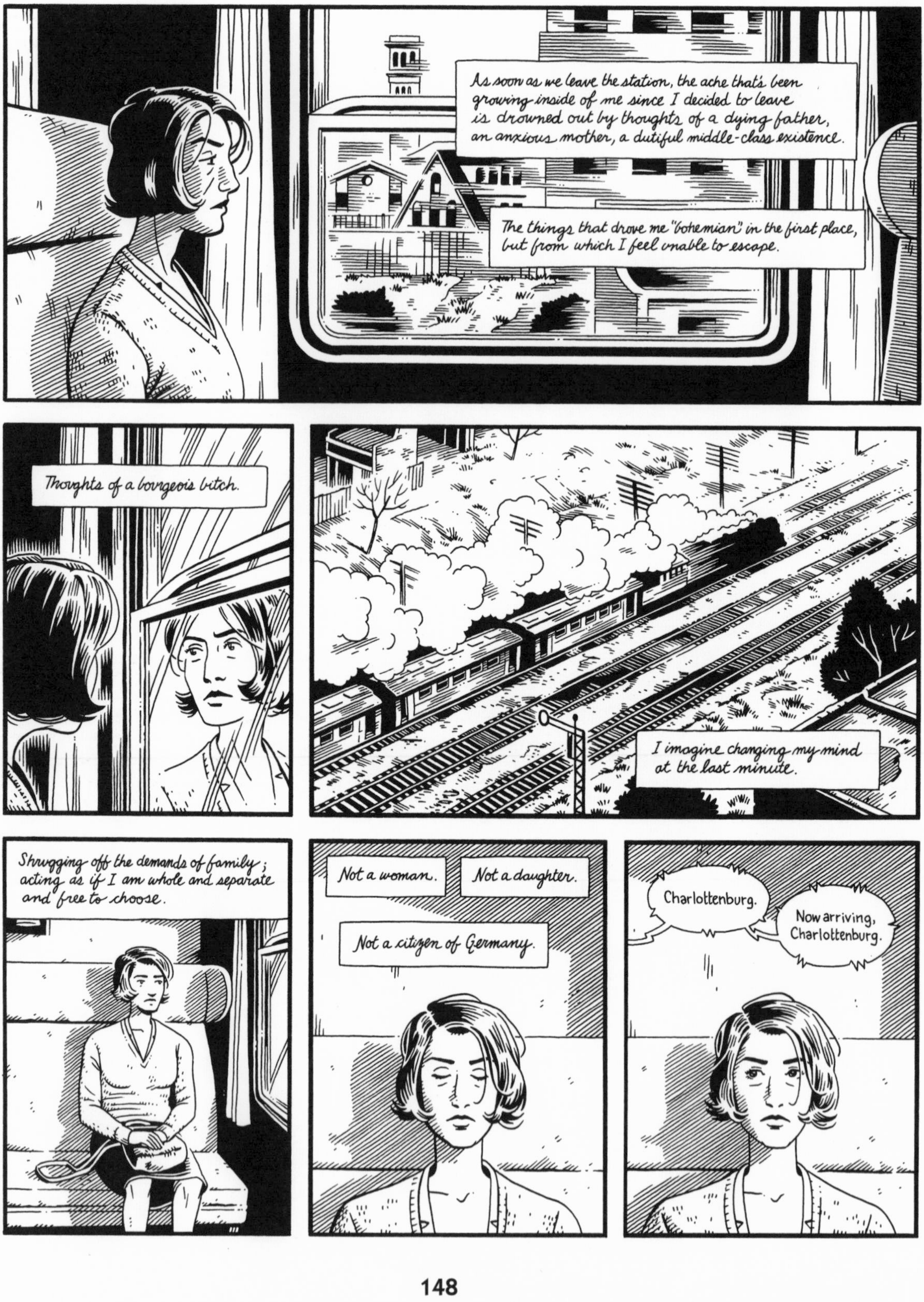
As soon as we leave the station, the ache that's been growing inside of me since I decided to leave is drowned out by thoughts of a dying father, an anxious mother, a dutiful middle-class existence.
The things that drove me "bohemian" in the first place, but from which I feel unable to escape.
Thoughts of a bourgeois bitch.
I imagine changing my mind at the last minute.
Shrugging off the demands of family; acting as if I am whole and separate and free to choose.
Not a woman.
Not a daughter.
Not a citizen of Germany.
Charlottenburg.
Now arriving, Charlottenburg.

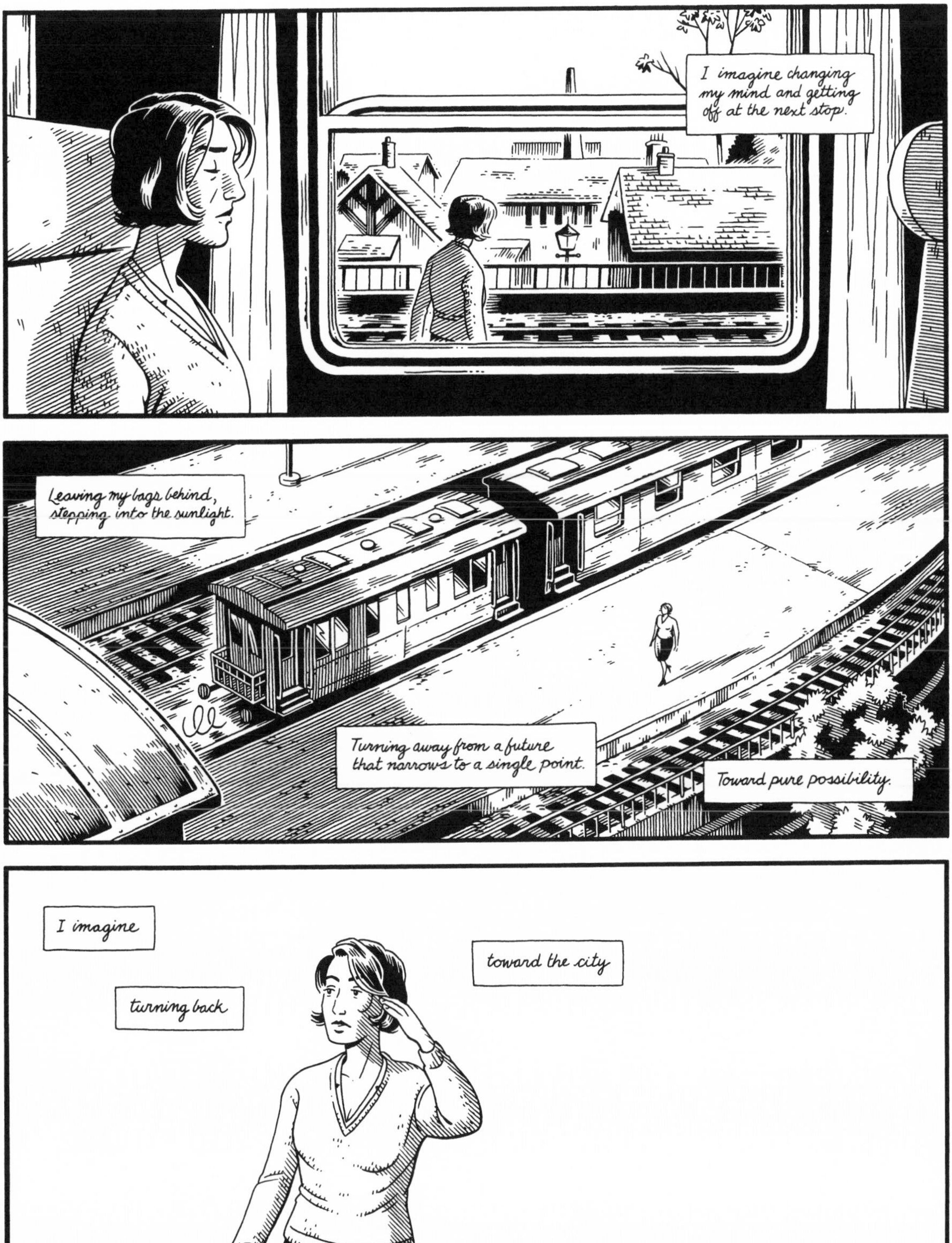
I imagine changing my mind and getting off at the next stop.
Leaving my bags behind, stepping into the sunlight.
Turning away from a future that narrows to a single point.
Toward pure possibility.
I imagine
turning back
toward the city

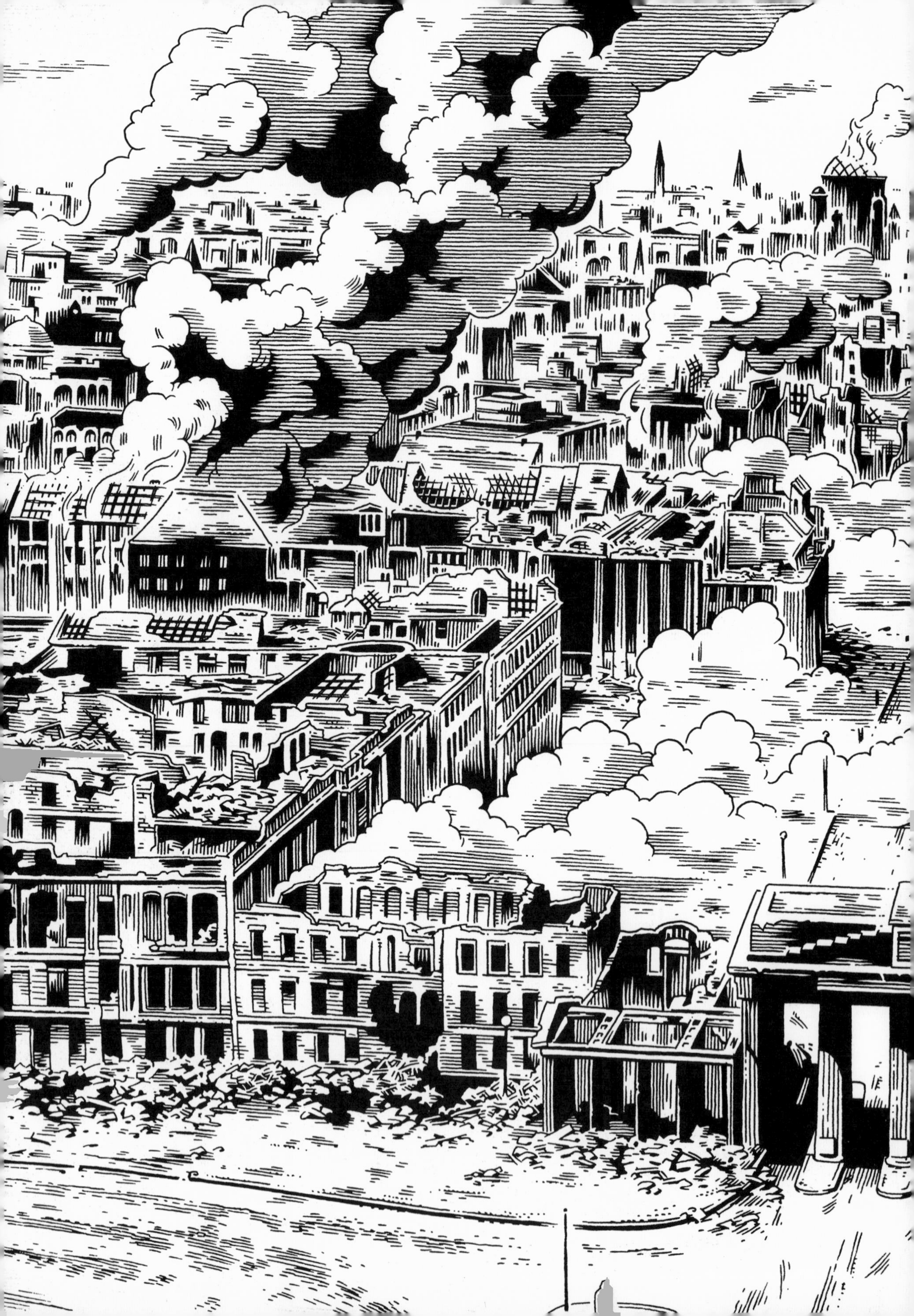

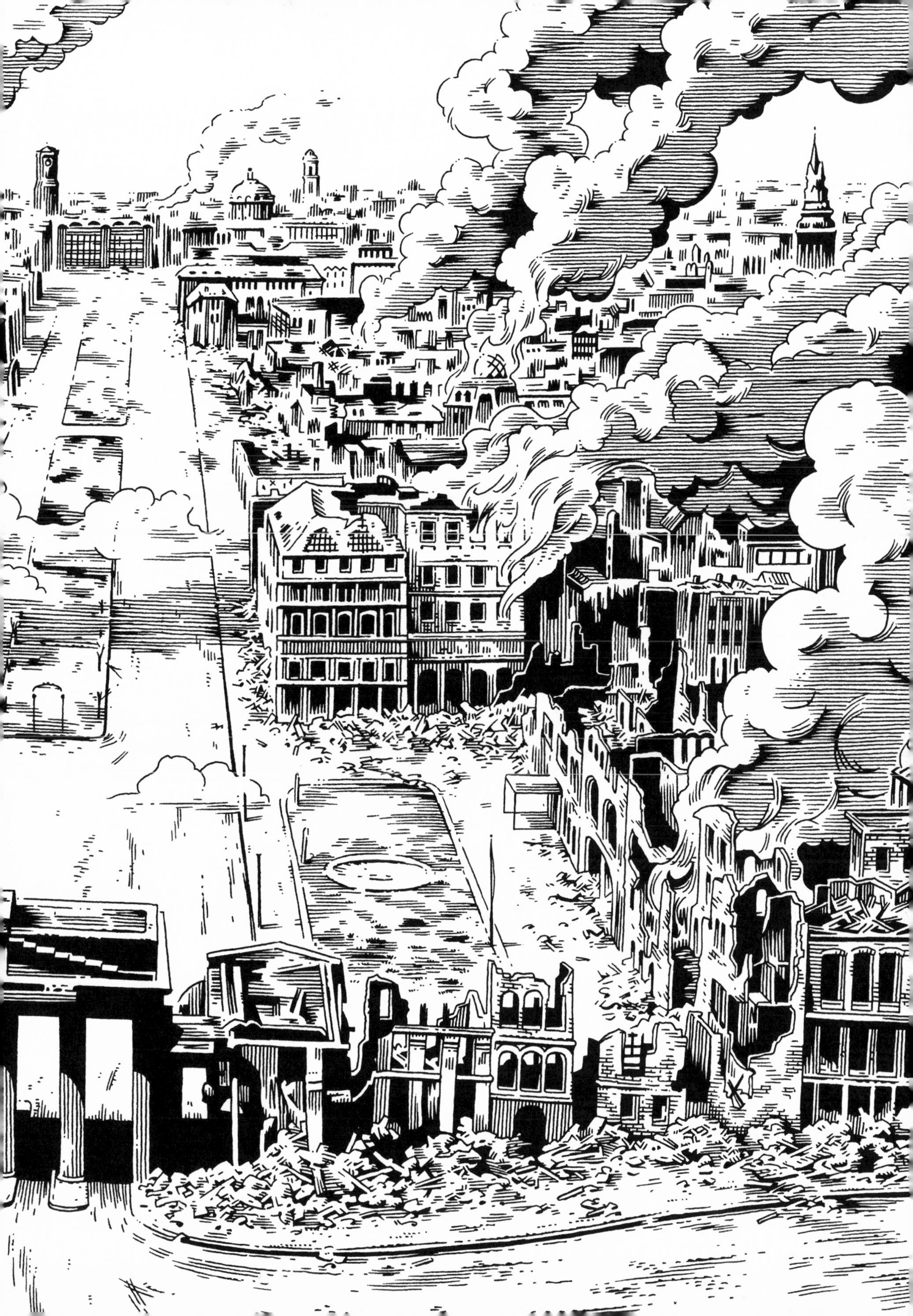

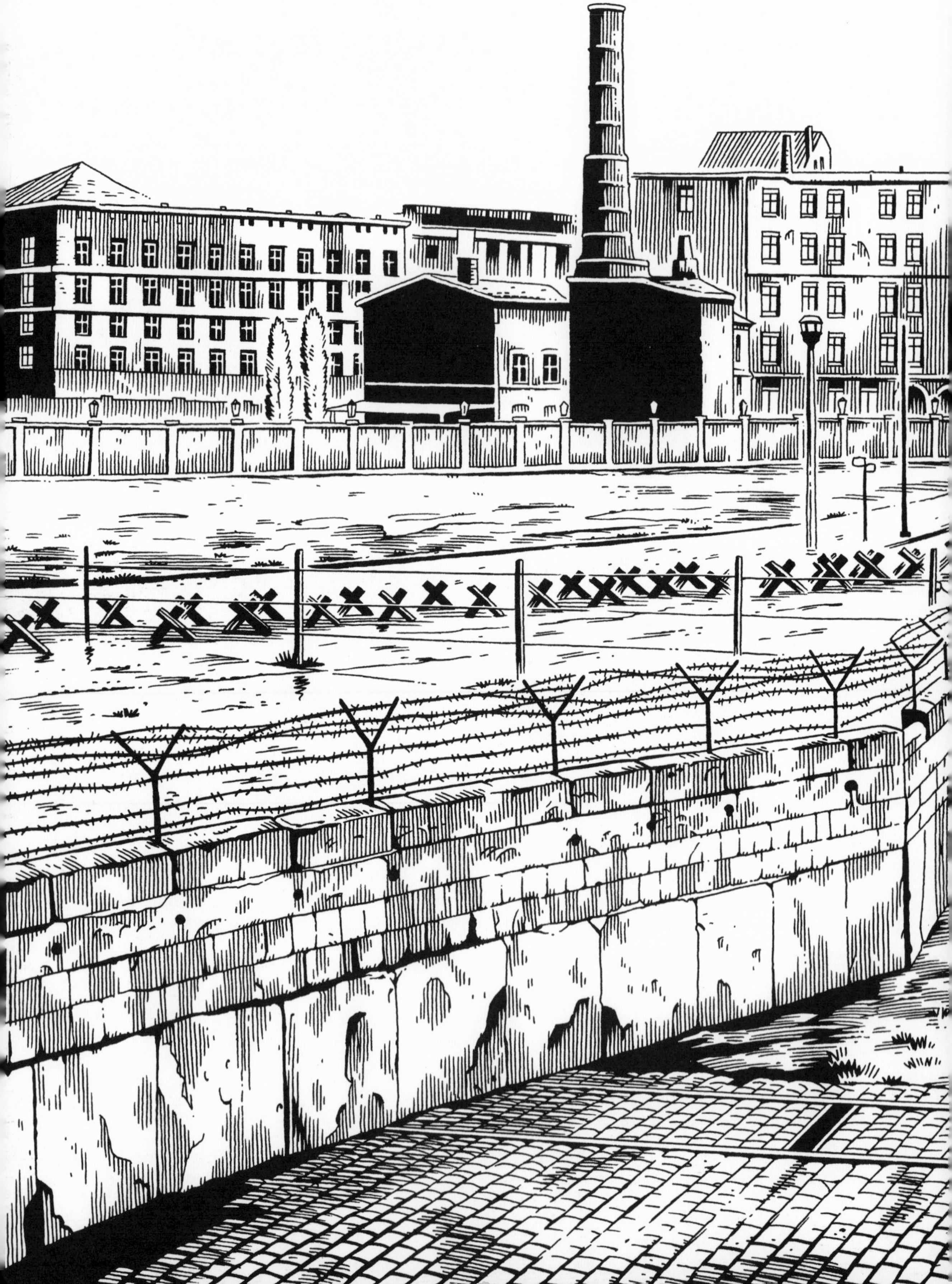

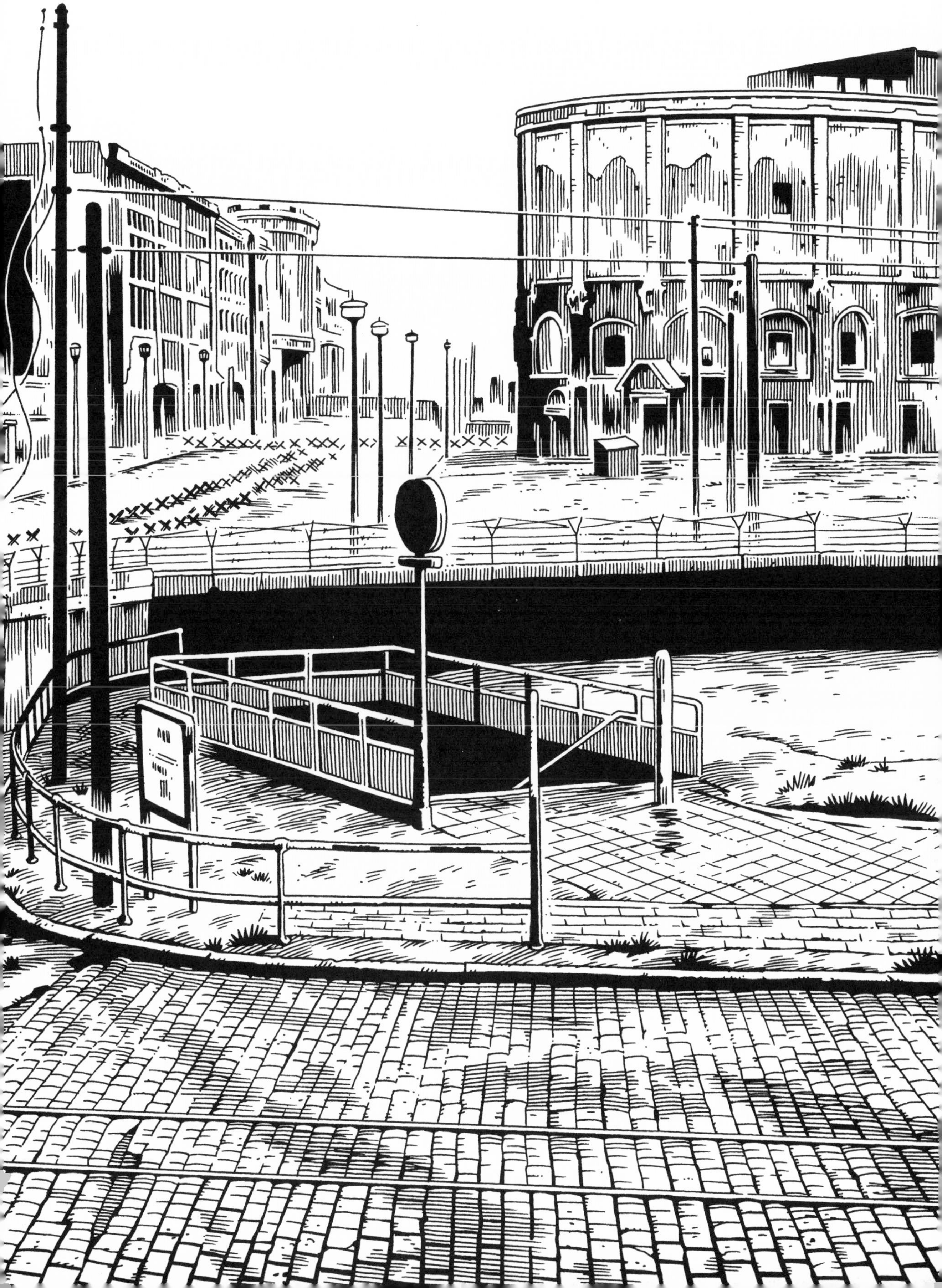

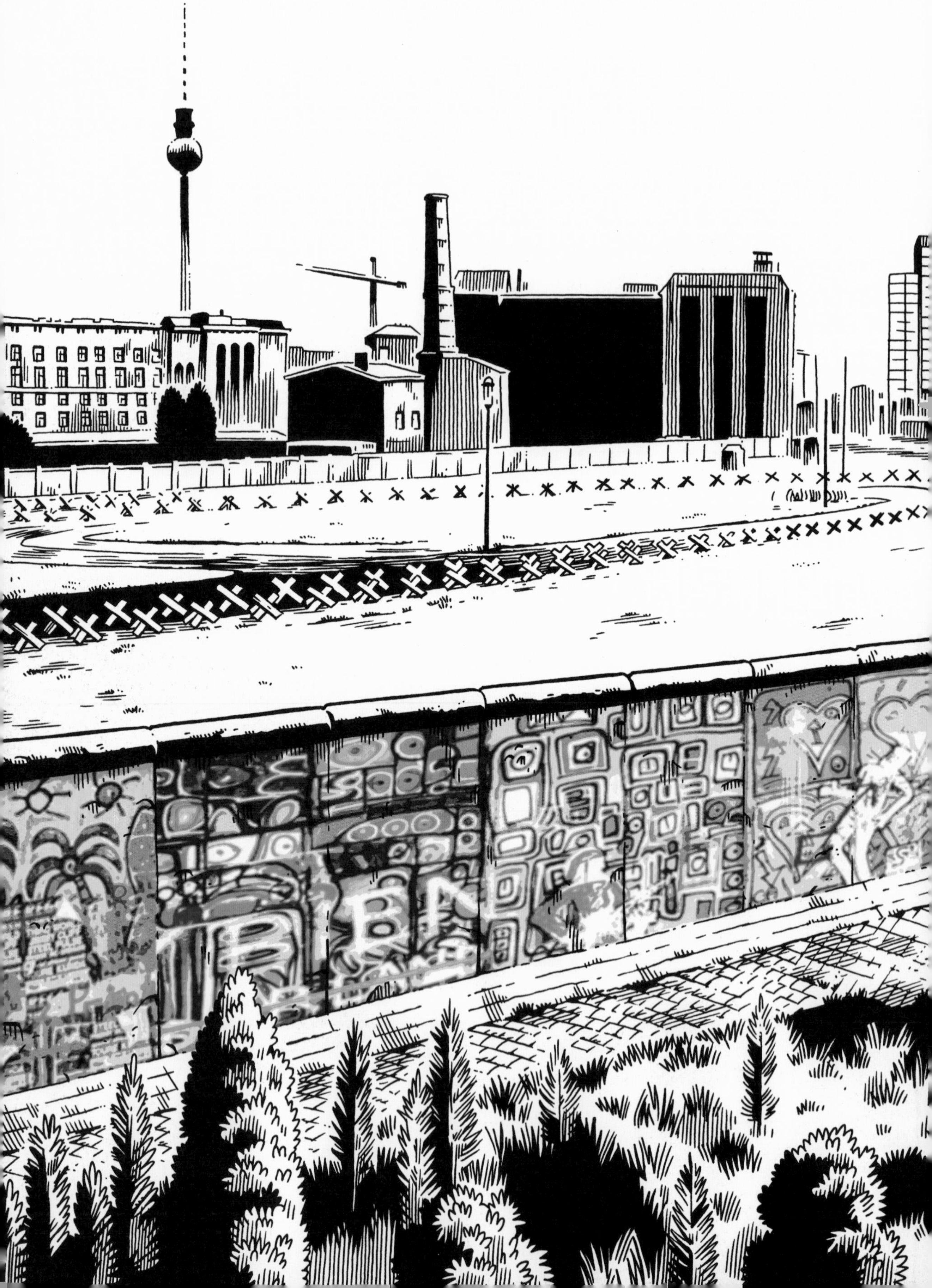

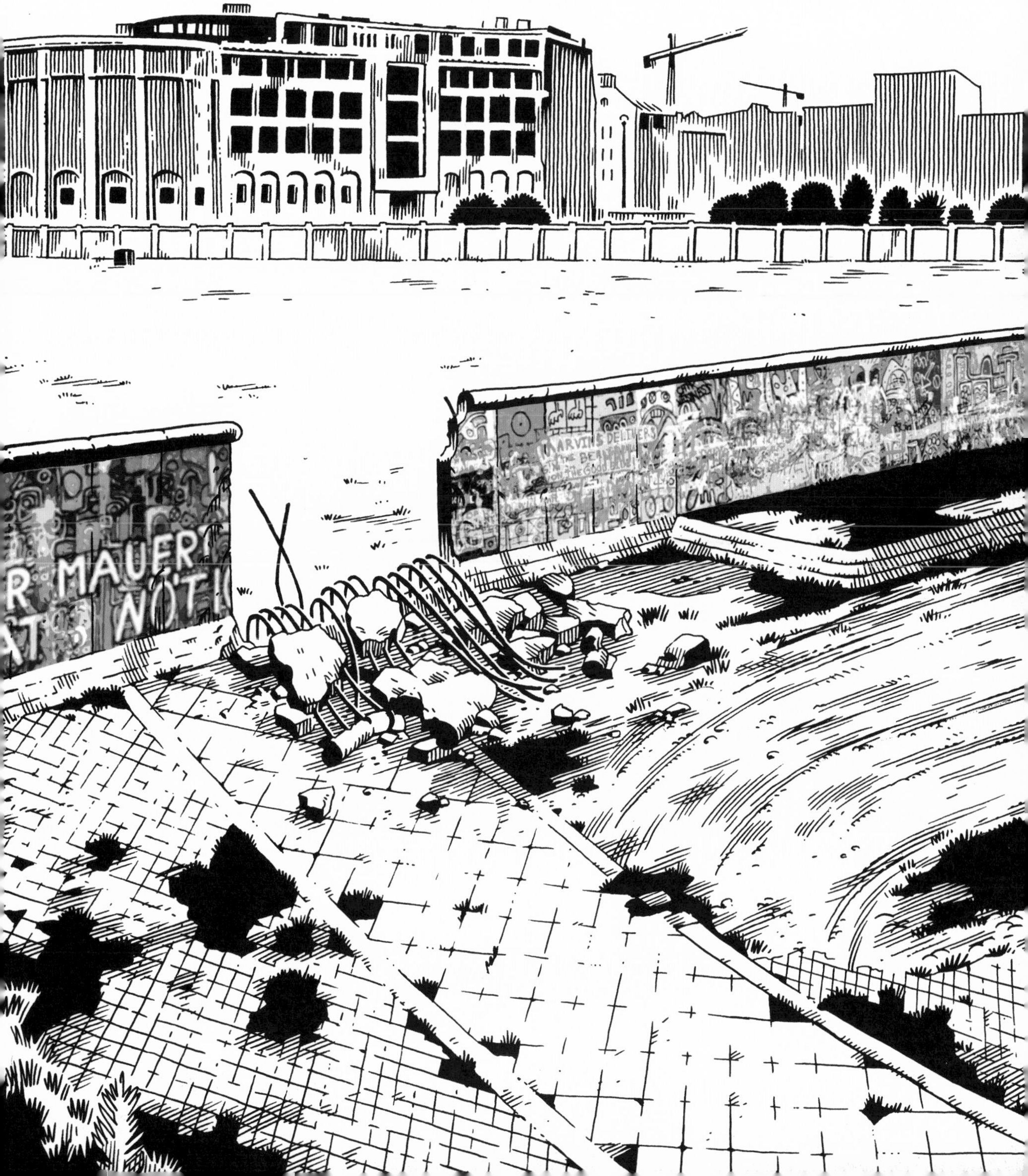
MAUER
MARVINS DELIVERS

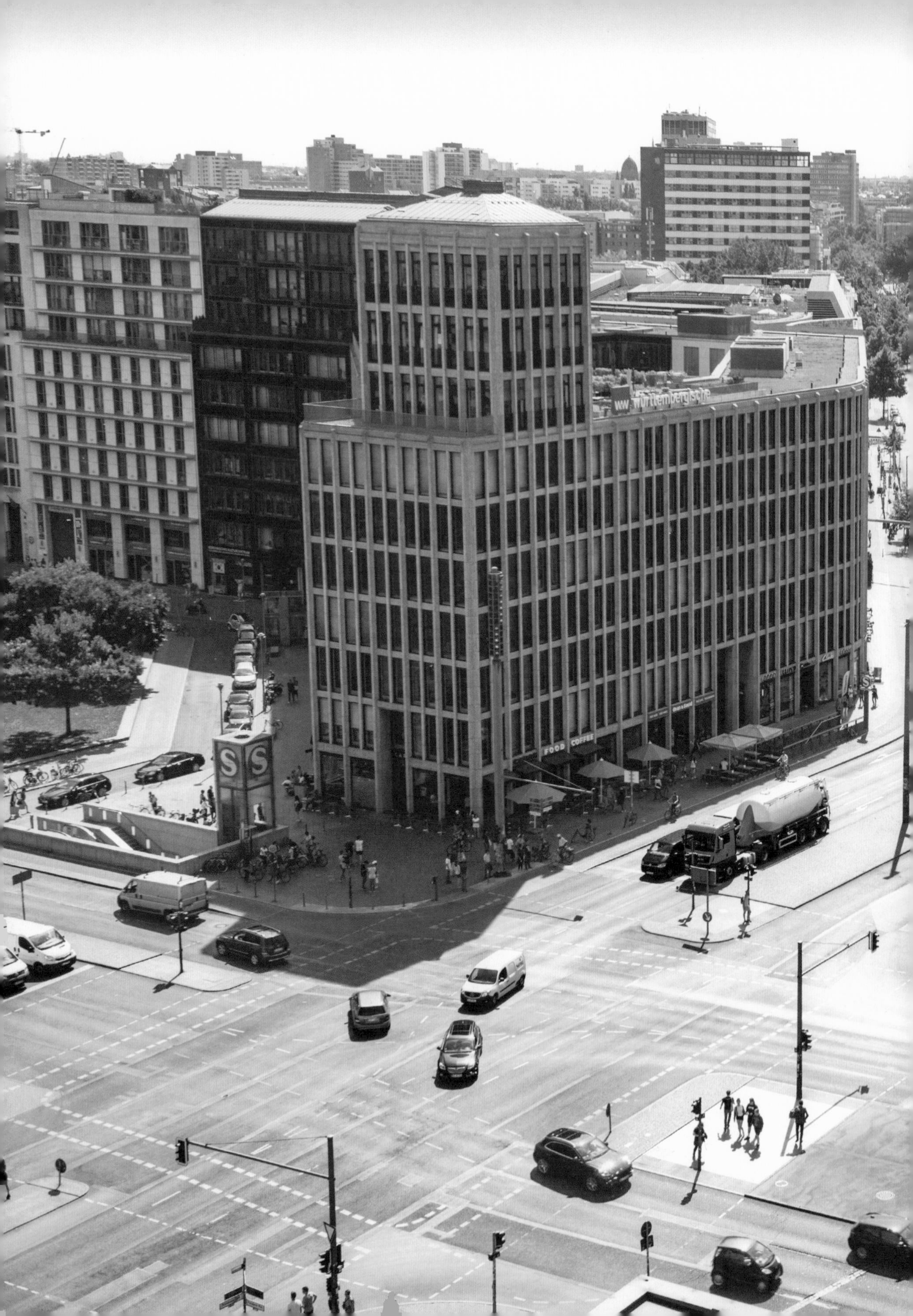
www.württembergische
FOOD
COFFEE
S
S

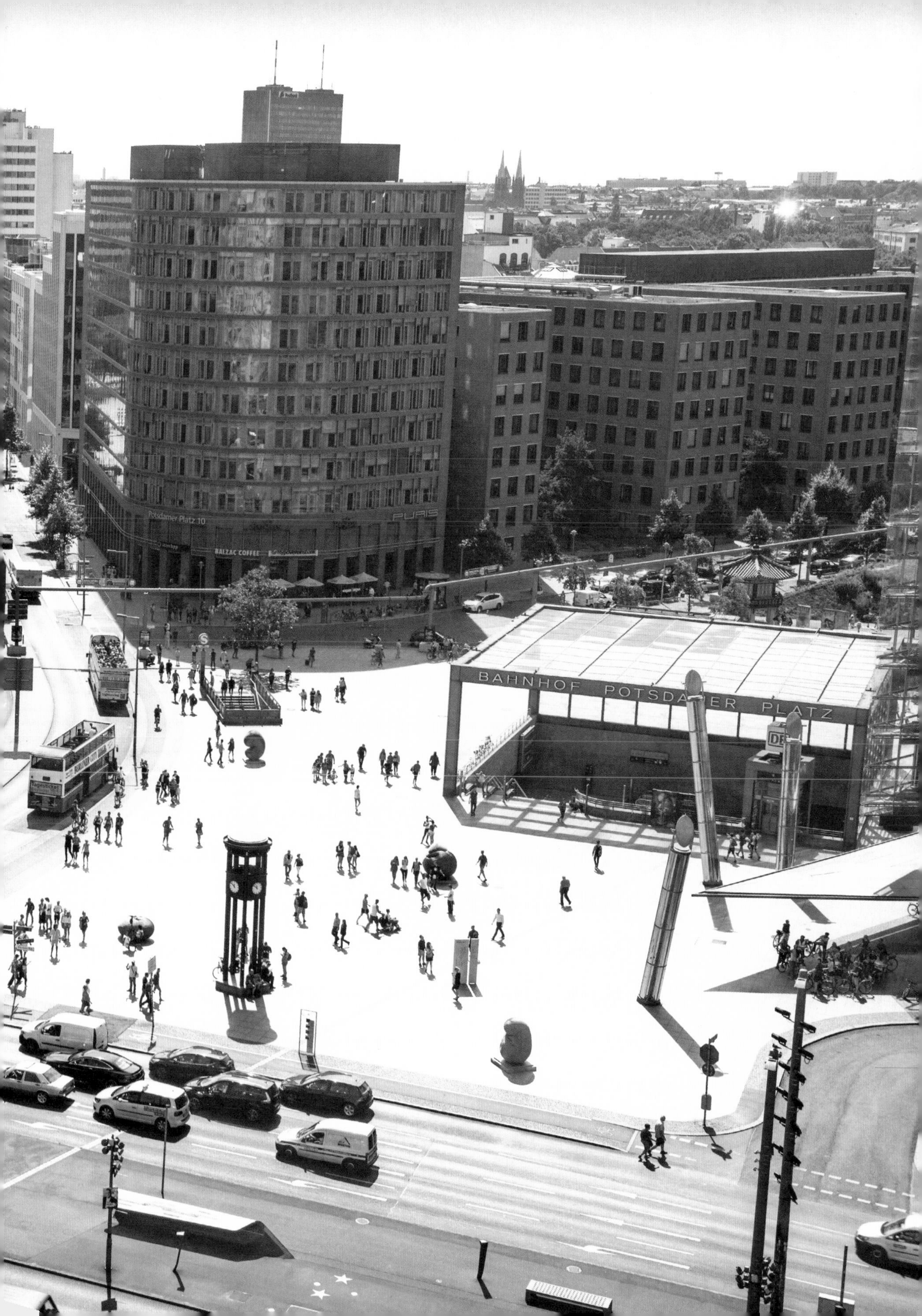
Potsdamer Platz 10
BALZAC COFFEE
BAHNHOF
PLATZ

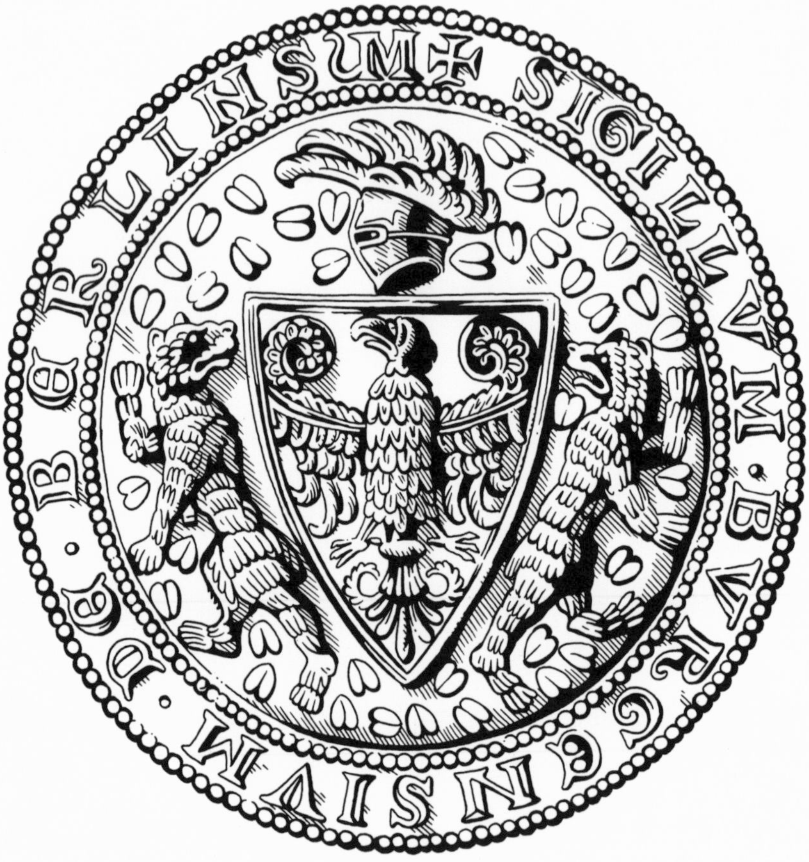
+ SIGILLVM·BVRGENSIVM·DE·BERLINSVM

Carl von Ossietzky served eighteen months in Tegel Prison, but continued his public criticism of the Nazi Party upon his release. After the Reichstag Fire in February of 1933, Chancellor Adolph Hitler ordered political dissidents arrested without charge. Ossietzky was again imprisoned.

In 1935, while detained in the Esterwegen concentration camp, he was awarded the Nobel Peace Prize, prompting the German government to forbid German citizens from accepting the prize in the future.

Suffering from tuberculosis and complications from abuse and deprivation, he died under supervision of the Gestapo at Nordend Hospital in Berlin-Pankow on May 4, 1936. He was 48 years old.

References & Inspiration

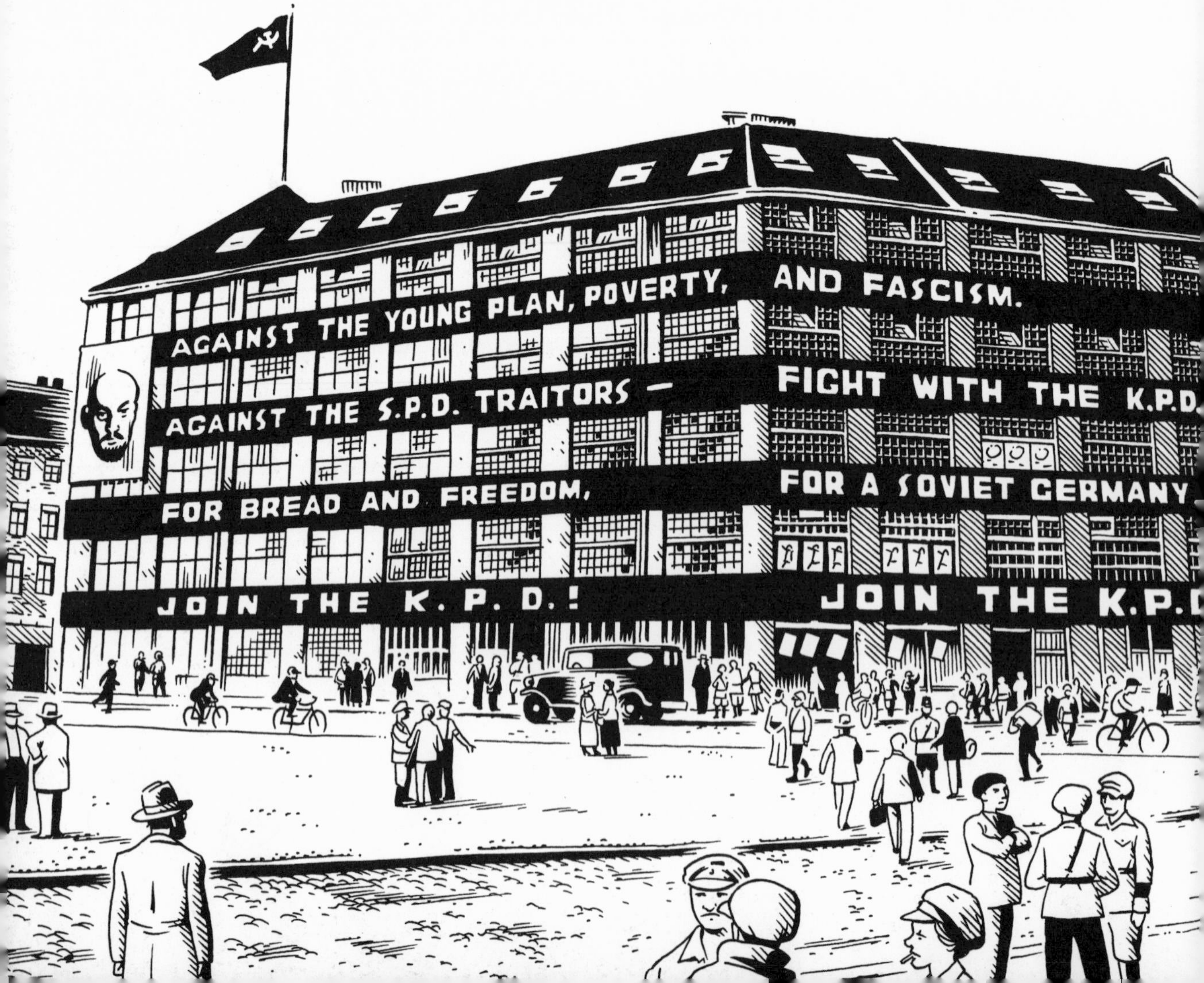

AGAINST THE YOUNG PLAN, POVERTY, AND FASCISM.
AGAINST THE S.P.D. TRAITORS — FIGHT WITH THE K.P.D.
FOR BREAD AND FREEDOM, FOR A SOVIET GERMANY
JOIN THE K.P.D.!
JOIN THE K.P.D

NON-FICTION

Barron, Stephanie and Tuchman, Maurice, *The Avant-Garde in Russia 1910–1930: New Perspectives*. Los Angeles County Museum of Art, 1980.

Barzun, Jacques, *Darwin, Marx, Wagner: Critique of a Heritage*. 1941. Doubleday & Company, Inc., 1954.

Booth, William, compiler. *Salvation Army Music*. The Salvationist Publishing & Supplies, Ltd., 1880.

Craig, Gordon A., *The Germans*. 1982. Penguin Books, 1991.

Crankshaw, Edward, translator. *I Was a German*. By Ernst Teller. 1933. Paragon House, 1991.

Crosland, Margaret, translator. *Germany*. By Joseph Rovan. E. Hulton & Co., Ltd., 1959.

Deak, Istvan, *Weimar Germany's Left-Wing Intellectuals: A Political History of the Weltbühne and Its Circle*. University of California Press, 1968.

De Jonge, Alex, *The Weimar Chronicle: Prelude to Hitler*. New American Library, 1978.

Edgeworth, Edward, *The Human German*. Methuen & Co. LTD, 1915.

Elso, Robert T., *Prelude to War*. Time-Life Books Inc., 1977.

Fitzpatrick, Sheila, *The Russian Revolution 1917–1932*. Oxford University Press, 1982.

Friedrich, Otto, *Before the Deluge: A Portrait of Berlin in the 1920s*. Fromm International Publishing Corporation, 1986.

Garraty, John A., *The Great Depression*. Anchor Press/Doubleday, 1987.

Gay, Peter, *Weimar Culture: The Outsider As Insider*. Harper & Row, 1968.

Gottwaldt, Alfred, *Das Berliner U- und S-Bahnnetz: Eine Geschichte In Streckenplänen*. Argon, 1994.

Greer, Thomas H., *A Brief History of the Western World*. 1968. Harcourt Brace Jovanovich, 1987.

Hallen, Andrea, and Müller, Bernhard. *Berlin zu Fuß: 22 Stadtteilstreifzüge durch Geschichte und Gegenwart*. VSA-Verlag, 1987.

Hampson, Norman, *The First European Revolution 1776–1815*. Harcourt, Brace & World, Inc., 1969.

Horne, Alistair, *Death of a Generation: From Neuve Chapelle to Verdun and the Somme*. American Heritage Press, 1970.

Huelsenbeck, Richard, editor. *The Dada Almanac*. 1920. Atlas Press, 1993.

Isenberg, Noah, editor. *Weimar Cinema*. Columbia University Press, 2009.

Jelavich, Peter, *Berlin Cabaret*. Harvard University Press, 1993.

Hofmann, Michael, translator. *What I Saw: Reports from Berlin 1920–1933*. By Joseph Roth. 1996. W. W. Norton & Company, Inc., 2003.

Hertzberg, Arthur, editor. *Judaism*. George Braziller, 1962.

Kaes, Anton; Jay, Martin, and Dimendberg, Edward, editors. *The Weimar Republic Sourcebook*. University of California Press, 1994.

Liang, Hsi-Huey, *The Berlin Police Force in the Weimar Republic*. University of California Press, 1970.

McKinnon-Evans, Stuart, translator. *Women in German History: From Bourgeois Emancipation to Sexual Liberation*. By Ute Frevert. Berg Publishers, Limited, 1989.

Meyer, Alfred G., *Communism*. Random House, 1960.

Noren, Catherine H., *The Camera of My Family*. Alfred A. Knopf, 1976.

Pascal, R., editor. *The German Ideology*. By Karl Marx and Frederick Engels. 1932. International Publishers Co., Inc., 1960.

Russell, Daniel, translator. *The Art of Bertolt Brecht*. By Walter Weideli. New York University Press, 1963.

Saperstein, Marc. *Jewish Preaching 1200–1800: An Anthology*. Yale University Press, 1989.

Taylor, Simon, *The Rise of Hitler: Revolution and Counter-revolution in Germany, 1918–1933*. Universe Books, 1983.

Tucker, Robert C., editor. *The Marx-Engels Reader*. W. W. Norton & Company, Inc., 1978.

Weidenfeld & Nicolson Ltd., translators. *In the Twenties: The Diaries of Harry Kessler*. By Harry Kessler. 1961. Holt, Rinehart and Winston, 1971.

Weitz, Eric D., *Weimar Germany: Promise and Tragedy*. Princeton University Press, 2007.

Winston, Richard and Clara, translators. *The Diary and Letters of Käethe Kollwitz*. By Käethe Kollwitz, Northwestern University Press, 1988.

Woods, John E., translator. *A People Betrayed: November 1918: A German Revolution*. By Alfred Döblin. 1948. Fromm International, 1983.

FICTION

Bentley, Eric, translator. *The Jewish Wife and Other Short Plays*. By Bertolt Brecht. 1943. Grove Press, Inc., 1964.

Isherwood, Christopher, *The Berlin Stories*. 1935. New Directions Publishing Corporation, 1954.

Jolas, Eugene, translator. *Berlin Alexanderplatz*. By Alfred Döblin. 1929. Frederick Ungar Publishing Co., 1983.

Powers, Richard, *Three Farmers on Their Way to a Dance*. McGraw-Hill Book Company, 1985.

Remarque, Erich Maria, *All Quiet on the Western Front*. 1928. Fawcett World Library, 1956.

Vesey, Desmond and Bentley, Eric, translators. *The Threepenny Opera*. By Bertolt Brecht. 1928. Grove Press, Inc., 1964.

FILM

Fassbinder, Rainer Werner, *Berlin Alexanderplatz*. Teleculture, 1980.

Ruttmann, Walter, *Berlin: Die Sinfonie der Großstadt*. Deutsche Vereins-Film, 1928.

Wenders, Wim, *Wings of Desire*. Road Movies/Filmproduktion/Argos Films/Westdeutscher Rundfunk, 1987.

VISUAL RESOURCES

Album von Berlin: 3 grosse Panoramen und 49 Ansichten nach Momentaufnahmen in Photographiedruck. Globus Verlag GmbH, 1904.

Appelbaum, Stanley, *Simplicissimus: 180 Satirical Drawings From the Famous German Weekly*. Dover Publications, Inc., 1975.

Behrens, Alfred, and Noth, Volker. *Berliner Stadtbahnbilder*. Verlag Ulstein GmbH, 1981.

Cabarga, Leslie, *Progressive German Graphics 1900–1937*. Chronicle Books, 1994.

Die Straßenbahnen Berlin: Eine Geschichte der BVG und ihrer Straßenbahnen. Alba Buchverlag GmbH + Co KG, 1974.

Eisler, Colin T., *German Drawings: From the 16th Century to the Expressionists*. Little, Brown and Company, 1963.

Fragen an die deutsche Geschichte: Ideen, Kräfte, Entscheidungen Von 1800 bis zur Gegenwart. German Bundestag Press and Information Centre, 1984.

Frecot, Janos, editor. *Erich Salomon: "Mit Frack und Linse durch Politik und Gesellschaft:" Photographien 1928–1938.* Schirmer/Mosel, 2004.

Friedrich, Thomas. *Berlin: A Photographic Portrait of the Weimar Years 1918–1933.* Tauris Parke Books, 1991.

Gordon, Mel, *Voluptuous Panic: The Erotic World of Weimar Berlin.* Feral House, 2008.

Grosz, George, *Ecce Homo.* 1923. Dover Publication, Inc., 1976.

Grosz, George, *Love Above All and Other Drawings.* 1930. Dover Publication, Inc., 1971.

Grunfeld, Frederic V., *The Hitler File: A Social History of Germany and the Nazis 1918–45.* Random House, 1974.

Hagemann, Otto, *Berlin the Capital.* Arani Verlags-GmbH, 1956.

Harvey, R.C., editor. *Cartoons of the Roaring Twenties Volume 1: 1921–1923.* Fantagraphics Books, 1991.

Heiting, Manfred, editor. *August Sander 1867–1964.* Taschen, 1999.

Hürlimann, Martin, *Berlin: Königsresidenz, Reichshauptstadt, Neubeginn.* Atlantis, 1981.

Karcher, Eva, *Otto Dix 1861-1969: His Life and Work.* Taschen, 1988.

Mänz, Peter, and Maryška, Christian, editors. *UFA Film Posters 1918–1943.* Umschau Braus Verlag, 1998.

Meyer, Annika and Bagley, Nigel, translators. *Cabaret Berlin: Revue, Kabarett and Film Music between the Wars.* Edel CLASSICS GmbH, 2005.

Michalski, Sergiusz, *New Objectivity: Painting, Graphic Art, and Photography in Weimar Germany 1919–1933.* 1994. Taschen, 2003.

Olian, JoAnne, editor. *Authentic French Fashion of the Twenties: 413 Costume Designs from "L'Art et la Mode."* Dover Publications, Inc., 1990.

Palmér, Torsten, and Neubauer, Hendrik, *The Weimar Republic: Through the Lens of the Press.* Könemann Verlagsgesellschaft mbH, 2000.

Ranke, Winfried, *Heinrich Zille: Photographien Berlin 1890–1910.* Wilhelm Heyne Verlag, 1975.

Robertson, Michael, translator. *Face of Our Time.* By August Sander. 1929. Schirmer's Visual Library, 1994.

Schneede, Uwe M., editor. *George Grosz: Vita e Opere*. Gabriele Mazzotta Editore, 1977.

Schrader, Bärbel, and Schebera, Jürgen, *The "Golden" Twenties: Art and Literature in the Weimar Republic*. Yale University Press, 1988.

Strache, Wolf, *Berlin: eine Erinnerung*. DSB Verlag, 1961.

Titzenthaler, Waldemar, *Berliner Interieurs: 1910–1930*. Nicolai, 2001.

Ulrich, Barbara, *The Hot Girls of Weimar Berlin*. Feral House, 2002.

Von Eckardt, Wolf, and Gilman, Sander L., *Bertolt Brecht's Berlin: A Scrapbook of the Twenties*. 1974. University of Nebraska Press, 1993.

Willett, John, *The Weimar Years: a Culture Cut Short*. Thames and Hudson, 1984.

Yapp, Nick, The Hulton Getty Picture Collection: 1930s. Könemann Verlagsgesellschaft mbH, 1998.

Zille, Heinrich, *Hurengespräche*. 1921. Schirmer/Mosel, 2000.

Zille, Heinrich, *Komm, Karlineken, Komm!* 1925. Schirmer/Mosel, 1983.

Zimmer, Petra and Peter Quirin, *Szene Typographie 1930*. Universitätsdruckerei und Verlag H.Schmidt, 1988.

Acknowledgments

Thanks to Ed Brubaker, Michael Buckley, Mike Christian, Stefano Gaudiano, Tom Hart, Megan Kelso, David Lasky, Jon Lewis, and James Sturm, for being the best creative community an aspiring cartoonist could hope for.

Thanks to Art Spiegelman and Françoise Mouly, for exploding the spectrum of possibility.

Thanks to Dale Yarger, for being a kind and generous mentor.

Thanks to Scott McCloud, for giving me a leg up when I really needed it.

Thanks to Michel Vrána, for publishing my first book, and for making all of my books look beautiful.

Thanks to Chris Oliveros, for inviting me into the Drawn & Quarterly fold; and Peggy Burns and Tom Devlin, for not kicking me out.

Thanks to the rest of the D&Q crew for their excellent work and support: Tracy Hurren, Julia Pohl-Miranda, Sam Tse, and Rachel Nam.

Thanks to Lynda Barry and Chris Ware, twin stars in the firmament.

Thanks to Jonathan Lutes, who knows Berlin better than I ever will.

Thanks to the good people at Carlsen Verlag, past and present, for their extraordinary patience and work on my behalf: Klaus Humann, Michael Groenewald, Claudia Jerusalem-Groenewald, Antje Haubner, Nico Hübsch, Joachim Kaps, Björn Liebchen, Kai-Steffen Schwarz, and Winnie Schwarz.

Thanks to Heinrich Anders and Lutz Göllner, for convincing German readers that I have a strong grasp on Berliner dialect.

Thanks to Lena Ganssmann for capturing in the real world an image I had in my head.

Thanks to the faculty, staff, and students at the Center for Cartoon Studies, who inspire me to make the best comics of which I am capable.

Thanks to Richard and Sarah Warren, for sustenance and stability.

Thanks to Carolyn Lutes, for being my first letterer, and for not balking at my decision to become a cartoonist.

Thanks to Rachel Bers, for all things unconditional.

This book is dedicated with love to Rebecca Warren, for believing in me over the 23 years it took to write and draw it; and to Clementine and Max Warren-Lutes, for being the best reasons possible to miss deadlines.

Jason Lutes was born in 1967 and grew up reading Hergé's *Tintin* along with American superhero and Western comics. In 1977, he discovered the tabletop role-playing game *Dungeons & Dragons*, which proved a major influence on his creative development. He received a BFA in Illustration from the Rhode Island School of Design in 1991 and started writing and drawing *Berlin* in 1994. His other books include *Jar of Fools*, *Houdini: The Handcuff King* (with Nick Bertozzi), and *The Fall* (with Ed Brubaker). He currently teaches at the Center for Cartoon Studies in White River Junction, Vermont.

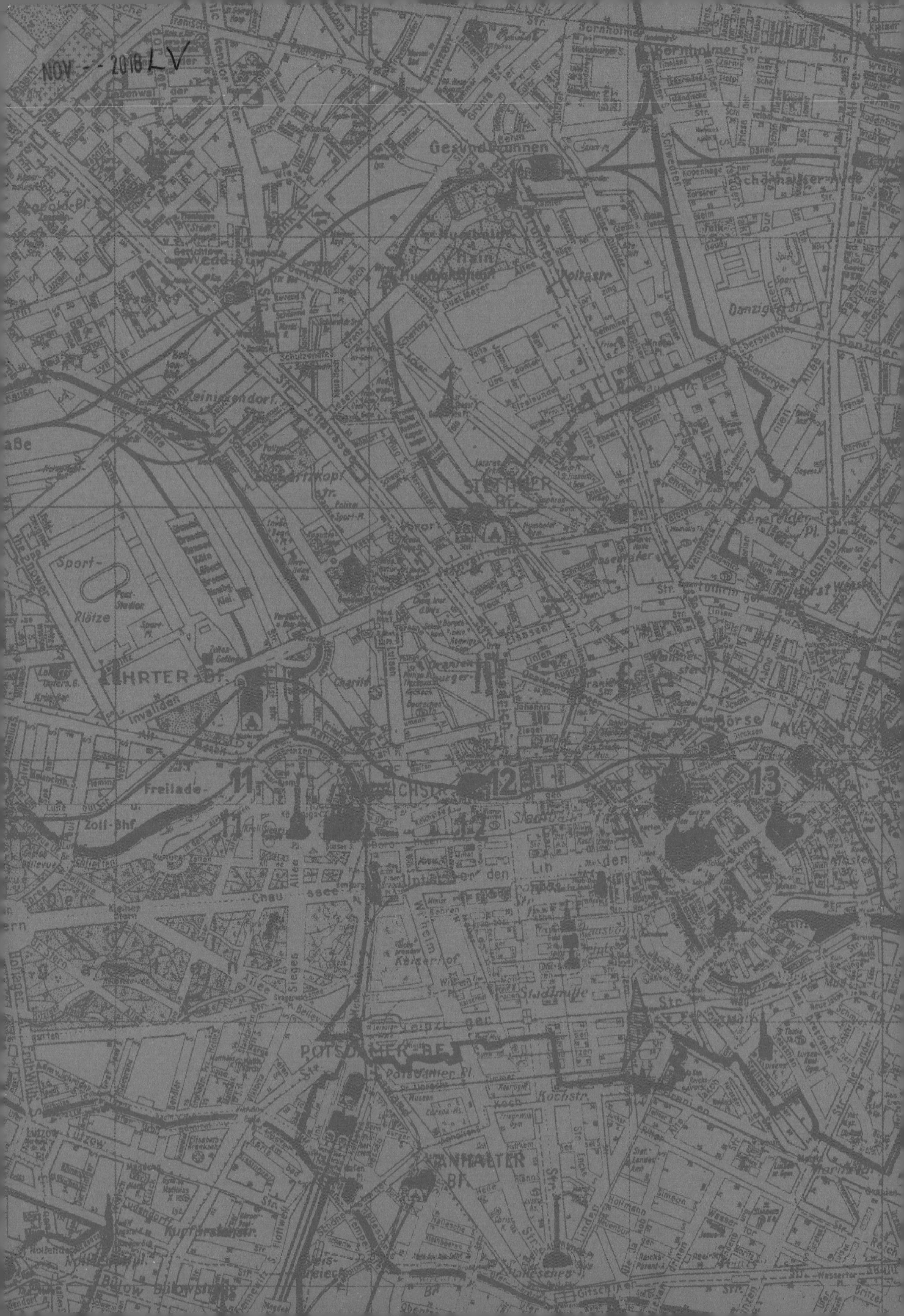
Bornholmer Str.
Gesundbrunnen
Schönhauser Allee
Danziger Str.
Reinickendorf.
Chaussee
Stettiner Bf.
Sport-
Plätze
EHRTER Bf.
Invaliden
Charité
Freilade-
Zoll-Bhf
11
12
13
Börse
Kaiserhof
Stadtmitte
POTSDAMER BF.
Potsdamer Pl.
Kochstr.
ANHALTER Bf.
Gitschiner